Raising Bilingual–Biliterate Children in Monolingual Cultures

Curriculum & Language Access Service (CLAS)

BILINGUAL EDUCATION AND BILINGUALISM
Series Editors: Professor Nancy H. Hornberger, *University of Pennsylvania, Philadelphia, USA* and Professor Colin Baker, *University of Wales, Bangor, Wales, Great Britain*

Recent Books in the Series
Language and Literacy Teaching for Indigenous Education: A Bilingual Approach
  Norbert Francis and Jon Reyhner
The Native Speaker: Myth and Reality
  Alan Davies
Language Socialization in Bilingual and Multilingual Societies
  Robert Bayley and Sandra R. Schecter (eds)
Language Rights and the Law in the United States: Finding our Voices
  Sandra Del Valle
Continua of Biliteracy: An Ecological Framework for Educational Policy, Research, and Practice in Multilingual Settings
  Nancy H. Hornberger (ed.)
Languages in America: A Pluralist View (2nd edn)
  Susan J. Dicker
Trilingualism in Family, School and Community
  Charlotte Hoffmann and Jehannes Ytsma (eds)
Multilingual Classroom Ecologies
  Angela Creese and Peter Martin (eds)
Negotiation of Identities in Multilingual Contexts
  Aneta Pavlenko and Adrian Blackledge (eds)
Beyond the Beginnings: Literacy Interventions for Upper Elementary English Language Learners
  Angela Carrasquillo, Stephen B. Kucer and Ruth Abrams
Bilingualism and Language Pedagogy
  Janina Brutt-Griffler and Manka Varghese (eds)
Language Learning and Teacher Education: A Sociocultural Approach
  Margaret R. Hawkins (ed.)
The English Vernacular Divide: Postcolonial Language Politics and Practice
  Vaidehi Ramanathan
Bilingual Education in South America
  Anne-Marie de Mejía (ed.)
Teacher Collaboration and Talk in Multilingual Classrooms
  Angela Creese
Words and Worlds: World Languages Review
  F. Martí, P. Ortega, I. Idiazabal, A. Barreña, P. Juaristi, C. Junyent, B. Uranga and E. Amorrortu
Language and Aging in Multilingual Contexts
  Kees de Bot and Sinfree Makoni
Foundations of Bilingual Education and Bilingualism (4th edn)
  Colin Baker
Bilingual Minds: Emotional Experience, Expression and Representation
  Aneta Pavlenko (ed.)

For more details of these or any other of our publications, please contact:
Multilingual Matters, Frankfurt Lodge, Clevedon Hall,
Victoria Road, Clevedon, BS21 7HH, England
http://www.multilingual-matters.com

BILINGUAL EDUCATION AND BILINGUALISM 57
Series Editors: Nancy H. Hornberger and Colin Baker

Raising Bilingual–Biliterate Children in Monolingual Cultures

Stephen J. Caldas

MULTILINGUAL MATTERS LTD
Clevedon • Buffalo • Toronto

Library of Congress Cataloging in Publication Data
Caldas, Stephen J
Raising Bilingual–Biliterate Children in Monolingual Cultures/Stephen J. Caldas.
Bilingual Education and Bilingualism: 57
Includes bibliographical references and index.
1. Second language acquisition. 2. Bilingualism. 3. English language–Acquisition.
4. French language–Acquisition. I. Title. II. Series.
P118.2.C35 2006
306.44'6–dc22   2005027401

British Library Cataloguing in Publication Data
A catalogue entry for this book is available from the British Library.

ISBN 1-85359-876-3 / EAN 978-1-85359-876-0 (hbk)
ISBN 1-85359-875-5 / EAN 978-1-85359-875-3 (pbk)

Multilingual Matters Ltd
UK: Frankfurt Lodge, Clevedon Hall, Victoria Road, Clevedon BS21 7HH.
USA: UTP, 2250 Military Road, Tonawanda, NY 14150, USA.
Canada: UTP, 5201 Dufferin Street, North York, Ontario M3H 5T8, Canada.

Copyright © 2006 Stephen J. Caldas.

All rights reserved. No part of this work may be reproduced in any form or by any means without permission in writing from the publisher.

Typeset by Saxon Graphics.
Printed and bound in Great Britain by the Cromwell Press Ltd.

Contents

List of Tables and Figures ix
Acknowledgements xi
Preface xiii

1   Introduction and Focus of the Book.. 1
    In the Beginning … 2

2   Bilingualism in America 10
    Introduction 10
    Historical Overview 10
    Educational Issues 12
    The Language Revival 16
    The Special Case of Louisiana 16

3   Methodology: Taking the Measure of the Project 22
    Introduction 22
    The Case Study 23
    Fieldnotes 24
    Audiotape Recordings 25
    The Bilingual Preference Ratio (BPR) 26
    Videotape Recordings 29
    Edelman's Contextualized Measure of Degree of Bilingualism .. 29
    French Proficiency Survey 30
    Children Administered French Proficiency and Bilingual Self-
        perception Surveys 31

4   Bilingual Antecedents 33
    Introduction 33
    An Unlikely Meeting … 33
    A Union of Cultures 37
    The Inspiration 39
    Social Class 39

5   Home and Community 41
    Introduction 41

v

Implementing the Plan: John 41
One System or Two? 43
Valerie and Stephanie 44
The Community 45
Which Language to Discipline in? 54
Profanity 55
The Summertime Linguistic Community of 'Le Québec' 57
Language Politics 60
Pre-adolescence, Fluency, and Language Conflict 62
Vive les vacances! (Long Live Vacations!) 64

6   The School 69
Introduction 69
Early Schooling 69
Which Language to do Homework in? 70
Cajun Country School French Immersion 71
First Québec Schooling Experience 76
Suburban School French Immersion 79
Second Québec School Experience 81
Summer Camp and French Literacy 82
Language Proficiency and Academic Placement 83
French Proficiency Surveys 85
Comparison of Children's and Teachers' Perceptions of
    French Proficiency 87

7   Recreational Reading, Media, Hobbies and Games 90
Introduction 90
The Foundation: Reading 90
Vive la télévision française! (Long Live French Television!) 93
Videocassettes 99
Hobbies: The Trojan Horses 101
Games 104
The Library 104

8   The Psychology of Pre- and Early Adolescent Bilingualism 106
Introduction 106
Adolescence and Bilingualism 106
Bilingual Preference 107
The Louisiana Context in Adolescence 109
Cajun 'Country' Culture 110
Early Adolescence and John's Language Shift 112

	John's Shift is Complete	117
	The Twins' Early Adolescent Language Shift	118
	The Québec Language Context in Adolescence	120
	The Accent Issue	122
	Quick Shift Back	125
	Early Adolescent Identity Construction	126
9	The Psychology of Middle Adolescent Bilingualism	129
	Introduction	129
	Summertime Changes	129
	Peer Influence and Accent Loss	130
	'Crossing Over'	133
	No Residual Effect	135
	'Weird Language Crap'	137
	No Peers, No Language Influence	138
	Summer of 2000	139
	No French	140
	No Parental Language Influence	141
	Lord of the Rings	143
	Summertime English	144
	End in Sight	144
	Approaching Fluency	145
10	Emerging Bilinguistic Identities	147
	Introduction	147
	A New Phase	147
	Decreasing Linguistic Self-consciousness	148
	Increasing Linguistic Self-confidence	149
	Society Stronger than Will	150
	Beyond Peers	151
	Bilingual Self-perceptions	152
	Accents	159
	Concluding Thoughts on Bilingualism in Adolescence	160
11	Taking the Measure of Bilingualism	164
	Introduction	164
	Measures of Bilingualism	164
	Bilingual Preference Ratios (BPRs)	165
	Correlation between John's and the twins' home language	
	preferences (BPRs)	170
	Edelman's Contextualized Measure of Degree of Bilingualism	172

French Proficiency Surveys 178

12 Lessons Learned, Broader Implications and Guidelines for
Parents 186
    The End of One Journey and the Beginning of Another 186
    How Do We Know? 187
    The Power of Society 187
    Importance of Societal Immersion 189
    Adolescence 190
    Implications for Parents 191
    Lessons from a School French Immersion Program 192
    What We Accomplished 194
    Authentic Societal Language Immersion 194
    Input=Output 196
    No Language Penalty 199
    What's the Best Bilingual Program? 200
    Suggestions for Immigrants to the United States and Canada .. 201
    So, How Do You Ensure Fluency in your Child's Minority
        Tongue? 202
    The Power of Media 204

Bibliography 207

Appendices 222
    Appendix 1: French Proficiency Survey 222
    Appendix 2: French Proficiency Survey
        (translated from French) 222
    Appendix 3: Children's French Proficiency Survey 223
    Appendix 4: Children's French Proficiency Survey
        (translated from French) 224
    Appendix 5: Bilingual Self-Perception Survey 225

Index 226

Tables and Figures

Tables

1. Descriptive statistics of family members' Bilingual Preference Ratios 168
2. Correlations between BPRs of family members 169
3. Descriptive statistics for John's Edelman's coefficients 173
4. Descriptive statistics for Stephanie's Edelman's coefficients 173
5. Descriptive statistics for Valerie's Edelman's coefficients 173
6. Bivariate correlations between Edelman's home coefficients for each child 177
7. Bivariate correlations between Edelman's school coefficients for each child 177
8. Bivariate correlations between Edelman's neighborhood coefficients for each child 177
9. Bivariate correlations between average Edelman's coefficients for each child 178
10. Descriptive statistics of French Proficiency Survey scores 179
11. Paired sample t-test comparisons of average self-report scores on children's French Proficiency tests at Time 1 and Time 2 181
12. Correlations between John's average French Proficiency Survey scores at Time 1 and Time 2, and average teacher scores 182
13. Correlations between Stephanie's average French Proficiency Survey scores at Time 1 and Time 2, and average teacher scores .. 183
14. Correlations between Valerie's average French Proficiency Survey scores at Time 1 and Time 2, and average teacher scores .. 184

Figures

1. Monthly Bilingual Preference Ratios of all family members: December 1994 to December 2000 166
2. Children's Louisiana Bilingual Preference Ratios 167
3. Children's summer Québec Bilingual Preference Ratios 167
4. Parents' language preferences: Québec and Louisiana 168
5. Bilingual Preference Ratios of John and twins: Superimposed by age 171

6. John: Edelman's coefficients of bilingual dominance 174
7. Stephanie: Edelman's coefficients of bilingual dominance 174
8. Valerie: Edelman's coefficients of bilingual dominance 175
9. John, Stephanie and Valerie: Average Edelman's coefficients of bilingual dominance 178
10. John's teacher French Proficiency Survey scores 180
11. Stephanie's teacher French Proficiency Survey scores 180
12. Valerie's teacher French Proficiency Survey scores 181

Acknowledgements

This book is based on 19 years of participant observation research during which time the author and his wife reared their three children – the subjects – to be biliterate and bilingual in French and English. Though I am the author of record for this book who actually typed these words on a computer, this project was very much a collaborative effort. Suzanne and I worked together very closely as husband and wife on the strategies we developed, implemented, and assessed together. The project required both of our concerted, conscientious, and consistent efforts, and I could no more have accomplished this project alone than a river can flow without water. Therefore, I must acknowledge a very deep debt of gratitude and love to a wonderful wife, mother, and colleague. She worked selflessly to rear not only bilingual-biliterate children, but well-rounded, intelligent and compassionate individuals who are all very likely to make this troubled world a more humane place in which to live.

The children themselves were marvelous subjects. We were very frank with them early on about our project to rear them as biliterate-bilinguals. They were mostly very indulgent and cooperative of our efforts to carefully document how they were learning to read, write, and speak two languages. They traveled with me to professional conferences where I presented research on their cases, and not only politely answered questions of other curious researchers, but worked my audiovisual equipment as well. When I sat down to write this book, after our children had already begun departing from 'the nest', it was with a lump in my throat that I reflected back on the project, and on just how quickly it was coming to an end. It had only seemed like yesterday that we watched in wonder as the toddlers uttered their first English or French words.

I would also like to thank several reviewers who provided many useful suggestions for improving this book. These include the helpful suggestions of Annick De Houwer of the University of Antwerp and Elizabeth Lanza of the University of Oslo. Another anonymous reviewer provided very extensive, useful, and insightful feedback which significantly improved this book. I appreciate Fred Genesee's giving selflessly of his limited time to read this volume and prepare appropriate and insightful remarks for the book's Preface. Roy Lyster provided many useful sources into which I could more deeply delve into the at times elusive issue of accents. Professor Jim Flaitz of the University of Louisiana has always given selflessly and graciously of his limited time to advance my projects. His help in formatting this manuscript is but another example of his professionalism and generosity. Thanks Jim. Denise Klein of McGill University not only took time to patiently explain some of the intricacies of the brain research in which she was engaged, but she even gave me a personal tour of the Montreal Neurological Institute to help me better grasp the technological complexities of her specialized field. I'm indebted to my father, Col. John J. Caldas, Jr. (USMC, retired) for his careful proofreading of every word in this manuscript. Karl Fontenot, a sound engineer with KRVS 'Radio Acadie', a station dedicated to preserving French Louisiana music, helped restore sound on aging, substandard audiotapes. I thank Janelle Jackson for long ago effectively teaching me French fundamentals from the discipline's 'first book'. Likewise, I deeply appreciate the effort put forth by all of the children's French and English teachers. Be assured that your hard work on their behalf has paid off. I'm especially appreciative of the professionalism of my children's French teachers and counselors who agreed to complete the French Proficiency Survey on each child. Your responses have provided useful data in writing this book. Finally, I'm deeply moved by the many Cajuns who passionately shared their stories of linguistic discrimination with me and allowed me to retell their sad tales. An effort to slow the demise of French in Louisiana was part of the motivation for this project. May we never forget.

Preface

The language acquisition research community has seen a great deal of interest recently on the subject of children who grow up learning two languages – children whom Jürgen Meisel (1986) has referred to aptly as bilingual first language learners. The fruits of research efforts on this topic have appeared in scientific journals that report the results of focused research projects and in book-length reports of case studies of bilingual first language learners (see De Houwer, 1991, for one of the first such publications, and Deuchar and Quay, 2000, for a more recent example). Each of these formats has its own strengths – journal articles provide highly focused and reasoned slices of the puzzle of bilingual first language acquisition, while book-length reports of case studies provide broad, encompassing insights about this form of language learning. Case studies have played an extremely important and highly respected role in scientific studies of language learning – witness Roger Brown's pioneering research on Adam, Eve, and Sarah, the results of which are still widely cited, even today (Brown, 1973). *Raising Bilingual – Biliterate Children in Monolingual Cultures* by Stephen Caldas in the Department of Educational Foundations and Leadership of the University of Louisiana, Lafayette, is a welcomed addition to case study reports of bilingual first langauge acquisition.

Caldas tells the story of his three children, John, Stephanie, and Valerie, growing up learning English and French from early childhood to late adolescence. In addition to the opportunities that the children had to learn and use English and French in Louisiana, their primary residence, they were fortunate to have spent many summer months in Quebec, Canada, where they were exposed to French spoken by monolingual francophone children of the same age. Caldas describes in a disarming way the efforts and strategies that he and his wife Suzanne took to ensure that their children acquired full competence in oral and written forms of both languages.

Their story is, on the one hand, very personal, since French is Suzanne's first language (Suzanne is from Quebec) and 'Steve' has French in his Cajun background, although he acquired English as his first language. The personal narrative is enriched considerably by the contrasts and similarities in how their three children individually respond to their bilingualism, a dimension of bilingual acquisition that is seldom reported (except see Vihman, 1998). At the same time, the personal narrative is richly embedded in other scientific and scholarly works on bilingualism, language learning, adolescence, and education. It is the counterpoint between personal and scholarly that makes for such an engaging and informative volume and a useful read for both researchers and other parents.

Caldas's treatment of language in this volume is broad in scope, with little detail about specific aspects of lexical and morpho-syntactic development. Those who are interested in the minutiae of language development are advised to examine other volumes (e.g., De Houwer, 1990; Deuchar & Quay, 2000, and Lanza, 1997) and the numerous reports that have been published in scientific journals. Rather, Caldas focuses on the children's general language proficiency and usage over the course of childhood and adolescence in home, school, and community contexts. He pays special attention to accent, not in a technical sense as one might find were this topic examined by a specialist in phonology, but rather as a barometer of the children's own views of their language competence and their efforts to fit in with their anglophone peers in Louisiana and their francophone peers in Quebec. He uses the children's experiences in Louisiana and Quebec to great advantage to illustrate the power of context in bilingual first language learners' social and language development – accent serves as an interesting gauge of the learners' own reactions to context and 'fitting in'. The data that Caldas reports here are best revealed through a detailed case study such as this, and indeed would be difficult to collect otherwise.

There is significant coverage of the children during their adolescent years, from 11 to 19 years of age. This is a period of bilingual development that has not been examined carefully by others (except see Zentella's (1999) work with Spanish-English adolescents in the U.S.) so that Caldas's contribution in these sections is particularly valuable to both parents who aim to raise their children bilingually and researchers who aim to understand bilingual first language acquisition across critical developmental periods. It is during Caldas's discussion of his children during adolescence that the primary themes of the book – family, school, and society, come together as he describes the critically important intersection of these factors in the children's construction of adolescent identity. Caldas documents how his and Suzanne's influences on their children's language development waned drastically during adolescence as peer influences grew, a not uncommon phenomenon. Peer influence grows during adolescence as teenagers actively seek to become part of the peer group. This can have significant consequences for the choices that teenage dual language learners make with respect to language and, indeed, their very decisions to continue with both languages or not, decisions that can mark the rest of their lives. The adolescent years present significant challenges not only to parents, like the Caldas-Caron family, but also to educators who strive to build bilingual programs that promote bilingualism across the secondary school years. Caldas reminds us that bilingual acquisition does not exist in a socio-cultural vacuum and that adolescence poses particular socio-cultural challenges. While Caldas does not provide concrete solutions to these challenges, he compels us to face them.

The distinctive feature of this book and its real strength is its focus on many issues that are given short shrift in other publications on bilingual first language acquisition – issues related to peer influence, cultural context, and the construction of language-related identities during adolescence. Those of us who work in bilingual first language acquisition areas are often cognizant of these issues, but usually focus elsewhere (except see Döpke's (1992), and Lanza's (1997) work on parental interaction and discourse styles). The general neglect of these topics is undoubtedly related, in part, to the difficulty in studying these issues. The bilingual acquisition researcher (student or professor) will find much of interest here that warrants further, focused investigation – for example: What role does language play in the identity of children raised bilingually? Is this the same for adolescents from minority and majority communities? How is cultural identity constructed in different language communities?

The challenges that peers and communities pose for raising children bilingually also represent the rewards of bilingual development. John, Stephanie, and Valerie have clearly been challenged in their dual language learning by their peers and by the pressures to integrate socially and culturally in Louisiana and in Quebec. In confronting these challenges, John, Stephanie, and Valerie, each in their individual ways, are changed and they become different from their peers who have lived their lives in monolingual communities with no or little contact with other language groups. These challenges were not easy, for these teenagers or for their parents, but the rewards appear to have been considerable. The future will reveal the full rewards and the reader cannot help but be curious about the lives of these young adults as they grow beyond their school years. Perhaps there will be a sequel ....

Fred Genesee
McGill University
June 17, 2005

References

Brown, R. (1973) *A First Language: The Early Stages*. Cambridge, MA: Harvard University Press.

De Houwer, A. (1990). *The Acquisition of Two Languages from Birth: A Case Study*. Cambridge: Cambridge University Press.

Deuchar, M. and Quay, S. (2000) *Bilingual Acquisition: Theoretical Implications of a Case Study*. Oxford: Oxford University Press.

Döpke, S. (1992) *One Parent One Language: An Interactional Approach*. Amsterdam: John Benjamins.

Lanza, E. (1997) *Language Mixing in Infant Bilingualism: A Sociolinguistic Perspective*. Oxford: Clarendon Press.

Meisel, J.M. (1986) Word order and case marking in early child language. Evidence from simultaneous acquisition of two first languages: French and German. *Linguistics* 24, 123–83.

Vihman, M. (1998) A developmental perspective on code-switching: Conversations between a pair of bilingual siblings. *International Journal of Bilingualism* 2, 45–84.

Zentella, A.C. (1999) *Growing up Bilingual*. Malden, MA: Blackwell.

Chapter 1
Introduction and Focus of the Book

Rearing children in two monolingual environments to be simultaneous biliterate-bilinguals who will speak their two languages with native-like fluency is a big challenge. The author and his wife experienced the challenge first hand, rearing three children from the cradle to young adulthood to be fluent French-English bilinguals who are functionally biliterate. Additionally, the children speak the target dialects of their languages with native-like fluency. In other words, maternal speakers of their varieties of French and English are likely to identify the children as native speakers of the language as well. What we have done is not at all unusual. Literally millions (perhaps even billions) of families have reared bilingual and even trilingual children (Romaine, 1995), and research studies have documented the many psycho-social dimensions of children acquiring multiple languages simultaneously (De Houwer, 1990; Deuchar & Quay, 2000; Fantini, 1985; Leopold, 1949; Okita, 2002; Ronjat, 1913; Saunders, 1982, 1988). What makes our experience unique is that we artificially orchestrated both the strategies, and to the extent possible, even the children's environments to ensure the success of our project. Additionally, we carefully documented our progress using a variety of research instruments and methodologies, including audiotape and videotape recordings, author constructed teacher and child French competency surveys, interviews with teachers, ethnographic fieldnotes, psychological and diagnostic testing, and standardized assessment instruments. This book draws from all of these sources to organize, present, analyze, and finally theorize about the process of rearing bilingual and biliterate children in two monolingual cultures through late adolescence. What we discovered in some instances validates existing linguistic theory, and in other cases squarely contradicts current conceptions about how, why, and when children learn to read, write, and speak two languages.

The vast majority of the world's multilinguals speak more than one language because of the circumstances of their lives. Most learned their languages effortlessly. Where parents have had to exert effort to ensure their children learned two languages, success has not been automatic (Okita, 2002). Had we made no efforts to ensure that our children learned to read, write, and speak two languages, they would likely be monolinguals like most American children, though perhaps able to speak a few French words and phrases, and recognize some written French. What I would like to do in this book is describe and analyze our very deliberate family bilingual-biliteracy project so that others might benefit from our experience, as well as to expand the body of research on what bilingual strategies work and why.

Based on our scientifically documented experience, I am able to validate certain specific strategies, which when carefully planned and faithfully executed, help in the formation of biliterate-bilingual children in the context of a monolingual society. This does not mean that such an endeavor would be easy for all families in all circumstances. In fact, given the very particular circumstances of our family's two social contexts, which are not typical of many immigrants around the world, some of the specifics of the strategies we employed would not be directly applicable or reproducible in other families. Still, many of the general principles that we validated, clarified, or discovered, would apply to most children in most families. Our project was in essence an extended social science laboratory experiment. There were costs and sacrifices associated with carrying out our project that some families either cannot or will not make. However, we were motivated by science in ways that would not move most families to action.

Depending upon the family and the specific environment, some costs to ensure that children become fluent biliterate-bilinguals can be very high indeed (Okita, 2002). It is also true, though, that the fruit of such an effort is priceless. To paraphrase a French saying: *'Une personne qui parle deux langues vaux deux personnes'* (A person who speaks two languages is worth two persons).

In the Beginning . . .

As important as a school foreign language immersion program could be to reviving and perpetuating an endangered tongue, an even more effective strategy is to pass along the tongue in the child's first, and for a time, most important social milieu – the family. Study after study has validated the critical importance of learning a language in infancy if one is to learn the language with native like-fluency and annunciation.[1] Our studies, too, have validated this linguistic reality. However, few studies have followed up on infant bilinguals to see what happens linguistically to these children as they move into, through, and out of adolescence. Do their language skills degrade? Can they 'forget' one of their two languages? How do they perceive their bilingualism? How does peer pressure affect their propensity to speak the minority language? Are they proud of the fact they can speak two languages, or do they hide this extraordinary ability?

These pages carefully document our family project to rear three bilingual-biliterate children in two different cultures – essentially monolingual English-speaking Louisiana, and totally monolingual French-speaking Québec. Importantly, the majority of our children's time, especially in their most linguistically formative years, was spent in English-speaking Louisiana. As a native French-speaking Canadian, and a native English-speaking American, my wife and I struggled to learn each other's language while in our twenties, long after the time acknowledged by neurobiologists and child psychologists to be the optimal period for second language acquisition. Being educators, and later researchers as well, we knew the importance of early socialization in learning anything fluently, including languages. So we started the linguistic socialization process from the first day in each of our children's lives.

The critical importance of early language acquisition was poignantly driven home to us in a single incident that ultimately proved to be the spark for this book. We were starry-eyed newlyweds, crossing the English Channel that separated the two countries that gave birth to our respective mother tongues. While idly observing a three-year-old boy happily playing between his two seated parents on the gently rocking ferry, our attention was drawn to the curious conversation taking place between the mother, who spoke to her child in English, and the father, who was addressing him in French. The young child would answer the mother in English, then immediately turn to the father and speak to him in French. My wife and I exchanged wide-eyed glances. After all, we were barely beyond the phase in our relationship where we had worn out well-thumbed French-English dictionaries in romantically inspired efforts to understand each other. But here, before us, was a child who could not have been speaking for much more than a year, if that long, and yet he had already mastered two entirely different linguistic systems!

We believe that the flash of inspiration struck us at that wondrous, 'teachable moment'. We decided to rear our yet-to-be-born offspring in exactly the way this Frenchman and his English wife appeared to be rearing their child. Before we reached Calais, it was settled: I would only speak English to our progeny, and my wife would only speak French. This is more formally known as the 'one parent, one language' approach (Döpke, 1992). Thus was born our project, which after 19 years of continuous, concerted, and conscientious effort, and some duly documented modification, is essentially completed. Our three children are fluent French-English biliterate-bilinguals, who indeed speak both languages with more facility than either of the authors (Caldas & Caron-Caldas, 1992, 1997, 1999, 2000, 2002).

It is important to clarify up-front that even before our children were born we had determined to rear them to speak Québécois French and American English with native-like fluency. That is, we agreed to employ whatever strategies we could to ensure that our children learned to speak each dialect like monolingual speakers of these respective languages. Both my wife and I had identifiable accents in our second tongues, and we wanted to rear our children to speak both of their languages without our 'linguistic markers'. Perhaps our goal was unrealistic, misplaced, or even naive, but it was still an explicit goal we both shared. The study of accents – how they are acquired, changed, and lost – is a legitimate field of study in linguistics (Moyer, 2004). More than scientific, though, ours was originally a personal goal. On the one hand, we wanted the children to be able to speak so well in either tongue that native speakers of their respective dialects couldn't tell they weren't natives. But as a social scientist, I was (and remain) quite interested in how the children's environments were influencing their developing accents. I had also intended to gauge the accomplishment of this objective, but discovered some years into the project that my instruments were too imprecise and impressionistic, and I didn't really have the linguistic expertise to apply the proper measures.

However, since the issue of 'accents' reared its head continuously, in ways I'll describe in this book, I could not ignore it. Indeed, the children themselves raised the issue so often that avoiding a discussion of 'accents' would result in an incomplete picture of our family project. Moreover, I discovered that there truly is an 'impressionistic', subjective dimension to how individuals perceive accents. Thus, rather than treating the issue of accent acquisition from a morphological perspective, that is, measuring precisely how the children were pronouncing French and English words at various times, this study approaches the issue sociolinguistically. I try to longitudinally document the following: (1) how we the parents, friends and family perceived the children's changing accents, (2) how the children's francophone teachers in Louisiana and Québec perceived the children's accents, and (3) how the children themselves perceived their own accents and how their attitudes towards having an accent changed over time. What I discovered about 'perceptions' seems worthy of reporting in and of itself, regardless the 'reality'. My own perceptions of accents changed over the course of this project, as I came to understand just how subjective this dimension of speech really seems to be: we don't all hear each other the same way.

Our having chosen to rear children who speak French and English like native, monolingual speakers is in no way meant to imply that those who speak accented versions of a language (like my French, for example) speak an inferior version of the language. We were, quite simply, interested in determining what factors account for an individual's learning to speak two languages simultaneously like a native. According to Ada and Baker (2001), only a minority of bilinguals achieve this level of bilingualism, and we wanted to know why this was the case.

I wholeheartedly subscribe to Zentella's (2004) emphasis on the importance of diversity and inclusion, acknowledging that one does not need to speak a 'standard' or 'unaccented' version of a language to either be considered bilingual, or to have one's membership in a social group validated. Three of my four grandparents spoke English with an accent influenced by another tongue (Portuguese and French), yet all were American citizens who were quite proud of this fact. I consider it absolutely reprehensible to discriminate against any individual for the way they speak (or do not speak) any language. I share Zentella's (2004: xi) concerns that:

> ... if we judge our proficiency in either of our languages against an unrealistic monolingual norm, inevitably we find ourselves wanting. For many members of ethnolinguistic minorities in the United States, whose ability to speak two languages may be the only advantage they enjoy over English monolinguals, debilitating feelings of linguistic insecurity can affect the development of their home language and of English, as well as their academic progress.

'Debilitating feelings of linguistic insecurity' describes well the psychological injury left behind in the wake of intolerance towards French-speaking Cajuns in Louisiana. Sensitive to my ancestors' tragic history, I recognize that the task of trying to rear perfectly bilingual children does not necessarily entail rearing children who speak the target language exactly like a native. Again I reiterate: We undertook this goal in part as a scientific experiment, curious which factors we would have to manipulate to achieve our pre-specified objectives, one of which was rearing children to speak two languages like monolingual native speakers.

Ensuring that the children learned to read, write, and speak English turned out to be the easy part for us. Actually, it was almost effortless on our part. This is in spite of the fact, as we will discuss in Chapter 4, that English would be spoken with much less frequency in our home than was French for the most formative part of our children's lives. Even given the emphasis placed on French in our home, periodic French language immersion in Québec, and the glorification of our French-speaking heritage in every milieu in which our children have lived and gone to school, none of these influences have been stronger than the children's adolescent peer cultures. This became painfully clear to us when we asked our son, who is two years older than our identical twin girls, if he spoke French with other French-speaking students in his American middle school. John's answer was an unequivocal, flat, 'no'. His reason? 'It's not cool' (age 11;10). Chapter 8 delves into the dynamics of early adolescence on the children's changing language preferences.

To us, one point became increasingly clear: in spite of our best efforts to Gallicize him, our son was turning out to be a pretty typical all-American boy, albeit a clandestinely bilingual one while around his American peers (during middle school, anyway). During the same time-frame that our son let us know that French-speaking was not 'cool' at his school, our twin girls, who had been in an elementary school French immersion program for the previous three years, not only spoke significantly more French at home, but had a decidedly more favorable attitude toward bilingualism than did our son (Caldas et al., 1998). We credited their staunch *'Parlez Français!'* retorts to his taunting 'English! English! English!' outbursts to their school French immersion program – of which John attended for only one semester. We were in for a surprise.

Two years later, much to our mutual chagrin, we watched the twins adopt almost wholesale their brother's indifference and at times even hostile attitude toward French speaking in the Louisiana context, especially around their *French-immersion* peers (Caldas & Caron-Caldas, 2000). Thus, we began to soberly reassess the limits of a school language immersion program, especially when it came up against adolescence in America. We discuss our children's school French-immersion experiences in Chapter 6, and draw several salient lessons from our observations, some of which run counter to scholarly thinking about these programs.

However, before the reader concludes, quite wrongly, that English won the day, our study included a second, non-English-speaking milieu: French-speaking Québec, Canada. It was in this decidedly non-anglophone environment that we saw our children put aside their English, hide it even–and pick up the French standard. Moreover, they continued to wave this French-speaking, *fleur de lis* standard just as vigorously, if not more so, as they moved into and through adolescence. Indeed, it was due to Québec that we were able to confirm beyond any measure of doubt that our experiment to raise perfectly biliterate-bilingual children had succeeded. Still, we once again have to give the children's peers – francophone in this case – much more credit for influencing John, Valerie, and Stephanie's linguistic behavior than we, the parents, had over our children during adolescence.

Our study includes several longitudinal qualitative and quantitative measures of French-speaking, reading, writing, thinking, and attitudes toward French-English bilingualism from which I develop my conclusions and recommendations. I elaborate more on these measures in some detail in my methodological discussion in Chapter 3, and again in Chapter 11 where I present detailed analyses of our quantitative measures. Non-specialists can easily gloss over or even skip these chapters and still get the main points of the book. As ethnographers know all too well, quantification is not everything (to put it mildly). When I watch my children carrying on fast-paced conversations in French with native speakers, and then observe them shift immediately back into English without missing a syllable, I 'know' at another, less quantifiable level, that I am observing the fruit of years of conscious, though at times indirect, effort. It is this conscious, concerted, systematic approach to rearing bilingual and biliterate children, and documenting the consequences of our approaches, which sets our experience apart from the linguistic experiences of literally tens of millions of multilingual individuals throughout the world.

The vast majority of multilinguals learn their respective languages as a result of necessity. These include the Spanish-speaking Mexican child whose parents immigrate to the U.S. and enroll her in an all-English-speaking school, the Vietnamese college student who decides to pursue an advanced degree at a university in Paris, or an Albanian refugee from the Balkans' conflict who flees to Germany and finds work in an all-German-speaking factory. These individuals essentially had no choice but to learn a second language. And they do. If I have learned anything about acquiring a language, I have learned that output is roughly equivalent to input. In general, the more one hears a tongue spoken (input), the greater the likelihood that one will speak the tongue (output), and speak it correctly (or at least in the same way that it is 'inputed'). As obvious as this simple maxim may seem to many readers, otherwise perfectly intelligent academics have suggested that there is no relationship between how much a language one is exposed to, and one's proficiency in that language (Crawford, 1998). This very sensitive issue has arisen in the context of bilingual education in the United States. While the findings of this case study cannot be directly generalizable to broader populations of students in either the U.S. or Canada, our findings can still provide useful insight into how individuals learn to speak two languages. A central finding of our research is that the children learned to speak their two languages as a consequence of being immersed in French and English with native speakers of both tongues, with extended periods of little or no recourse to the other language. Moreover, I demonstrate a direct correlation between the degree of immersion in a given language (input) and the degree of proficiency in that language (output).

The situation in our family was different from the above international scenarios in an important way: had we never made any conscious effort to rear biliterate-bilingual children, they would be essentially monolingual English speakers. Oh, they might have picked up the odd French word from their mother, or perhaps even a few Cajun words out of curiosity. But they would not be French speakers, and even less, readers and writers of Voltaire's tongue. As is explained in detail in the Chapter 7 discussion of the use of media, we continuously battled the English assault on our children in the U.S. context, to the extent of controlling their exposure to American television, radio, film, and videocassettes. We forced ourselves to speak French, even when around English-speaking relatives, and even though we knew we risked being viewed as rude and impolite (and indeed, probably were considered ill-mannered at times). Most individuals 'go with the linguistic flow'. Not us: we bucked it – that is, as long as it seemed a fruitful course to follow. There did come a point in our project, though, when we realized that 'bucking' English in the American context was likely to be counter-productive. This point came during our children's adolescence, an interesting and essential dimension to our project that we relate in some detail in Chapters 8–10. Adolescence and the children's peer environments were, ironically, the variables that ensured the fluent acquisition of French by the children.

Given the enormous amount of time, effort, research and money that we had to invest to rear bilingual children in an essentially monolingual environment in the U.S., to suggest that it is somehow criminal to speak to children at home in a language other than English, as a Texas judge did ('Woman Ordered', 1995), does not seem entirely rational. The judge ruled that it constituted child abuse for a west Texas mother to speak only Spanish to her five-year-old daughter, since it might doom her to a life as a monolingual Spanish-speaking maid. This judge's approach to languages seems as likely to fuel xenophobic fears as it is to perpetuate the speaking of English in the U.S. The next chapter frames these and related issues in the larger historical context of language in the United States.

Knowledge of the facts, and the dissemination of that knowledge, would go far to dispelling myths about language and language acquisition. This is a central rationale for this book. It has been well documented that the vast majority of immigrants to the United States are eager to learn English. Indeed, second generation children are not only competent speakers of English, but many no longer even prefer to speak the mother language of their immigrant parents (Bankston *et al.*, 1997; McCollum, 1993; Portes & Schauffler, 1994). Most third generation descendants of immigrants do not even have a choice of which language to speak, since they are effectively monolingual English speakers.

It is hard to study the linguistic history of North America and conclude that English speaking in either Canada or the United States is, or ever has been, somehow threatened. One need simply broach this issue with just about any Québécois or Cajun, both of whom will be more than happy to clarify the hegemony of English for you. Moreover, as an indicator of just how hegemonic English truly is, the Cajun is the more likely of the two to answer you in Shakespeare's tongue. In some parts of the United States in particular, what is threatened is the bilingualism that many American children bring to school. This is examined in more detail in the next chapter. We, in our own small way, decided to buck the tide and fight the good fight to preserve one of America's endangered languages. Chapter 10 focuses on the ultimate fruit of this effort, documenting the emerging linguistic identities of the children in middle and late adolescence as they moved toward linguistic identity achievement, and beyond the 'imaginary audiences' of their early adolescent peer groups (Enright *et al.*, 1979; Lapsley *et al.*, 1988). This period was marked by a diminishing self-consciousness in the spontaneous use of their two languages, increasing competency in the use of both languages, and an increasing linguistic self-confidence and pride in themselves as bilinguals. This book details the strategies, the battles, the milieus, the assessments and measures, conclusions, lessons, and ultimately, the project's success.

Note

1. See Döpke, (2000), for several in-depth studies highlighting the facility with which infants and young children learn two languages simultaneously – and effortlessly.

Chapter 2
Bilingualism in America

Introduction

Bilingualism in the United States has been under attack. Within the past two decades more than a dozen states have moved to legally declare 'English' as their official state language, bringing to 23 the total number of states that have done so by the turn of the new century (Barker *et al.*, 2001). The 'English-only' movement has also been active on the national American political scene as well. In 1983, after failing to get a national amendment to the U.S. constitution making English the official national language, Senator Samuel Hayakawa (D-HI), along with John Tanton, formed the advocacy group *U.S. English* to promote the 'official English' cause. At the turn of the 21st century, it boasted a membership of about 1.4 million, and included many well-known celebrities (U.S. English, 2001). As recently as the 106th Congress, there were four 'English-Only' bills pending in the House of Representatives (Barker *et al.*, 2001) which would mandate making English the official language of the federal government of the United States, and effectively limit all government business and printing to English. Even former senator Bob Dole (R-KS) endorsed the move to make English the official language of the United States during his unsuccessful run for president in 1996 (Facts on File, 1996).

It is important to place this 'movement' in its broader historical context, as such crusades are nothing new in the U.S. Moreover, the casualties of these sporadic linguistic pogroms – lost bilingualism – are not a new phenomenon either. Louisiana, one of the two settings of the current study, is a particularly interesting case in point, and one to which I shall return shortly. The Bayou State has been through the entire cycle of official bilingualism, rabid anti-bilingual xenophobia, and finally, a rediscovered emphasis on the value of the bilingual child.

Historical Overview

The current fear among some Americans that English is threatened as the predominant language is older than the country itself. As early as 1753, the venerable Benjamin Franklin expressed concern over the degree of

German spoken in Pennsylvania (Castellanos, 1992). Our family has crossed Pennsylvania twice a year for more than a dozen years, and we have yet to hear a single word of German. So, we suspect Franklin's fear was a bit exaggerated.

Since the country came into existence in 1776 with its Declaration of Independence from Great Britain, language xenophobia in the United States has waxed and waned depending on such factors as immigration, war, the perceived threat of communism, the economic climate, and now, probably terrorism too. The most recent 'English-only' movement, which began in the 1980s, is closely linked to the country's newest wave of massive non-English-speaking immigration to the United States, during which literally millions of new immigrants flocked to the U.S. This influx of immigrants marks the largest movement of people to North America since the beginning of the 20th century, when two of the author's non-English-speaking ancestors arrived from Italy and Portugal. Evidence that language xenophobia has reached a fevered pitch in the United States is revealed in actions like a recent court decree handed down by the aforementioned state district judge in Texas.

English has traditionally been viewed as a primary tool for assimilating new immigrant groups into American society (Gordon, 1964). Indeed, English was seen as the fire that brought the 'melting pot' to a boil. Theodore Roosevelt put this sentiment bluntly, immediately after the greatest wave of immigration ever to the U.S.: '... we have room for but one language here, and that is the English language, for we intend to see that the crucible turns our people out as Americans, of American nationality, and not as dwellers in a polyglot boarding house' (cited in Edwards, 1994: 166).

The disturbing aspect of the current English-only movement and previous nativist movements in the U.S. is not the emphasis on the importance of English. A common language is a very important national asset. Indeed, it is perhaps the most important factor in uniting nations and peoples, facilitating business, trade, education, and upward mobility. What is potentially injurious is the historical American viewpoint that proficiency in English and abandoning one's non-English native language go hand in hand (as hinted at by Teddy Roosevelt). One can see this 'monolingual' attitude in the American government's historical treatment of Native Americans. For example, in a model government boarding school set up for Native Americans in Pennsylvania in 1879, students were forbidden to speak their native tongues, and were physically punished when they did (Portes & Schauffler: 1994:96). Neither has the 'English-only' mania been limited to Americans. As colonial missionaries in Africa, our English cousins not only banned African languages in the universities they founded on that continent, but even forbad the 'drum languages', a form of communication which reproduced native speech tones (Gaines, 1996).

Educational Issues

While the belief that monolinguism is somehow preferable to bilingualism may seem narrow, quaint, and outmoded, the belief that bilingualism hinders academic achievement seems to be more widespread (discussed in Makin *et al.*, 1995; Portes & Schauffler, 1994, 1996). Once again, this perspective is not uniquely American. As far back as the 1920s, the Danish linguist Jespersen (1922) argued that bilingualism was a disadvantage because a child could learn neither language as well as he could learn just one. Jespersen justified his position by speculating that learning two languages unnecessarily taxed the brain. As outrageous as this position might seem, one of the children in the current study, in a moment of frustration with schoolwork, paraphrased Jespersen's argument 80 years later when he declared, 'I have twice as much stuff in my head as everyone else. I have to remember twice as much as everyone else. Jeeez, it isn't fair!' (John, aged 14;4. Discussed in Chapter 9).

Reynold (1928), a German, stated that bilingualism led to language mixing and language confusion, which in turn resulted in a decreased ability to think clearly. This perception still lingered some 40 years later, as evidenced by Weisgerber's (1966) stance that bilingualism was detrimental in part because humans were basically monolingual, and that being bilingual was like trying to belong to two religions at the same time. Even the Association of (English-speaking) Catholic School Principals of Montreal published an official statement as recently as 1969 that read: 'We are of the opinion that the average child cannot cope with two languages of instruction and to try to do so leads to insecurity, language interference, and academic retardation' (p. 12).

More recently, some of the impetus behind California's proposition 227, limiting bilingual education, stems from a concern that maintaining a child's minority language hurts his/her academic achievement in English (Hakuta, 1999). Indeed, this position has gained much ground in the United States, and fuels the anti-bilingual education movement in the U.S. This movement has spread beyond California to states like Massachusetts, which passed a referendum in 2002 severely restricting bilingual education. There is a major debate raging about whether some bilingual programs for limited English proficient students in the U.S. may hinder the child's acquisition of English. Whether or not this is true is not germane to the position that being bilingual hurts one's academics. Toward the end of the book I will make some general observations about the efficacy of bilingual education programs based on what we've discovered in our project. The bilingual education debate is more complex than either side usually admits.

Historically, in spite of xenophobia, speaking more than one language has almost always been viewed as an advantage. For example, in the 1600s, the philosopher John Locke advocated teaching English children a second language (preferably French) as soon as they learned English, sometime around age three (from 'Some Thoughts Concerning Education' as cited in Ozmon & Craver, 2002). After they learned the second language, which he believed should only take a year or two (a position that has since been validated scientifically), Locke proposed that they should commence learning a third tongue. Benjamin Franklin, in spite of his concern over German-speaking Pennsylvanians, credited his ability to speak French as a major advantage in his life (Franklin, 1932). Indeed, Franklin's ability to effectively persuade the French – *in French* – that the American colonies needed France's help during the Revolutionary War is a major reason there even is a United States of America today (Schiff, 2003).

Contrary to the belief that speaking more than one language is somehow damaging to thinking processes, a body of current research is emerging which suggests that multilinguals may actually have more highly developed cognitive abilities than monolinguals (Ben- Zeev, 1977; Bialystok, 1988, 2001; Diaz, 1983; Hakuta, 1986; Lambert & Tucker, 1972; and Peal & Lambert, 1962), though some point out that the research is not conclusive (Jarvis *et al.*, 1995). Balkan (1970) discovered that early bilinguals (before age four) scored significantly higher on tests of numerical aptitude, verbal flexibility, perceptual ability, and general reasoning than either later bilinguals or monolinguals. Peal and Lambert (1962) noted that bilinguals who were matched with a control group of monolinguals performed significantly better than the monolinguals on both non-verbal and verbal IQ tests. They stated, '… it appears that our bilinguals, instead of suffering from mental confusion or a "language handicap" are actually profiting from a "language asset"' (p. 15). Scott (1973) found that bilingual English-Canadians demonstrated greater 'divergent thinking' than a control group of monolinguals. Carringer (1974) reported that Spanish-English bilinguals scored higher than a control group of monolinguals in all aspects of creativity, verbal and figural fluency, flexibility, and originality. Turnbull *et al.* (2001) reported that third grade French immersion students in Canada who were instructed in French performed as well on tests in English – including Math – as their peers taught only in English. In a study of

French-immersion students in Louisiana, Caldas and Boudreaux (1999) found that native English-speaking students who are taught academic subjects only in French scored significantly higher on Math and English standardized achievement tests administered *in English* than did their counterparts immersed in English-only classes. Döpke's (2000) volume is replete with the marvelous abilities of very young bilingual children to quickly sort out two complex language systems and produce language specific structures as early as 18 months old – an amazing cognitive feat by any measure.

Though our data on this point are largely subjective and impressionistic (and therefore not conclusive), the children in the current study seem to have in no way suffered as a result of being reared simultaneous bilinguals from birth, and, we suspect, have benefited academically and cognitively as a consequence of their biliguality (they've certainly benefited socially and culturally). Their bilingualism definitely seems to have inspired their interests in other tongues, and facilitated the acquisition of Spanish for Valerie and Stephanie, and a fourth tongue, German, for Valerie. Though linguists are still pondering the reasons for the enhanced cognitive functioning of bilinguals, one intriguing theory links the superior academic performance of bilinguals to their earlier and greater awareness of the arbitrariness of language – apparently liberating their thinking processes (Ianco-Worrall, 1972). This is indeed what the current study discovered with regard to the children's flexible attitudes towards French and English profanity, discussed in detail in Chapter 5.

A noted linguistic psychologist also suggested that since multiple languages are stored in the same small part of the brain, the increased number of neural connections and interconnections in the brains of bilingual children could explain their superior cognitive abilities (F. Genesee, personal communication, May 12, 2001). Some brain research using functional magnetic resonance imaging (fMRI) has more quantitatively determined that the neural substrates of bilingual brains are different from individuals who function in only one language (Wartenburger *et al.*, 2003), and that the brains of bilinguals handle two languages simultaneously in neurologically very sophisticated ways (Rodriguez-Fornells *et al.*, 2002). Bialystok (2001) suggests that very young bilinguals have extensive practice exercising language inhibitory functions (i.e., mentally stopping one language to speak in another), and that this practice carries over to processing in other cognitive domains. Bialystok speculates that a bilingual's brain, therefore, may differ from a monolingual's in those regions that are involved with tasks requiring this specific type of process (e.g. executive function, inhibition and control).

Klein et al. (1994), and Klein et al. (1995) were the first to use functional neuroimaging techniques to examine language organization in bilingual individuals. They found common cortical substrates for highly proficient English-French bilingual speakers when they conducted searches within and across languages. In a follow-up study of English-Chinese bilinguals, Klein et al. (1999) explored how their original findings might generalize to very different languages. Their findings contradict the view that second language learners process language in a different way from monolinguals, even when the languages are distinct. Using positron emission tomography (PET) on a French-English bilingual, Klein (2003) also found evidence that at least at the single-word level, age of acquisition is not a significant factor either in determining functional organization in the brain, results which tend to contradict Wartenburger et al.'s (2003) findings. However, Klein et al. (1994, 1995) and Klein et al. (2001) did observe activity in the left basal ganglia when native English speakers produced words in their L2 French, possibly due to the greater cognitive effort required. Speaking on the state of the research in her highly specialized field, Klein does agree that it is plausible that increased neural networking in bilingual brains could have beneficial cognitive effects. However, she is inclined to believe that any benefits would more likely apply to specific areas of thought processing rather than in the more global fashion that has been suggested in earlier research (personal communication, D. Klein, September 9, 2003). As for contradictory research findings, Klein comments that there are still major methodological issues to work out in the field of neurolinguistics, including better experimental controls, before more definitive conclusions can be drawn about the effects of bilingualism on cognition.

As for the hypothesis that monolinguals can somehow focus academically in ways that bilinguals cannot (ostensibly due to 'interference' from the dormant second language), research suggests that the complete linguistic assimilation of immigrant groups in the U.S. does not necessarily ensure they will perform better in English schooling. For example, second generation bilingual Vietnamese in New Orleans have more success in school than their fellow immigrants who speak only English (Bankston & Zhou, 1995; Zhou & Bankston, 1998). Moreover, not only do these students perform better than their linguistically assimilated counterparts, but bilingual Vietnamese even do better on standardized tests than native-born Louisianans (Bankston et al., 1997).

Why is it important to establish a possible strong link between multilingualism and higher cognitive functioning? One reason is that if such a link truly exists, it may then place the impetus on educators and policy makers to not only tolerate bilingual children, but to even foster bilingualism as a way of helping individuals to develop to their fullest intellectual capacities. Plus, if there is a bilingual advantage, then there is yet an additional benefit to those educational programs whose aims are to preserve, maintain, and re-establish the speaking of a second language among young people. Of course, establishing a strong connection between bilingualism and doing well academically does not necessarily give the global stamp of approval to all bilingual education programs, a point to which the book returns in the concluding chapter.

The Language Revival

In spite of the language xenophobia of some, there has been an ethnic awakening in the United States, with a newfound interest in reviving and maintaining non-English languages (Fishman, 2001). This American 'revival' may in part be linked to a larger global 'ethnic revival', of which there are many examples of efforts to preserve and pass on endangered languages. These include efforts to preserve Gaelic in Ireland, ensure the hegemony of French in Québec, and save Welsh in Wales. Of course, the re-establishment of Hebrew in Israel following a 2000-year lapse is perhaps the best example of a success-story to revive an ancient language and enshrine its usage in everyday life. This 'language revival' movement has also visited Louisiana. One of the major reasons for rearing the three children in this study to be French-English bilinguals was a desire to preserve the French language and heritage of Louisiana. Another was to pass on the ancestral language of both the author and his wife. Heritage is a powerful motivator for learning a language (Caussinus, 2004; Noels & Clément, 1989; Oxford & Shearin, 1994), and was used as a strategy with some success in the present study up to the point of the children's adolescence – at which time it became a completely ineffective motivator (discussed in Chapter 8). Heritage was probably a much stronger motivator for the author to learn to speak French than for his children (discussed in Chapter 4).

The Special Case of Louisiana

Louisiana has traditionally been a bilingual state. Indeed, it is the only state in the American union that is officially French-English bilingual (Mazel, 1977). Moreover, unlike many other parts of the U.S., there is no movement to declare English as the state's official language. In 1990, roughly 25% of the population of 4.3 million Louisianans identified their ancestry as French, Acadian, or French Canadian, and more than 260,000 Louisianans indicated that they spoke French at home (U.S. Census

Bureau, 1990). This number shrunk to 198,784 Louisiana francophones in the 2000 Census, as the last of the large generation of native, traditional French-speaking Cajuns decreases due to mortality.

Historically, France claimed the territory of Louisiana as her own in 1682, and French settlers began arriving in a steady stream shortly thereafter. The largest single migration of French speakers to Louisiana occurred from 1759 to about 1785, when thousands of exiled Acadians (including another of the author's ancestors) began arriving in what was then a Spanish colony. The Acadians had been expelled from areas of Canada now called New Brunswick, Nova Scotia, and Prince Edward Island, in part because they refused to become model English subjects and abandon their language and religion. These Cajuns, a derivation of the word Acadian, and other French-speaking Louisianans, maintained their French language even after the colony was purchased from Napoleon by the United States in 1803 (Louisiana was again temporarily French from 1800 to 1803). In 1806 there was another massive migration of French-speaking individuals to Louisiana, this time about 9000 Creoles, 6000 of whom were black, fleeing the revolution in Haiti (Brasseaux & Conrad, 1992).

Louisiana's first governor, monolingual English-speaking William Claiborne, lamented, 'not one in fifty of the old inhabitants appear to me to understand the English language' (cited in Crawford, 1992: 40). When Louisiana became a state in 1812, it was the first and last U.S. state admitted in which native English-speakers were in the minority (Crawford, 1992).

Many of the French-speaking communities in Louisiana were tight-knit, and located in isolated, lowland areas of the state, one of which was a venue for 10 years of the current study. These communities clung tenaciously to their language and heritage, referring to the English-speaking settlers who began arriving in the state as 'Les Américains' well into the 20th and even 21st centuries. Indeed, at the turn of the 21st century there were still a few elderly native-born Louisianans who spoke only French. Throughout the 19th century and until about roughly 1920, entire communities in south Louisiana were filled with white Cajuns and black Creoles who coexisted happily together speaking no English. When the legendary Huey Long campaigned for governor in 1924 and 1928, he needed the aid of a French interpreter when he gave his stump speeches in the southwest region of Louisiana called Acadiana (Williams, 1969).

French language threatened

Following the end of World War I, isolationist and anti-foreign sentiment in the United States was particularly strong. There was growing momentum throughout state legislatures across the country to limit the teaching of foreign languages in schools. In the Mid-West this sentiment was primarily anti-German (Alexander & Alexander, 1998; Crawford, 1992) and resulted in the Nebraska legislature passing legislation forbidding teaching in any language other than English. The Nebraska legislation stated in part that:

> Section 1. No person, individually or as a teacher, shall, in any private, denominational, parochial or public school, teach any subject to any person in any language than the English language. (As cited in Alexander & Alexander, 1998: 254).

In Louisiana, the xenophobia immediately following WWI was decidedly anti-French. However, the Bayou State went one step further than most, and actually enshrined its anti- 'foreign language' sentiment in its state constitution. Article 12, Section 12 of the 1921 Louisiana state constitution stated that:

> The general exercises in the public schools shall be conducted in the English language. (West's, 1977: 696).

French was the primary language of instruction in many Acadian south Louisiana schools when this constitutional prohibition was passed. This prohibition against teaching in French, combined with growing popular anti-French-speaking sentiment, marked the decline of the language in what is still an officially bilingual state.

Numerous older Cajuns who paid the price for this 'anti-foreign' sentiment have shared with the author their experiences of being physically punished and mentally humiliated for speaking French while on school grounds. One Cajun woman described how a Catholic nun ridiculed her on a regular basis for her thick French accent at school (Mme. Blanchard, personal communication, November 1, 1992). She was also punished for using the French word '*mais*' (but) which she habitually used to preface her English sentences. She was forced to write the phrase 'I will not say "*mais*" in school', hundreds of times, and often wrote the phrase even before she was punished – because she was sure she would slip up and say it anyway. As recently as April 2004, the author observed two elderly Cajun women speaking English to each other at an Acadiana Wal-Mart store, but prefacing their sentences with 'mais' and 'cher' (dear). Other Cajuns told the author tales of being paddled, kneeling on rice, or of having to put their nose in the corner of the classroom for speaking French at school. Some told of whispering to each other in French, lest a school official overhear them, and punish them.

A college professor told the author the story of how his Cajun grandfather quit school in the fourth grade in the 1920s rather than stop speaking French. The girl seated in front of him in his rural, southwest Louisiana one-room schoolhouse whispered to him in French. The teacher overheard the French, and demanded to know who spoke it. When no one would 'turn in' the young girl, the teacher lined up all the boys and 'switched' them one-by-one. Before it was his turn to be punished, the man jumped out the classroom window and never returned to school again. He started a life of trapping the next day (I. Esters, personal communication, May 2, 2001).

Those who spoke French in Louisiana during this period of anti-foreign passion were made to feel inferior to English-speaking Louisianans. The daughter of an elderly French-speaking woman explained to the author that her mother so closely associated the French accent (of which the mother had a heavy one) with ignorance, that she could not understand why bilingual Cajun governor Edwin Edwards was not ashamed to speak publicly with such heavily accented English (S. Starling, personal communication, November 12, 1991). Moreover, many Cajuns came to believe that not only was their English sub-standard, but so was their French. To this day, it is hard to initiate a conversation with a French-speaking Cajun or Creole without first hearing an apology for the way they speak. Their conversations often begin with, 'I don't speak the good French, *non*', or the equivalent expression in French, '*Je parle pas le bon français*'. What many Louisiana French speakers have never been told, however, is that their way of speaking is unique and has been classified as a language all its own: an indigenous language of Louisiana with its own dictionary (Daigle, 1984).

Resurgence of French pride

Since the mid-1960s, there has been a transformation in the way the Cajun French culture and language are viewed. Where there was once hostility to native French speakers, there is now a sense of urgency to preserve the threatened language (Caldas, 1998; Caldas & Boudreaux, 1999; Caldas & Caron-Caldas, 1992; Lowy *et al.*, 1985). This is due in part to the formation of a state government agency in 1968 called 'The Council for the Development of French in Louisiana' (CODOFIL). Its primary goal is to promote French speaking in Louisiana for the 'economic, cultural, and tourist benefit of the state' (Elaine Clément, personal communication, November 6, 1997). CODOFIL initiated a major push to teach French in all elementary schools. Hundreds of French teachers have been brought into the state from francophone countries. Indeed, the author met his wife and frequent co-author as a consequence of a CODOFIL exchange program. In fall 2003, for example, Louisiana brought to the state 108 teachers from Belgium, 107 teachers from France, 67 from French-speaking Canadian provinces, 28 from francophone Africa, and 6 from Haiti (D. Côté, personal communication, April 30, 2004). Moreover, French immersion programs have sprung up in several Louisiana parishes, where thousands of Louisiana children are now instructed primarily in French. The three children who are the subject of the present study, but especially the twin girls, have benefited from these programs. Thus, though practically an entire generation of French speakers was lost due to official and unofficial harassment of French speaking, a new generation of French-English bilinguals is arising – and, incidentally, flourishing academically (Bankens & Akins, 1989; Caldas & Boudreaux, 1999). The big question is whether they will speak French outside of class. Based on the findings of this study, it appears not to be the case. This issue is addressed in more detail in Chapter 6.

The resurrection of French in Louisiana is taking place within the greater, emerging world view that maintaining minority languages is a social justice imperative of government (Corson, 1992), and that government language policies can indeed help save endangered languages (Hornberger, 1998). The example of Law 101 in Québec, which dictates precisely how large the font size should be on English and French commercial signs, is a dramatic case for just how far government can go to protect a minority tongue. As noted above, it is becoming more difficult for governments to justify refusing students' dual language instruction on pedagogical grounds. There is an accumulating body of research which points to the effectiveness of foreign language immersion programs in not only teaching a second language (Genesee, 1987; Lambert & Tucker, 1972), but, as mentioned earlier, in promoting higher cognitive abilities in children. The same success has been noted for 'two-way 'bilingual programs, which in 1994 were operating in a total of 169 U.S. schools, and which are primarily focused on Spanish-English (Christian, 1994). By 2003, this number had grown to 271 programs in 24 states and the District of Columbia (Center for Applied Linguistics, 2003). (Two-way bilingual programs are much like Louisiana's French-immersion programs, differing principally in that they include students from the target language [e.g., Spanish] as well as English backgrounds.)

So, what can be concluded about situations like Louisiana's, where children fluent in English are being taught in French, and are thus becoming bilingual and biliterate in the second language while learning the regular school subject matter? Quite simply, if preservation of the second, endangered language is the goal, then there is probably no better way to ensure its survival, especially if the threatened tongue is no longer spoken in the home. Moreover, there is a plethora of research reports that point to the academic competence, and even supremacy, of the bilingual products of immersion programs (Bankens & Akins, 1989; Boudreaux & Caldas, 1998a, 1998b; Caldas & Boudreaux, 1999; Christian, 1994; Snow, 1990). Still, as will be demonstrated from the findings in this study, learning to speak the minority language and actually speaking it is not necessarily the same thing.

Louisiana has come full circle: from a predominantly French-speaking state, to an officially bilingual one, to one which was aggressively extinguishing its French, and finally, to a state that has decided to preserve its French-speaking heritage. Other states too, like California and Massachusetts, are wrestling with issues related to bilingualism, though their circumstances are somewhat different – as are the solutions they have chosen. Areas in the United States which have been experiencing massive non-English-speaking immigration are struggling with how to teach immigrant children to read, write, and speak fluent English, while maintaining the child's native minority language. The challenge facing Louisiana is taking native English-speaking children and producing a 'balanced bilingual' who will read, write, and speak fluent French.

Adolescence poses a formidable threat to the attainment of bilingualism and the speaking of a minority tongue, as students feel strong societal and peer pressure to conform linguistically (Caldas & Caron-Caldas, 1999, 2000, 2001, 2002; Christian, 1994; Landry & Allard, 1991). Getting children to spontaneously speak a non-English language with their teenage American peers is perhaps the ultimate test of success for any program dedicated to preserving a 'foreign' language on American soil. The research shared in this book suggests that this is a test which few programs, including Louisiana's French-immersion programs, are likely to pass. Even Louisiana's notorious Gallic stubbornness is unlikely to provide the edge that would no doubt be needed to help the state pass this important linguistic milestone on the way to preserving its rich linguistic heritage.

Thus, we now return to the much more specific issues with which the present volume deals: a detailed description, analysis, and interpretation of a project to rear bilingual and biliterate children in two monolingual cultures who will speak their two languages with fluency. The next chapter discusses the methodology employed in this participant-observation case study to measure the consequences and effectiveness of our project.

Chapter 3:
Methodology: Taking the Measure of the Project

Introduction

This chapter outlines the research methodologies employed in this participant-observation case study. The chapter is one of two technical chapters; the other is Chapter 11, where the results are presented from the quantitative measures used to measure various dimensions of the children's bilingualism and biliteracy. Those readers either not interested in the technical aspects of this study or not versed in statistics can safely skip over this chapter and Chapter 11 without missing the most salient findings of this bilingual project. The quantitative measures are used in part to help validate the qualitative and more accessible findings, and are summarized throughout the book with references to where more detailed technical information can be found.

The study uses a mixed methods approach, employing a variety of qualitative and quantitative research measures over the 19 years of the project. Mixed methods approaches provide a broader, more rounded, and multifaceted perspective of the complex reality of social settings than either just quantitative or qualitative approaches alone (Tashakkori & Teddlie, 1998). Measures used by this study include the following:

- fieldnotes of author observations;
- audiotape recordings;
- videotape recordings;
- French Proficiency Survey: an author-developed standardized measure which solicited teacher input on several dimensions of the children's French competency over a four-year period;
- Children French Proficiency Survey: a variation of the teacher survey which solicited the children's perceptions on several dimensions of their French competency;
- Bilingual Self-perception Survey: solicited children's self-perceptions on their developing bilingualism at two points in time with a five-and-a quarter year interval;

- national and state standardized academic test scores administered in parochial and public schools;
- Torrance Creativity assessments: a professionally scored measure of the children's creativity at ages 11;10 (John) and 9;10 (twins);
- intelligence assessments (IQ tests): administered and scored professionally at two points in time by same psychologist with a three-year interval.

I used the following quantitative measures to gauge various dimensions of bilingualism or the validity/reliability of my instruments including:

- the author-constructed Bilingual Preference Ratio (BPR, a measure of language preference);
- Edelman's measure of bilingualism (measure of language dominance);
- average French competency scores from teachers' and children's surveys;
- the Pearson Product Moment Correlation – r;
- t-values.

First, I describe the validity of the case study in general as a powerful approach to understanding and explaining scientific phenomena. Next, I consider and describe in more detail each qualitative approach we used. Finally, I explain each of the quantitative measures we employed.

The Case Study

While the case study approach employed here has limitations, it also has some definite strengths. The chief limitation of the case study is its questionable generalizability. How do we know to what extent events in the Caldas family are comparable to those in other bilingual families? To address this limitation, we offer some comparisons with other families that have been the focus of case-study linguistic research (e.g., De Houwer, 1991; Deuchar & Quay, 2000; Fantini, 1985; Saunders, 1982, 1988). However, we acknowledge up-front the subjectivity of this research approach. According to Feagin *et al.* (1991: 6), a case study is 'an in-depth, multi-faceted investigation, using qualitative research methods, of a single social phenomenon'. It is the 'single' that is the limitation. However it is also the 'single' that can be a strength.

I might add that in our own case, I have employed quantitative methods as well, to analyze data that we have collected within the context of the case study. While problems of generalizability must be recognized, there are also some excellent justifications for the method of the case study. Feagin *et al.* (1991: 6–7) list several fundamental advantages in using the case study approach:

1. It permits the grounding of observations and concepts about social action in natural settings studied at close hand. 2. It provides information from a number of sources and over a period of time, thus permitting a more holistic study of complex social networks and of complexes of social action and social meanings. 3. It can furnish the dimensions of time and history to the study of social life, thereby allowing the investigator to examine continuity and change in lifeworld patterns. 4. It encourages and facilitates, in practice, theoretical innovation and generalization.

A limitation of the case study in general, and of participant-observation in particular, is subjectivity. I do not claim to have conducted an objective study. Indeed, it is the subjective nature of the study that is its strength. A case study's strong point is its in-depth and detailed look at a specific instance 'at close hand'. As participant-observers in this case study, Suzanne and I had the added advantage of being 'on-site' most of the time. We were there. We heard and saw what happened, and knew most of the antecedents of any particular 'fact' that we observed. We were also there to observe the consequences of most actions as well. In short, we 'saw' the whole story.

Parents, in particular, are perhaps in the best position to observe the linguistic development of their children. As Deuchar and Quay (2000: 4) noted, 'The parent can be present over a much wider range of situations than an investigator who makes scheduled visits ...'. We were 'on-site' virtually the whole time, with summer camp stays being the notable exception to this rule.

Of course simply 'being there' is not enough. If that were the only criteria to conduct science, then everyone would be a scientist. While 'there' the author 'saw' the story as a researcher trained to observe and analyze the particulars that he witnessed. While 'there' he employed a variety of common research tools available to both the qualitative and quantitative social scientist. Following is a description of each tool used and how it was employed.

Fieldnotes

The author kept a notebook within which he recorded events related to the children's acquisition of their two languages. I took notes in the two research milieus of Louisiana and Québec, and at times while in transit between these two locales as well. A sampling of the kinds of information I recorded include which television programs the children watched and how often they watched them, how they addressed each other, the parents, and non-family members, and incidents of cross-linguistic structures I heard in their utterances. Not simply a detailed analysis of the children's language structures, though, the notes are more sociolinguistic in nature than most linguistic case studies. They describe how the children acted and spoke in their many given social situations, which the author tried to accurately reconstruct and describe on paper (or computer).

Audiotape Recordings

The author began audiotaping the children's spontaneous conversations in August 1994 in various places, such as in the car, playing in the den, and at the dinner table. At this time the three children were aged 9;3 (John) and 7;3 (twins). In December 1994, I implemented a more systematic plan to tape weekly dinnertime conversations for 10-minute intervals, which continued through December 2000 in both Louisiana and during summertime and wintertime stays at the family's Québec cottage. January 1996 recordings are omitted from the study due to so few words on tape, as well as July and August 1998 due to a bad audiotape. This left me with just one recording from French Canada during the summer of 1998, a limitation revisited below. Also omitted are recordings in June 2000, due to the father's travels. However, data from recordings are included from as late as the summer of 2003. A total of 248 dinnertime conversations were recorded.

The audio recordings are 10-minute snippets of relaxed, natural family communications around the dinner table, usually at the evening meal. There were on average between three and four recordings per month. Family mealtime conversations are very important social contexts within which language socialization takes place (Blum-Kulka, 1994; Pan, 1995), and studying dinnertime bilingual speech has been employed in other seminal linguistic research (e.g., Lanza, 1992). Importantly, this is the sole context that remained constant for all five family members over the entire study period, regardless of which country we were in. Also, it is significant that there was no overt pressure on the children to speak any particular language in the home at the dinner table, as both parents are completely bilingual. Since only immediate family members were ever present at each taping, we created a bilingual setting that minimized inhibitions on speaking either language (Paradis, 1996). Thus, the children truly had free choice in which language they chose to speak. As Gut (2000: 203) notes, in conversation with other bilinguals, 'output control is relaxed and speakers are in the bilingual mode where code switching can occur'. During this six-year timeframe, the twin girls' ages spanned from 7;8 to 13;8, and the boy's age frame was from 9;8 to 15;8. On a cautionary note, much research has underscored the importance of 'topic' in influencing the choice of language, a variable that while not completely ignored, isn't a central focus in analyzing the tape recordings.

In the beginning, when the children asked about the recorder, I responded truthfully that I was taping their conversations to study how they were learning to speak both French and English. After a couple of weeks, they almost never seemed to notice they were being taped. Once the tape was rolling, I tended to forget as well, as the recorder occupied an inconspicuous spot next to the table. Thus, the 'principal of formality' – speech being influenced by systematic observation (Wardaugh, 2002: 18) – was probably not a factor in family conversations around the table, except for perhaps this book's author. Since I operated the tape recorder, turning it on was an automatic reminder of the family bilingual project, and our strategy to only speak French in the home.

The Bilingual Preference Ratio (BPR)

A construct I was particularly interested in measuring was the children's shifting preference for speaking either English or French over time. I wanted to know how their language preferences related to their changing ages and environments. 'Language preference', 'bilingual dominance', 'bilingual proficiency', 'fluency' and 'degree of bilingualism' are terms which have been loosely, and often interchangeably used in the areas of both linguistics and education over the last few decades. This has caused a good deal of muddled thinking, and, as Snow (1991) has noted, has created the need to clarify and define more precisely what we mean when we make statements such as ' ... he speaks Spanish like a native', or ' ... she's a perfect bilingual' (p. 63). This is increasingly true as bilingual school populations in the United States continue to burgeon. School officials have sought out instruments to accurately measure a student's 'degree of bilingualism' to aid in placing bilingual students in appropriate educational programs, without always considering the distinction between a bilingual's 'language proficiency', for example, and his or her 'language preference'.

'Bilingual dominance', in particular, is a term that has been used to mean everything from 'degree of bilingualism' (Edelman, 1969; Burt & Dulay, 1978), to 'fluency' in one of a bilingual's two languages (De Houwer, 1991), to bilingual 'proficiency' (Edelman, 1969; Fantini, 1985; Genesee *et al.*, 1995; Nicoladis & Genesee, 1998; Saunders, 1982, 1988), to bilingual 'preference' (Caldas & Caron-Caldas, 1997, 2000; Dodson, 1985; Baetens Beardsmore, 1982) to language complexity (Döpke, 1992), to speaking one language 'dominated' by a second language's grammatical structure (Lanza, 1992) and/or vocabulary and idiom (Grosjean, 1982). Dodson's (1985) contention that a bilingual's dominant language is his/her 'preferred' language for a discrete area, or domain, of experience seems to come closest to capturing the true sense of what is often meant by the more vague term 'bilingual dominance'. Dodson's (1985) usage of the term in a contextualized sense has likewise been employed by other researchers (e.g., Caldas & Caron-Caldas, 1997, 1999, 2000, 2002; Berman, 1979; Lanza, 1992; Leopold, 1949). I propose that this later sense of the term 'bilingual dominance' is really referring to 'bilingual preference', a concept we more fully develop and utilize in Caldas and Caron-Caldas (2000).

Thus, there is general agreement in the literature that an individual can have more than one 'preferred' language, depending upon the language context and/or environment. However, it is not so much that a bilingual is 'dominant' in a given language, e.g., one of a bilingual's two languages always lords it over the other in some sense, but that he or she has a decided 'preference' for a given language that is context sensitive. The 'context', or language environment which influences one's speech, is sometimes referred to as a non-production factor (Deuchar & Quay, 2000; Petersen, 1988). We have operationalized the construct of 'bilingual preference' in our Bilingual Preference Ratio, or BPR (Caldas & Caron-Caldas, 2000) – the ratio we use to gauge the children's changing language preferences.

I create each subject's BPR from the words he/she utters on our audiotape recordings. Suzanne and I actively listened to five-minute snippets of each 10-minute recorded session from the six-year period of audiotapings, and tabulated the number of distinct, individual French and English words (tokens) uttered by the boy separately, and the girls together. (We recorded our tallies separately.) Trying to make a distinction between the twins' audiotaped speech proved too difficult. However, we believe that it makes sense conceptually to view the twins together. For one, they are the same age, and have been spoken to by us in French since birth (whereas the father addressed the boy exclusively in English until age one and a half). Also, the girls were almost inseparable in play at home, and at school have been in the same French immersion classrooms. Moreover, they are identical twins, and are as physically and genetically similar as two human beings can be, with quite similar voices.

In order to have an objective measure of how much French each parent was speaking, and to have some indication of whether or not we were speaking more French than English in the household (as was the plan), we went through the same procedure for both parents. We listened to the tapes, and separately tallied the number of French and English words which we detected each of us speak.

After the tallying was completed, we added together the total number of French and English words heard separately by each of us, for each month and for each subject in the study. Next, I ran paired-sampled t-tests on each pair of tallies (i.e., French words tallied for John by each author) to determine if there was a statistically significant difference in the number of words each of us tallied for each subject. I found statistically significant t-values ($p < 0.05$) for the following: the number of French words tallied for the father, and the number of English words tallied for John and the twins (though the twins' t-value was only barely significant at $p = 0.045$). Then, I conducted an additional check on interrater reliability (or determination of 'the consistency of the observations over raters', Crocker & Algina, 1986: 143) and correlated the tallies of each of us for each month, in French and English, using Pearson's r as an interrater reliability coefficient (Linn & Gronlund, 2000: 83). I generated separate reliability coefficients for each of our tallies of John, the twins, the mother, and the father. Each reliability coefficient was $r = 0.92$ or greater, except for French tallies for John and the father, which still had relatively robust coefficients of $r = 0.75$ and $r = 0.71$, respectively. Even nationally normed standardized tests consider a reliability coefficient of 0.80 to be robust (Linn & Gronlund, 2000).

In an effort to further reduce measurement error, I created an average of the two researchers' total word counts for each month (Linn & Gronlund, 2000). For example, I added together the number of words I heard the boy utter on tape in a given month (e.g., 200) and the number heard by Suzanne (e.g., 250), and divided by two (e.g., 225). Finally, I used a formula developed by Edelman (1969) to calculate a French to English proportion, or ratio, in order to determine overall language preference for each month (the BPR). The algorithm used is as follows:

Number of individual French words (tokens) − number of individual English words (tokens)
☐ Larger of the two   ☐ + 1 . 2

Values can range from 0 to 1.0. Coefficients greater than 0.5 indicate French preference; coefficients less than 0.5 indicate English preference. A value of 0.50 would indicate a perfect balance between French and English words (50% in each language), a situation we believe comes closest to approximating 'balanced bilingualism' (Caldas & Caron Caldas, 2000).

I use the individual monthly BPRs in my correlational analyses. However, in order to more clearly present the children's language preferences while both in Louisiana, and in Québec, I calculate average BPRs for each child, and each parent, for each year, in each separate language context–Louisiana and Québec. In this way, it is easier to clearly see, compare, and interpret broad trends. Finally, a total ratio for the Louisiana and Québec language contexts is computed to give us a global index of French language preference for each family member.[1] To explain shifting BPR's, I use both child and teacher surveys, as well my fieldnotes, to help understand what causes language preferences to shift over the six-year period.

Videotape Recordings

I randomly videotape recorded eight sessions of interaction among family members from October 1985 to 2000. The tapings ranged from about 15 minutes to 45 minutes in length, and only included immediate family members. Though these tapings were neither frequent nor systematic, they do provide a snapshot of family communications at various times over the history of the project when we were away from the dinner table and the author did not suspect that one day the data would be used in this study. Additionally, they provide the only recordings, audio or visual, of the period before 1994 (when the children were aged 9;4 and 7;4, respectively), and offer some interesting examples of the children's language mixing and code-switching in their early childhood years.

Edelman's Contextualized Measure of Degree of Bilingualism

I also utilize Edelman's formula, coupled with his original technique to measure what he termed 'degree of bilingualism' (Edelman, 1969). This measure is very different from our BPR, and ostensibly measures 'bilingual dominance', rather than 'preference'. Like Lanza (2000), we believe that language dominance 'is essentially a psycholinguistic phenomena closely intermeshed with sociolinguistic parameters . . '. (p. 237). The sociolinguistic parameters would be social context. We believe 'dominance' implies one language's greater degree of subliminal influence over the other. Lanza (2000), who argues convincingly that the concept of 'dominance' is still a useful one, describes it as meaning that 'one language is somehow stronger than the other and affects the processing of the other' (p. 228). Edelman argued that his measure identified which language was 'dominant' in three areas of an individual's life: the home, the school, and the neighborhood. The measure is employed by asking a child to name as many things he or she can think of, in 45 seconds, in each of these three domains. This is done separately for each of the two languages, and the researcher tallies the results. Edelman's formula is used to calculate a ratio of French to English dominance (according to the algorithm previously noted). Numbers greater than 0.5 indicate French dominance; numbers less than 0.5 indicate English dominance.

I employed Edelman's bilingual dominance measure with each of the three children on 20 separate occasions from February 1996 through May of 1998 (see Appendices 4, 5, and 6 for longitudinal graphs of all coefficients for each child). The twins ranged in age from 9;9 to 11;0, and John ranged in age from 10;9 to 13;1. By the last administration, it was clear that the children (especially the budding teenager, John) increasingly viewed the exercise of spouting off words in each language as childish and senseless, and I decided to discontinue the practice.

I analyze these Edelman's bilingual dominance coefficients for longitudinal trends. Additionally, I use Pearson's r to determine the correlation between the children's Edelman's bilingual dominance coefficients and our own BPR coefficients over the same time period. This allows me to determine if there is a relationship between bilingual dominance and bilingual preference. I also correlate each child's coefficients in each domain (home, school, and neighborhood), as well as correlate the average child's coefficient for each month (all three domains together) with the other children. This allows us to see if the environment is affecting the children's bilingual dominance in the same way. The results indicate which language is 'dominant', and reveals statistically significant patterns.

French Proficiency Survey

This study also uses data that were compiled from the author-constructed French Proficiency Survey. This survey was completed by the children's numerous native French-speaking teachers, both in Louisiana and in Québec, over a period of three years for John, and four years for the twins (see Appendix 1 for original French version and Appendix 2 for English translation). The surveys were designed to solicit from the children's French teachers their perceptions of the children's written and spoken French, and French-comprehension. Gardner and Tremblay (1995) noted that these domains were central to measuring the capacity of the learner in the target language. The teachers were asked to compare the children's competencies on these three dimensions with native French-speaking children of the same age. There were 10 survey questions each followed by a Likert scale with values ranging from '1', very inferior, to '5', very comparable. A space for additional comments was provided at the bottom of the survey. As an overall global measure of French proficiency, we calculated an average for each child's rating on each question, by adding them together and dividing by the total number of survey questions (10). This is a valid approach, since each question is phrased such that the higher the Likert value, the greater the proficiency in some aspect of French. A perfect score would be 50 (10 × 5). The surveys were all written and administered in French.

The children spent at least one month with each teacher surveyed. The twins had seven Louisiana French immersion teachers (four Canadians, one Cajun, and two citizens of France), and three French teachers in Québec (two for a month each in an elementary school, one during one month of summer camp). John's French Proficiency Surveys were completed by his one French immersion teacher in Louisiana (a Belgian), two French teachers and one camp counselor in Québec, and one French teacher (a Québécoise) in Louisiana (see Table 10 on p. 179 for descriptive statistics).

Children Administered French Proficiency and Bilingual Self-perception Surveys

When the children were aged 12.10 and 10.10 respectively, and then five and a quarter years later when they were 18;1 and 16;1, we asked them to complete a modified version of the teacher French Proficiency Survey (in French and modified to address the questions to the children) soliciting the children's perceptions of their French competency (see Appendix 3 and 4 for the French and English versions of this survey). This was done to determine if the children's perceptions of their proficiency in French varied from how other native French-speaking educators perceived them, and also to gauge how the children's perceptions of their proficiency in French changed over time (see Table 10 for descriptive statistics).

The children were administered the author constructed Bilingual Self-perception Survey at the same two times that they took the French Proficiency Survey. This survey was in English, and included seven open-ended questions (see Appendix 5). The open-ended items were designed to solicit from the children how they viewed their bilingualism in relation to English-speaking Americans and French-speaking Québécois. In constructing the survey, I wanted to get at the question of how the children viewed themselves culturally and linguistically, in light of their two languages and nationalities. This, I believed, would also indirectly reflect how they perceived the predominant linguistic norms of the U.S. and Québec. Also, the results from the open-ended items were compared over the six-year period to gauge how the children's perceptions of themselves as bilinguals in two monolingual cultures changed from early adolescence to middle/late adolescence. In an attempt to get the children to share their views on bilingualism in a structured, yet relaxed and non-threatening way, I asked the children to complete the surveys on their own, emphasizing the importance of complete honesty. The children were not able to collaborate on their answers. On both occasions, the children seemed to take the task of completing both surveys quite seriously. This is indicated by the gravity of their written responses.

The next chapter turns from the technical aspects of the study to the decidedly non-technical genesis of the entire project. The chapter introduces the author's mono-linguistic past, and the 'bilingual meeting' between the author and his spouse (and frequent co-author) that changed this. I discuss the bilingual dimensions of our budding relationship and outline our own efforts to attain biliteracy and bilingualism. Finally, I share the emergence of 'the plan' to rear our yet-to-be-born children as biliterate/bilinguals.

Note

1. I only created BPRs for the parents from January 1997 to December 2000 – a period of four years. When I finally decided to go back and listen to the earliest tape recordings of the parents' speech, I discovered that the tapes had degraded too much to get an accurate measure of how much French and English they were speaking during the first two years. I even hired a sound engineer to help out. I'm hoping one day to decipher their speech with the use of the most sophisticated audiorecording software available.

Chapter 4
Bilingual Antecedents

Introduction

To better understand this project to rear three children to be French-English biliterate-bilinguals, it is necessary to first understand the history of the author and his wife's efforts to achieve biliteracy and bilingualism in these same two languages. This short chapter gives a brief overview of our efforts. The strategies we employed with our children were in part informed by our own subjective experiences of what worked, as well as by our objective research into what had worked for others.

An Unlikely Meeting ...

The author was 21 years old and eager to learn a new language. I liked foreign languages. I had lived in Japan during the fifth and sixth grades, and loved trying to speak with the Japanese shopkeepers who sold (what to me) were exotic goods and foods. As a college student, the new language I intended to learn was not my ancestral French – but Spanish. Though my mother was a Cajun whose parents spoke fluent French, I did not have as intense a desire to learn my ancestors' tongue as I did to learn America's second language. As the son of a military officer, I had moved around frequently as a child, and did not relate particularly closely to my parent's native state. In fact, apart from taking French in the ninth grade in South Carolina, I had never considered furthering my knowledge of Louisiana's second language, and (I confess) was fairly ignorant of my French roots.

I grew up speaking the very homogenized, standard American English of individuals who move around much and who are reared in a nomadic group with other individuals from all over the United States who also spent their lives in perpetual motion. This homogenized North American accent is sometimes referred to as 'Network English', after the national news broadcasters who speak it (Wardhaugh, 2002). My mother always spoke with the New Orleans accent typical of the city within which she was reared. I know this, because other military wives at our various duty stations outside of Louisiana often asked my mother if she was from

Brooklyn, the New York borough where residents speak remarkably like New Orleaneans. My father, also a native New Orleanean who was reared in the French Quarter, spoke with much less of an identifiably New Orleans accent than my mother. As an indication of just how important social milieu can be on accent formation, none of my five siblings grew up speaking English with the New Orleans accent of our stay-at-home mother.

In my quest as a college junior living in Louisiana to become bilingual, I had volunteered to have a Spanish-speaking roommate assigned to my dorm room. I was no linguist, but it just seemed to make sense that the way to learn a language was to have to speak it. Ofilio, a 40-year old pharmacist from Panama, became my new friend and roommate. The jovial Ofilio spoke little English, so my plan was to try to communicate with the Panamanian using the little Spanish I had picked up in one year of high school Spanish I. In return, I was going to help Ofilio learn English.

Since I had a car, a humble machine but one that normally ran, and my roommate did not, Ofilio and I spent many hours together visiting various sites and places around LSU's campus in Baton Rouge. Ofilio would ask me how to say something in English, and then I would ask Ofilio to tell me the same word or expression in Spanish. Ofilio seemed to love sharing his beautiful language, while also describing his beautiful country of Panama, to which he would be returning to his wife and children after the sweltering summer semester at LSU learning English. For my part, I felt my knowledge of Spanish was advancing nicely, and I was even making plans to take a course in Spanish before graduating. Ofilio made encouraging comments about how fast I was learning Spanish (always a good pedagogic practice, even if there's some exaggerating), and I had visions of one day carrying on fast paced conversations with native Spanish speakers in their own tongue.

Then *it* happened (the best laid plans ...). After about three weeks together, Ofilio and I filed into the dormitory cafeteria one evening for supper. We served ourselves in the cafeteria line and sat down to eat in the noisy room to continue our bilingual discussions. We had no sooner begun eating than a large group of French-speaking students of various ages began exiting the food line and walking among the tables looking for places to eat in the increasingly crowded cafeteria. Two young ladies in their twenties approached the only vacant spots at our table – across from Ofilio and me – and asked in heavily accented English if they could sit there. Of course, we graciously gestured that they could. The women put down their trays and took their seats, and though I spoke little French, I knew enough to recognize the language the two women were speaking with each other. So I ventured to break the ice and spoke about the only

French I remembered from ninth grade to the girl sitting across from me on whose nametag was written 'Suzanne'.

'*Parlez-vous français?*' (Do you speak French?) I dumbly asked the long, brown haired, pretty girl with the large brown eyes.

'*Mais oui, je parle français, et toi?*' (But of course I speak French, and you?) she answered happily.

'*Non, je ne parle pas le français*'. (No, I don't speak French.) I exhausted my limited French.

Suzanne laughed. Her friend and roommate, Dorice, sitting next to her laughed. Ofilio just shook his head. And thus was born a new friendship which would develop in ways no one seated at the table could have ever foreseen on that July day in 1979. In broken English and hand signals the two young ladies explained that they, like Ofilio, had come to Louisiana from Québec, Canada to learn English at an LSU summer program.

The four of us sat together the next night as well. I was quickly growing fond of the pretty Québécoise Suzanne, and following our second meal together I boldly (and clumsily, I'm sure) asked her out to eat at a restaurant off campus on the coming weekend. She said 'oui' – and the rest is history. My plans to learn Spanish came to a quick and abrupt halt, and would not be undertaken again for 24 years. As much as I liked Ofilio, I devoted an ever-increasing amount of my free time outside of class to walking across campus to the transient student dormitory to meet with my other new foreign student friend. From there, we would spend the late afternoon hours, when the temperature had fallen to tolerable levels, strolling around the expansive live oak studded campus, getting to know each other and our respective languages.

I spent much of the last three weeks of the all-too-short summer semester with this enchanting Québécoise reducing her French-English dictionary to tatters as we passed it back and forth between us in our clumsy, increasingly romantic efforts at communication. I took Suzanne in my car to visit various places in the countryside around Baton Rouge. My French vocabulary began to expand, as did Suzanne's English. She mentioned that she was learning more English from me than in the morning English sessions she attended on campus – an early presage of our then nascent philosophy of the importance of foreign language immersion.

Suzanne's intensive month of English language instruction and immersion quickly came to an end. We spent her last day in the Bayou State visiting New Orleans, and afterwards I drove her to the nearby international airport on that balmy midnight, and waved a profoundly sad goodbye as she boarded a charter jet for Québec with her group of fellow French Canadian teachers. She returned to Canada and resumed teaching physical education and English to elementary school students. We continued to communicate via letters (in English) for the next five months during which time our relationship grew in *absentia*.

During the Christmas break I flew for the first time in my life to snow-covered Québec City where I spent three weeks with Suzanne and her family, totally immersed in only French – and the politics of separation. It was 1979, only months away from a provincial referendum on the independence of Québec from Canada, and most of Suzanne's large family was for Québec sovereignty.

Ironically, Québec's independence movement sensitized me, for the first time, to the plight of the French language on the North American continent. My eyes were opened to the preciousness and precariousness of Louisiana's French. As an example of how oblivious I was to Louisiana's French language and culture, it took this first visit to Québec to discover the very popular Louisiana musician Zachary Richard. Here was a veritable pop star singing in French about bayous and Mardi Gras and *fait do do's* and other unique aspects of our state, and I had to go to another country to discover him. It was like an epiphany to me.

The Québécois were trying to preserve their vibrant tongue from the onslaught of English, and a grim future not unlike what had happened in my own home state, where English had virtually crushed Louisiana's first colonial tongue. Spending three weeks with no recourse to English also reinforced another important lesson: there is no better way to learn another language than to be immersed in it. My French speaking advanced significantly during this short period of time, as I had to interact with Suzanne's parents and six brothers in only French. I had what Gardner and Lambert (1972) proposed as the most powerful motivating factor to learn another tongue: 'integrative motivation', or a desire to perform well in another language in order to communicate with others who speak only the target tongue.

Suzanne's family was very indulgent of my fledgling efforts, and slowly repeated words for me, allowing me time to process what I was hearing. Suzanne and her immediate family spoke with the accent peculiar to Québec City, and it is exposure to this variant of French which ultimately influenced the pronunciation and accent I would develop. As the time for my departure drew near, I made it known that I wanted to buy souvenirs of my visit to distribute to my friends and family back in Louisiana. This led to the learning of another important object lesson about language and politics. The incident occurred while strolling through a souvenir shop with Suzanne and a couple of her brothers in the elegant hotel Chateau Frontenac, perched high on a cliff which the English once scaled to conquer

New France in the battle of Quebec. I loitered around the flag display, deciding that a nice maple leaf flag would be an appropriate souvenir to bring home with me. Even as I reached for the symbol of Canada, I felt myself being steered toward the adjoining flag display – the one containing the four white *fleur de lis* on a blue field (the *fleur de lis* is a lily which symbolizes French royalty, and decorates the four corners of the Québec provincial flag). That episode caused a flash of political and cultural insight into the 'Québec Problem' that all the political essays in the world may not have adequately conveyed to me.

My three weeks in the white winter wonderland of Québec quickly ended, and I dreaded the prospect of another long and uncertain separation from the delightful French-speaking woman to whom I had quite obviously fallen head over heels. Thus, in the very early morning hours of my last night in Canada, I quietly exited her brother's second floor apartment in which I had been staying, went outside into the freezing cold and snow, and knocked on Suzanne's frosty bedroom window on the ground floor of the same building. I signaled to my sleepy but startled host to meet me upstairs. She nodded puzzled agreement and came upstairs to see me. I proposed, probably in horrendous French – but she still accepted.

A Union of Cultures

Five hours later I was on a Louisiana-bound jet, and neither of us had any idea how we would ever realize our plans of a life together. We continued our earnest correspondence once I was back at LSU, but with a slight twist. To help me further my knowledge of written French, we agreed to write to each other in French only. To help my poor French letter writing in particular, and my acquisition of French in general, I enrolled in a five-hour French course at LSU. It was one of the best and most relevant courses I ever took. I cannot ever remember being so motivated to attend class and do the assigned homework. By comparison, four of the five semesters of Latin I had taken as a freshman and sophomore had been shear, unadulterated drudgery. What saved my last semester of Latin was an engaging, sympathetic professor who used Asterix and Oblelix comic books written in Latin! The pictures definitely helped. (More on the importance of comic books and literacy in Chapter 7.) Again, at a very personal level, we see the difference in power between Gardner's (1985) integrative motivation (learning a language to be able to communicate with someone) and academic motivation (learning a language because it is an academic requirement). In my case the former was a much more effective motivator than the latter.

John Dewey, the great Pragmatic Philosopher and proponent of hands-on learning, explained well that there was no substitute for a student's interest in inspiring them to excel at their studies (see chapter on Pragmatism in Ozmon & Craver, 2002, for good overview of Dewey's teaching philosophy). The distinguished economist Douglas Graham once told a colleague of mine that to create the best possible foundation when learning a discipline, one needed to become extremely familiar with the discipline's first book – from which everything else is derived (personal communication, M. Baillargeon, July 3, 2003). For me this meant learning the basic structure of the French language, including its verb conjugations. In retrospect, I credit that first semester of university French (and the dynamic teacher who taught the course) as the most important four months ever spent in my efforts to achieve French literacy. I have been an avowed Deweyite ever since.

Suzanne and I were determined to get together permanently, although we did not know whether it would be in the United States or Canada. We explored both the possibility of Suzanne moving to Louisiana, and my moving to Québec. À la Dewey, the prospect of moving to French-speaking Canada stoked the fires of my enthusiasm for the French language (again, integrative motivation), and gave me the best possible impetus to learn the language. For her part, Suzanne was reading and teaching English in Canada in the event fate would send her South – which is precisely what it did.

Suzanne returned to LSU in the summer of 1980 for a repeat of the English language program she had attended the previous year. She also landed a teaching position with CODOFIL – the Council for the Development of French in Louisiana – teaching elementary school French as a second language to Louisiana students as part of the state's efforts to preserve French in Louisiana. We were married in the sultry month of August, and except for summers, have lived in the Bayou State to the time of this writing.

From the beginning, we both very much wanted to become biliterate and bilingual, a feat which was going to be easier for Suzanne since she was now effectively immersed in her second language. Thus, to help me in my efforts to acquire French, we agreed to speak it in our home as much as possible. We also returned to Québec for Christmas and summer vacations, which gave me periodic societal immersion in French. Additionally, I began taking graduate level French courses toward a French minor in my Master's degree, as well as certification to teach k-12 French, both of which I attained in 1985.

During the period from 1980 to 1985, we gradually became 'fluent' in each other's language. Though we would not have been mistaken for native speakers of our second languages by native speakers, we were developing what Bachman (1990) referred to as 'pragmatic competence'. This includes 'sociolinguistic competence' (knowing how to use our second language in the appropriate context) and 'illocutionary competence' (having a functional usage of the language). Suzanne taught in an elementary French-immersion program in Baton Rouge, teaching second grade students their academic subjects only in French. Slowly, our linguistic philosophies developed and matured in the reality of pragmatic experience, and we both increasingly became proponents of the immersion approach to learning a second language – whether the immersion be in a family, a school program, or in society in general. After all, it was what was working best for the bilingual students who Suzanne was teaching, as well as for us.

The Inspiration

Attuned as we were to the difficulties and challenges of learning a second language, and considering the prospect of having our own children and rearing them to be biliterate-bilinguals, two seminal events occurred which helped shape the strategy we would employ for rearing our own yet-to-be-born children. The first, described in the introduction, was the incident we witnessed when crossing the English Channel during a European trip in 1982.

The second experience that would shape our family plan was Suzanne's teaching in the aforementioned elementary French immersion program in Baton Rouge. Her second grade students, with whom she spoke only French, were fluent enough after only a few months to hold a conversation in French. Therefore, by the time Suzanne was pregnant with our first born in 1984, we had adopted our strategy: I would speak to the newborn child in only English, and Suzanne would communicate with him in only French – the so-called 'one parent, one language approach' (Döpke, 1992).

Social Class

Before we continue any further, a word about social class is in order. Throughout the duration of our study, our family has lived in comfortably middle-class neighborhoods and homes in both Louisiana and Québec. Both Suzanne and I were raised in solidly middle-class environments with essentially middle-class incomes and values. Research has documented well the relationship between family socioeconomic status (SES) and school success (Caldas & Bankston, 1997; Coleman *et al.*, 1966; Grissmer *et al.*, 2000; Steinberg, 1997). The children to whom the rest of the book is devoted to studying have always had ready access to books, computers, and help with schoolwork if they needed it. Their peer-groups in both the U.S. and Québec have also been largely constituted of suburban children from advantaged SES backgrounds, for whom school-success is in general an important value. It is important to view all that we report about the home through this important conceptual lens. In subsequent chapters we examine more closely the influence of community, school, and peer groups on the children's developing bilingualism.

Chapter 5
Home and Community

Introduction

This chapter focuses on the specific influence of the home on the children's bilingualism. I discuss the implementation of our 'one parent, one language' strategy with the firstborn John, and our modification of this plan in light of our perception that the majority language (English) was too dominant. Then, I discuss the continuation of the plan with the birth of the identical twin girls Valerie and Stephanie two years after John's birth. After discussing the influence of the home milieu, the chapter turns to an examination of the community influences in Louisiana and Québec on the children's developing biliteracy and bilingualism.

Implementing the Plan: John

When son John was born in Baton Rouge, Louisiana on May 6, 1985, the first words he heard from his father, who was in the delivery room when his small wiggly body entered the world, were English. When his mother was finally able to speak to him shortly after his first exposure to American English, she introduced John to the differing phonology, lexicon, and syntax of the Québec French language. This was John's aural initiation to the world of two linguistic systems.

During the rest of that May and into the first summer of John's life, almost all of his time was spent in the presence of his mother, who stayed at home with him. I was teaching in the month of May, so I was away from home during most of the daylight hours. In June I commuted to two local universities to take French classes toward a teaching certificate in French, so again, I mostly saw John in the evenings and on weekends. In July I flew to France to spend the entire month taking additional classes in French at a French university to complete the teacher certification process. Thus, we can safely ascertain that John was very likely hearing much more French than English during the first three and a half months of his life. However, he heard English from me during the evening hours and on weekends during the first two months of his first three and a half months.

Also, he heard English from our TV set that only received American English programming at that time.

However, from the middle of August, when Suzanne returned to teaching her French-immersion class, John would be immersed for eight hours a day, five days a week, in English-speaking day care with other monolingual English-speaking children. Thus, except for summers, he remained in day care until he was four, at which time we enrolled him in an all-English-speaking pre-school. During John's first 18 months, we became increasingly aware that Suzanne's French communications with our son constituted only a fraction of the much greater volume of English to which he was exposed. In addition to day care, he was immersed in English through TV, neighbors, and his American relatives. So when John was aged 1;6 we reassessed our 'one parent, one language' approach, and made an important change. I, too, would begin to speak to John only in French to more equally balance his exposure to the two languages. Other bilingual parents who initially began rearing their children according to the 'one parent, one language' approach have reached the same conclusion as we did, and shifted to speaking only the minority language in the household (De Houwer, 1991; Gawlitzek-Maiwald, 2000; Gut, 2000). In these published case studies, the parents also felt the need to equalize their children's exposure to their two languages.

At about this same time, we also reassessed our own interpersonal communications that had grown increasingly sloppy during John's first 18 months. We were cognizant of our speaking to each other in a mixture of French and English, or 'Franglais'. Thus, we resolved to be more disciplined and try to speak to each other in only French. Thus, we consciously contrived to create an all-French-speaking home environment – except for the TV (more on television in our chapter on media).

Though John clearly understood both languages equally well, and we did not sense any developmental delay in his language comprehension, he had only barely begun to speak by the time he was 21 months old, uttering mostly one or two word sentences. From other research, we were aware that bilingual children might begin speaking later than monolingual children (Saunders, 1982), so we hoped that this was the case with our son. Döpke (1992) and van der Linden (2000) reported that their bilingual subjects, too, were late to speak. Our concerns were soon allayed. About the time John turned two he suddenly exploded in language. At first he frequently inserted lexical items (i.e. nouns) from one language into what was otherwise the matrix language, saying things like 'I'm *chaud*' (I'm hot) or 'Je veux *candy*' (I want candy), a cross-linguistic structure referred to as 'language mixing' (Lanza, 1997), and a common phenomenon among infant bilinguals (Lanza, 1992). However, he fairly rapidly sorted out his two tongues between the age of 2 and 2;6, and only occasionally language mixed after that age.

One System or Two?

We did not begin audiotaping our children's speech until much later, when John was 9;4, and can therefore not make any scientifically valid statements about our infant children's cross-linguistic structures. (Our analysis of taperecordings begins at that later age.) However, I sense, again with no empirical justification, that almost from the beginning – if not *before* the beginning – of John's speaking, he knew he was 'confronted with two different language systems simultaneously' to use van der Linden's (2000: 40) expression. Those who have postulated and hypothesized about whether a bilingual child's first utterances constitute 'a fused' system, or 'two separate systems' base their judgments on an analysis of actual uttered speech. Though we cannot probably ever know precisely what children are thinking before they speak, is it not entirely conceivable that pre-speech bilingual infants have entirely separated out the input from the two language systems before they are able to verbalize their two systems? Is it not true that most bilinguals who learn their second language later in life are able to understand words and phrases in their second language before they are able to actually verbalize these same words and phrases? Are not the processes of infant bilingualism and second language acquisition later in life at least somewhat analogous?

I share the skepticism of some other researchers (Caldas, 2004), like all 10 scholars in Döpke's (2000) edited volume on this topic, that children start out with a fused language system (though there is some recent research suggesting that very young children [<2] do not show pragmatic differentiation (Nicoladis & Genesee, 1996). I am relatively certain that even in John's earliest speech, he was producing the expected target structures in both languages. Suzanne, on the other hand, senses (again, with no empirical evidence) that John (and later his sisters) believed they were initially dealing with one language system, not two. Regardless our opposing viewpoints, we both agree it is impossible to know how a child perceives language prior to his or her first speaking it. Thus, it may be impossible to ever know for sure whether a child, in his or her earliest stages of cognitive, pre-speech development, perceives that their bilingual parental interlocutors are speaking one language or two. That controversy aside, our tapes do empirically indicate that our children were language mixing even as late as adolescence. Their parents are still language mixing into middle age.

Valerie and Stephanie

Valerie and Stephanie, identical twins, were added to our growing family two years after John, in May 1987. We continued what seemed a successful strategy of speaking only French in the family. Thus, in theory anyway, the girls were exposed to even more French from their parents than was John during their first year and half, since I spoke to them in French during this most formative linguistic period (something I did not do with John). However, unlike John, the twins were exposed to an important additional English influence during their first two years – an English-speaking brother. The twins could communicate with each other and with John, which meant that in essence the twins had two live-in peers that John did not have during his first two years. John, of course, now also had two new peers at home.

Like John, the girls stayed home with Suzanne for their first three and a half months. When Suzanne returned to her teaching post in mid-August, the twins entered all-English-speaking day care with their brother. Thus, they were with John almost all the time from their birth until they were two years old and John started pre-school. At four years of age, the girls would also eventually attend the same English-speaking university pre-school as did their brother. They even had the same teacher as he had. So, in many ways, John and the twins lived in quite similar environments from the very beginning. The two major differences – and they should not be minimized – were that John had no siblings for his first two years, and I did not speak French to John until he was 18 months old.

After John turned two, his French and English vocabulary began to expand quickly, though he had a decided and obvious preference for speaking English. This was somewhat troubling to us, because we had expected him to respond to us in French. This confirmed our suspicions that English was the more predominant force in John's environment, and that our combined French speaking was still not enough to counteract the otherwise monolingual English world John lived in. As we discussed the situation, we realized that John perceived his environment as essentially an English one – much like we did. Indeed, had we made no effort to speak French, we would have been speaking English as well. This was the crux of the issue – essentially all the environmental forces surrounding our family validated, encouraged, and rewarded English speaking. Suzanne and I were the only mouthpieces for French, and this was only because we made a concerted and continued effort to speak it. Had we been around John all the time, the influence of French would have undoubtedly been greater. But with both of us away from home much of the day, English reigned during the children's waking hours.

The Community

'Communities' serve the very important function in every society of integrating individuals into the larger social structure (Durkheim, 1951). We all live and work within multiple communities, be they neighborhoods, villages, towns, cities, countries, or indeed, the international community. Communities give us our sense of 'shared identity' (Putnam, 2001: 18). We conform, to one degree or another, to the social norms of our various communities. These include the linguistic norms. Indeed, it is this very conformity that gives us regional accents, dialects, and languages. I now shift from the brief overview of the early home environment, to a description of the various communities within which the children have lived, played, vacationed, and attended school, and how these communities have influenced the development of their French and English. These communities were in anglophone Louisiana, Cajun Louisiana, and French Canada.

Anglophone Louisiana

Until the fall of 1994, when the children were 9;7 and 7;7, we lived in an almost entirely anglophone part of southeast Louisiana. The parish was a mostly suburban bedroom community of the state capital Baton Rouge. The 1990 Census indicated that only 6.5% of the population of this parish spoke a language other than English at home. Since only one-fifth of this number spoke Spanish, and only about 1% of the population was foreign born, it can be surmised that the large part of this 6.5% were undoubtedly French speakers. Still, we rarely met them.

Though monolingual English speakers surrounded us almost entirely, we never felt uncomfortable speaking French publicly with our children, as fully 37% of the population indicated they were of French ancestry (U.S. Census, 1990). This contrasts with the Japanese mothers in Okita's (2002) study who felt uncomfortable speaking Japanese to their children in the UK. Typical of the kind of reaction we received to our speaking French in public was an incident during a trip to Baton Rouge when the whole family went to Kinko's Printing so the children could have their passport pictures taken. When the two women working there learned that the children – ages 9;4 and 7;4 – spoke French, they began to compliment their bilingualism and asked the children to give them a demonstration. On several occasions strangers who heard us speaking French to our children would stop us in stores and comment on how they wished their Cajun parents or grandparents had taught them French. Thus, we were not confronted with the hostility that other language minorities in the U.S. have faced. Consequently, neither of us was particularly hesitant to speak French in public, something which we believe contributed to the early success of our project. Nevertheless, we did assume that when we spoke French in stores or at the park, that those who did not know us would assume that we were foreigners.

Due to the positive reaction of the public to our children's bilingualism, we believe that the children have never acquired the negative stereotype formerly associated with French-speaking Louisianans. In fact, we have made a concerted effort throughout our project to reinforce the idea that they are fortunate to speak French, and that many monolingual Louisianans would gladly trade places with them. Many of the fathers' relatives have openly praised the children for their ability to speak French, and, at least until they were adolescents, the children spoke the language freely even when around their anglophone paternal relatives. We continually emphasized to the children their French-speaking heritage in both Canada and Louisiana. In essence, in the early days our strategy was to link French ethnicity and ethnicity's 'inevitable link with language in general, and language maintenance in particular', (Fishman, 1985b: 70). This strategy, however, did not work when the children entered adolescence, a point examined more carefully in Chapter 8.

Still, the only French the children were exposed to in this part of Louisiana came either directly from us, or from videocassettes and French books, of which we built a fairly sizable library. We bought, borrowed, or checked out literally dozens of the French versions of many feature-length films, including Disney films, which we played constantly. (We discuss our use of media in more detail in Chapter 7.)

Need for French linguistic cultural immersion

Since we knew the importance of the environment in determining which language someone spoke and how well they spoke it, we decided to conduct a little experiment. During the summer when John was three years old, he and Suzanne flew to Québec for a two-week stay with relatives. John spent the entire time surrounded by only French speakers. Upon his return to Louisiana, he was speaking noticeably more French. He continued to speak predominantly in French for a couple of months until he returned to English-speaking day care, at which time he shifted back into his predominantly English-speaking mode at home. Thereafter, he spoke mostly in English to his sisters and us until his next Québec trip the following year.

As for the twins, as they approached two years old, they understood our French and everyone else's English, just like their brother had when he was the same age. However, they were even slower to verbalize than John had been. Twins, on average, speak later than do singletons (Savic, 1980). This tardiness of twins to speak has been attributed to parents having less time to devote to each twin as an individual (Jones & Adamson, 1987; Tomasello *et al.*, 1986). This theory does make sense. If there is indeed less language input, for whatever reason, it is logical to expect that there will be less output. Thus, our twins had in essence two strikes against them: they had two languages to sort out and learn while being part of a twinship which researchers also note inhibits speech.

When the twins did begin to utter their first one to two word sentences around approximately age two, they imitated their brother's English, though they did not seem to speak nearly as facilely in either language as John at the same age. So it seemed that once again our French speaking was not enough to counter their otherwise dominant monolingual English environment. Indeed, the twins had the added inducement to speak English of having an older English-speaking sibling. Even more, the twins could also communicate with one another in English. We concluded as parents that we were in a sense 'out gunned'. What we now knew beyond the shadow of any doubt was that more trips to French-speaking Canada were in order.

Thus, in 1989 when John was 4;2 and the twins were 2;2 we set off for a two-week vacation in Québec. John's aunt volunteered to keep him with her and his nine-year-old (French from France) cousin. He had no recourse to English for two entire weeks. When we picked him up for our return to Louisiana we could hardly believe the transformation in John's speaking: he would only speak French for the next several months, even after re-immersion into an all-English-speaking environment.

The twins, too, stopped speaking what little English they were capable of, and began to speak only French at home (which we have recorded on videotape). When they re-entered day care at 2;3, however, they would speak only English to each other, and of course to their day care providers and the other children. However, at home French became their language of choice in conversing with each other, John, and us. We felt that our trip to Québec in 1989 was a watershed event in our bilingual family experiment, and the point at which we could truly point to the success of our combined strategies. Gut (2000) documented a similar dramatic increase in a 3;10 year old bilingual child's minority language (English) after a vacation in the UK. We never again missed taking a summer vacation in Québec through the end of our project, gradually extending our stays until the children were spending two months each summer in the French-speaking province. Suzanne and I now both shared a deep sense of satisfaction in having discovered what it took – and then doing it – to ensure that our children spontaneously spoke the minority tongue in our Louisiana home. Our evolving strategies were working.

In several videotapings made during the early years, the interactions are telling. In one of the first episodes in Louisiana when John was 3;4 (prior to the watershed Québec trip), the interactions between the father and son were all in English. Two years later, in a long videotaping when the twins were 3;6 and John was 5;6, virtually all the interactions between all five family members, at several different times of the same day, were in French. This included interactions solely between the children, with no prompts from the parents, and included interactions between just the girls, and each girl and John.

A year later in Louisiana, when the twins were 4;8 and John was 6;8 (and in first grade), we made two video recordings in two days. In one, most of the communications between the father and son were in English. The next day, most of the communications between the twins, the twins and the mother, and the twins and the father, were in French. Approximately half the communications between John and the father were in English, but almost all the communications between John and his sisters were in French. In one episode, John was reading to the twins from an English book (his first grade reading assignment), while the father behind the camera is addressing John in French. John is speaking to his sisters in English and French, while they are answering him in French. The mother then enters the scene, admonishing John in French to take his English reading seriously. He complains to her in French.

We made a roughly half hour videotape of the children playing outside in Louisiana when the twins were 6;6 and John was 8;6 (in the first and third grades, respectively). The large majority of their communications with each other and me were in French, though they occasionally uttered a phrase in English. I caution that we did not systematically begin recording our children's speech until they were 9;7 and 7;7, respectively, and so we cannot give precise ratios of their spoken French to English until that time. It can be said, however, that there was much French interaction between all family members when we lived in anglophone Louisiana.

The linguistic community of French Louisiana

In August 1994, I secured a teaching position at the University of Southwestern Louisiana (now the University of Louisiana) in Lafayette – located in the French-speaking heart of the state. However, Suzanne and the children remained in the anglophone part of the state until November, and I commuted back to be with the family on weekends. All of our fieldnotes and audiotape recordings (I began audiotaping their speech for the first time in August 1994) indicated the children (ages 9;4 and 7;4) were speaking almost only French during the month of August and into September following their return from two months in Québec. Indeed, the children indicated they had trouble speaking English, as I recorded in my fieldnotes on August 18:

> Today was the first day of school [fourth and second grades] for the three kids. Both Suzanne and I noticed that after school all the children spoke only in French. In response to my question (in French) of how her day went, Valerie volunteered that she at times had trouble speaking in English. John, overhearing her, immediately jumped in and said, 'C'est vrai, lorsque je parlais anglais des fois j'ai dit "oui, parce que"', sans penser. [It's true, when I spoke English sometimes I said 'yes, because' without thinking.]

As much French as the children were speaking, we were still worried it would not last long after they re-entered school in Louisiana. A month later, I noted on 9-19-94 that this was the first time I heard any extended English conversation between my children since we had returned from Québec six weeks earlier. We worried about the encroachment of English as a result of all of the activities we were then required to do in this language, such as homework, catechism, piano lessons, and karate lessons. In October 1994, I audiotaped the girls (7;5) playing in the living room for about 10 minutes. They only spoke English.

In November 1994, when the twins were 7;6 and John was 9;6, the rest of the family moved in with me in our new home in the southwest region of Louisiana called Acadiana. The name 'Acadiana' was formed in the mid-1900s through the fusion of the words 'Acadia' and 'Louisiana'. Acadia comes from the French 'Acadie', which is a variation of the name 'Arcadia' that the Italian explorer Verrazano gave to the beautiful countryside he discovered in what is today Nova Scotia. Verrazano thought that the forested region looked remarkably like the Arcadia region in Greece, which was famous for the peaceful, pastoral life of its contented people. The first French settlers in North America arrived in Acadie in 1604, and were dubbed 'Acadians'. The peaceful, pastoral lifestyle of the Nova Scotian Acadians would make Verrazano's choice of a name seem almost prophetic. As noted earlier, the deported Acadians who eventually landed in Louisiana morphed 'Acadian' into the word 'Cajun'. Though the name changed slightly, the Louisiana Cajuns would continue to enjoy the peaceful, country lifestyle that defines this ethnic group in both Canada and the U.S. to the present day.

According to the 1990 census, an estimated 50% of the census tract in the rural Acadiana community to which we moved spoke French (U.S. Census, 1990), though most of the French-speaking population throughout Acadiana was over 50 years old (Henry & Bankston, 1999). Indeed, according to the 1990 U.S. Census, one-third of the residents of our community indicated that they 'did not speak English well'. Fully 51% of the population of this largely rural parish and a large majority of the whites indicated that they were of French or French-Canadian descent in 1990. The way the questions on the 1990 census were worded, few blacks, who constituted roughly a third of the total population, would have indicated that they were of French descent. However, in reality much of the black population in our parish, who refer to themselves as Creoles, have French ancestry and speak a Creole-French dialect traceable to French Haiti of the early 19th century (Brasseaux & Conrad, 1992). Still, blacks and whites speak a dialect so similar that they interact seamlessly with each other in French.

We were immediately able to sense that not only was much of the community bilingual, but that there was a normative social structure which legitimized French speaking in some situations more than others. One is still able to hear French spoken in the local stores, post-offices, and at community functions. Several of our neighbors were happy to converse with us in their native tongue, unconditionally accepting us into their linguistic community once we established our 'ethnic connection' to them. Indeed, beyond the simple increase in our exposure to and usage of spoken French, we admitted to each other experiencing a sort of transcendental connection with our Cajun cousins (Suzanne, too, has Acadian roots). Such an 'authentic knowing', as Fishman puts it, is at the heart of 'being associated with ethnicity and language' (Fishman, 1985a: 9). Suzanne and I were also both aware that we were much more likely to speak French un-self-consciously in our new social environment. Unlike our interactions around Baton Rouge, storekeepers and librarians who got to know us in Acadiana would cheerfully great us in French when we encountered them. This was not the case when we lived in the anglophone part of the state, where few people could speak French. When strangers heard us speaking French in public in Acadiana, they would often stop us just to speak with us in French. However, neither my wife nor I were ever mistaken for a Cajun by French-speaking Cajuns. I was, however, because of my accent, often mistaken for a French Canadian.

There are also some local radio stations that broadcast at least part of the day in French, so I often tuned our radio to this Cajun programming – at least until my children decided that they preferred pop and alternative rock. Moreover, our new house had a parabolic antenna that allowed us to receive all-French TV programming from Québec. When we finally hooked up our aerial antenna a couple of years later, we discovered some local TV programming was in French as well. Thus, even though English still dominates all aspects of life in Acadiana, the 'cultural atmosphere' is decidedly different there, and we are convinced that it had a strong, positive influence on our project ... until adolescence.

In addition to our speaking French to adult members of our Cajun community, John and the twins were even occasionally speaking French to our then 14-year-old neighbor, who understood the language perfectly, but struggled a bit trying to speak it. His fluent Cajun French-speaking mother and father seemed thrilled that we were speaking French to their son, as they too wanted to perpetuate French speaking in their family. The mother, who was also our children's school bus driver, reciprocated by speaking French with our children as they boarded her bus in the morning and got off in the afternoon. We incorporated some Cajun words and phrases into our repertoire of French, like 'Pas de quoi', (you're welcome) and 'asteur' (now). At the university, I was able to speak French with several of my Cajun colleagues and a variety of support staff, white and African American, who were native to Acadiana.

Indeed, my own French improved as a result of moving to Acadiana. I learned several French words and expressions from local Cajuns that I had not known before, but were still spoken in either Québec or France. So, the move invigorated me as much as I felt it had invigorated the children's French. As for Suzanne, the move in a sense brought her closer to her roots. For example, after her French conversations with our neighbor, she would tell me that our neighbor used many words and expressions that Suzanne's grandparents in Québec would have used, but which are no longer spoken by Québec's younger generation. On occasion I would watch Suzanne speaking rapidly with our neighbor in only French, and marvel that the two could understand each other so well given that Louisiana French had been cut off from Canada for more than 200 years.

We listened to a local public radio station that broadcast in Black Creole French on Saturday mornings and Cajun French on Sundays. We spoke with local shopkeepers and bank tellers in French. We drilled into our children their linguistic heritage in a fairly melodramatic, perhaps even somewhat exaggerated fashion, trying to construct our family identity as French-Canadian-American. I recorded the following in my fieldnotes on August 30,1994 during one of our first visits to Acadiana:

we went to eat in a local restaurant called Poché's, located only a mile from our [new] house. On entering the restaurant one is greeted with a sign that says 'Ici on parle français'. [French is spoken here] Suzanne and I made a point of speaking with the elderly people seated at our table, all of whom spoke French. We were happy that our kids could see it, and made the point of explaining to them that in this part of Louisiana, most people could still speak French.

On another occasion two months later, Stephanie (7;6) came running up to me and handed me an envelope that our new bank had just mailed to us. She showed me under the bank's return address the phrase *'Parlons Français à la maison'*. [Speak French at Home]. After I got over my surprise, I said to her 'See, even the people at the bank want us to keep speaking French at home!'

At the end of 1994 (on 12-4), after fully moving into our new house in Acadiana, Suzanne summed up her feelings about the children's French speaking:

> Last night before sleeping, Suzanne commented that she thought the kids were speaking much more French this year than at the same time last year. She attributed this to the two months in Quebec. I believe that it's as much a function of the fact that we now watch more French than English programming on TV [via satellite], and live in a francophone area of Louisiana.

We noted how after only three weeks in our new Cajun community that John began to speak English with an obvious Cajun accent. Prior to moving to Acadiana, I had noted that he spoke English with the light Southern accent typical of Baton Rouge. I recorded the following in my fieldnotes after John returned home from a sleepover with a group of his new Acadiana schoolmates:

> Yesterday, I continued to notice John's (age 9;8) transformed accent in English. In fact, it was at times so obvious that his pronunciation of some English words had taken on such a pronounced Cajun accent that I was sure he was putting me on.

John's paternal grandparents came over for Christmas 1994, and also noticed John's Cajun accent. My father asked John if he were learning any Cajun French. John answered 'yes', then added, quite seriously, that he was learning a little 'Cajun English' as well. Though this may seem a humorous response, Dubois and Horvath (2003) have indeed studied and documented the peculiarities of 'Cajun English'.

Within a month, we noticed the girls picking up a bit of a Cajun accent too, though it would never be as pronounced as John's. Indeed, over the next three months that the children attended their Cajun country schools, we began to notice that their English was at times grammatically incorrect in the same way that Cajun English sometimes is. On several occasions Suzanne asked me, 'Are they talking right?' Of one thing we were relatively sure: they were not picking up the Cajun French accent when they spoke French, probably because they did not speak enough French with local Cajuns.

Still, in general, the children seemed much more at ease speaking French in our new Cajun community. When John was 9;8 I asked him if he felt more comfortable speaking French in the Lafayette area (in Acadiana) than where we had previously lived near Baton Rouge. He said 'yes'. Then he said [of his friends who heard me speaking French to him one day] that they all asked him what we had said to each other. He said he was proud that he was able to show them that he spoke another language.

The degree to which French had infiltrated not only the twins' speaking, but also their thinking is evidenced by an episode in March, when Valerie was 7;10, and in a second grade French immersion class. She was in the process of reading *Alice in Wonderland*, for her English-speaking teacher. While we were waiting for her bus one morning, I asked her to tell me what she had read so far. She began to recount the story to me in French, and did not shift into English the whole time that she excitedly explained the details to me. I was amazed – the book had never even been discussed in her French class.

I also made a big deal to my children of the fact that blacks in our community spoke French as well as whites. On one occasion, we donated a bed to a black family that lived a couple of miles from our house. Our Cajun neighbor knew the family, and we loaded the bed onto his pickup truck, and he, John and I drove over there early one evening. The black man, who appeared to be in his sixties, was called 'Pon Pon' (pronounced with a nasalized French accent). My neighbor and I spoke with him in French, and then I convinced John (9;7) to ask him something in French, which he did. Pon Pon seemed pleased that we understood his 'Creole', though I did have to ask our neighbor what a few of the words he said meant.

I made numerous references in my notes to which language I heard my children speaking at various times of the day, and especially in the morning as soon as they woke up. In general, I noted that they were speaking French much more often and spontaneously after we moved to Acadiana. Our sense was that the children truly felt like they were in a francophone environment. Suzanne and I were continually amazed by our linguistic and cultural good fortune, happy that we had discovered our own 'Acadie' of sorts in rural Louisiana in the midst of a hectic, fast-paced, modern America.

Which Language to Discipline in?

Of course, all was not always paradisiacal. One of the less pleasant, but necessary duties of a parent is to correct and discipline their children. This domain of child rearing proved to be even more complex for us due to our bilingual household. Logically, the language of discipline should ostensibly have been French since this was our declared home language. But, as we discovered, it was not that simple. In fact, I was painfully aware that we were as likely, if not more so, to correct our children in English. The following incident when John was 9;7, highlights my own personal struggle with this issue. I returned home from work one evening to be greeted at the door by my somber wife. John had lost his temper about something, and she had punished him in his room. She wanted me to have a 'chat' with him. I recorded in my notes that ...

> What I did was pull him off alone into my room, shut the door, and had him first explain everything that happened, and then I talked to him about the importance of self-control, especially in situations where one perceives that a wrong has been committed against oneself. Our talk lasted quite some time. I was fully aware that much of my communication to him was in English. On a couple of occasions I switched into French, but I think switched back into English relatively rapidly. I spoke predominantly in English, I believe, for several reasons. For one, I wanted to be as clear and precise in my speech to him as I possibly could. I was painfully aware that I did this better in English, even though I knew, with more effort, I could probably have done nearly as well in French. Which leads me to the second reason: I didn't want to expend the additional effort it would have required to speak only in French. The situation, I felt, was too important, and required all of my powers of concentration and presence of mind without having to devote additional energies to do it in French as well. Moreover, as I spoke, I was conscious that not all that long ago, I too was in his situation, when my parents had 'conferences' with me. Perhaps unconsciously as well, I knew that I was in part acting out a similar role as they had performed, and doing it in English sort of made it somehow 'valid' (I know that's not the best word [sic]). The

fact is, especially in situations like last night, I am still more spontaneous and 'natural' in English.

I noticed that Suzanne, too, was more likely to speak to the children in English when she was angry with the children. I would occasionally ask her to speak French when she scolded them, but it just never seemed appropriate to correct her when she was correcting the children. Moreover, when I did raise the cry 'Parle français!' when she was scolding the children in English, it just seemed to aggravate her more. In times like these, she usually ignored my admonition to speak French anyway.

Profanity

Ianco-Worrall (1972) postulated that bilingual children are more likely to see the 'arbitrariness' of language than are monolinguals. It is a given that an interesting phenomena of languages is that what might be socially acceptable in one language could be considered profane in another. Our experience lends support to the hypothesis that bilingual children are more likely than monolingual children to see this linguistic relativity.

For example, in French, the word for seal is 'phoque', which is phonetically almost indistinguishable from the English word 'fuck'. Moreover, my children learned this very early on. So early, in fact, that we had to tell them to be careful saying 'phoque' around people who speak only English, as they were almost certain to hear 'fuck' instead.

Which brings us to cursing. As early as eight years old, our children had picked up Suzanne's habit of saying 'merdre' and 'maudit' in French. The rough English equivalents of both words are 'shit' and 'damn', two words I never allowed my children to say around us in English. I considered these words socially unacceptable for American children to say (though, of course, they're said all the time by some American children, and have even been uttered by this author on occasion). So, at least when the children first started using 'merdre' and 'maudit' in French, I was a little uncomfortable, and discouraged them from saying these words. However, Suzanne assured me that they were not unacceptable in Québec French in the way they were in English in the U.S. Interestingly, though, 'maudit' seems to carry much the same punch in France that 'damn' does in the U.S. Anyway, Suzanne warned the children (ages 10;2 and 8;2) to stop saying the Québec expression 'maudit torrieu à merdre' (difficult to translate, but one can see the two questionable words in the expression).

So, I spoke with a Québec high school teacher I knew personally who taught a course equivalent to 'ethics' (J. Caron, personal communication,

June 17, 1995). I asked him specifically what words would be unacceptable to him if uttered by children on school grounds. His short answer was that there was essentially nothing so bad a student could say that would get him or her expelled from school for saying it. He did add that in his class, he would not accept a student saying 'Christ', but that it would be all right in most instances if a student said 'maudit' or 'merdre'.

So, I was ambivalent in my discouragement of the use of these two French words. Still, I know my displeasure registered with the children, because on at least one occasion one of the children (either John who was aged 10;1 or a twin, aged 8;1) corrected the other one for saying 'maudit' in my presence. Then, he or she (I didn't note who in my fieldnotes) looked to me for my approval. I think they sensed my ambivalence, because they continued to use these words around me as youngsters (and later as adolescents), whereas they almost never (unless they lost their temper) cursed around me in English.

When John was 10;1 and attending a Québécois elementary school (an experience elaborated on in the next chapter), I asked him if his Québécois schoolmates cursed. He answered 'pas beaucoup' (not much), but then the very next day told Suzanne that they say 'fuck' (not 'phoque'). The high school ethics teacher confirmed that students could say 'fuck' in his classroom without any sanctions, so clearly when a Québécois child says 'fuck', it does not carry nearly the taboo as when an American elementary child says it. Another Québécois fifth grade teacher, though, told me he would not allow his children to say 'fuck' in the classroom, and if he heard the phonetic equivalent, expected his students to add 'en Alaska' to distinguish the 'good' word from the curse word (M. Caron, personal communication, July 7, 2003). There is a popular Québécois song about a 'phoque en Alaska' (seal in Alaska).

The word is also used as a verb in Québec, as in 'Ma voiture est toute fucker' (My car does not run). Moreover, my children learned this distinction very quickly, as they were no doubt intrigued that so off limits a word was spoken so innocently by their young friends around their teachers. However, I do not remember them saying it in French before they were adolescents, and then only rarely. I suspect they just never got comfortable using the word in French around me. In fact, to my knowledge, I never corrected the children as teenagers for 'cursing' in French.

On the other hand, my children marveled that such words as 'tabernacle' (same as in English), 'osti' (host), 'baptême' (baptism) and other words associated with the Catholic mass were so forbidden in the Québécois lexicon. I used these 'curse' words as a pretext to teach my children both a history and a linguistics lesson. I explained to them that at one time the Catholic Church in Québec was extremely powerful and influential (the church has lost much of its influence in Québec since the 'silent revolution' of the 1960s), and so to use words from so sacred an institution gave the words a certain forbidden allure. For example, the aforementioned ethics teacher told me that he had corrected his son (aged 10;8) for saying something like 'tabernacle osti de Christ' the week before I had spoken with him. I was hoping my little lesson would shed light on how words assumed a certain 'taboo', and that it was society that decided which words were 'OK' and which ones were 'bad'. However, before I come across as Mr. Relativist, I confess that I corrected both my son and daughters as late as 19;6 and 17;6, respectively, for using certain English curse words around me. Moreover, before one thinks my wife was liberal in allowing the children to say the equivalent of 'damn' in French, she was complaining to me about the kids' habit of using 'maudit' a month after she first said it did not sound that bad in French. She told me it had gotten out of hand and made them sound low class. Obviously, we were not always models of parental consistency.

The Summertime Linguistic Community of 'Le Québec'

From the time the children were in the first grade, we enrolled them in a daylong all-French-speaking summer camp in the Province of Québec. The camp is located on a lake popular with Québécois vacationers in an Appalachian mountain community not far from Québec City. The lake is surrounded with summer cottages and second homes. Several members of Suzanne's family either have chalets (cottages) on the lake, or live in the county that encompasses the lake. We purchased a cottage on this lake in 1994 in order to be able to spend longer periods of time in Québec with the children, thereby immersing them in French. According to Statistics Canada (1996), only 0.5% of the residents in the county speak English as a first language, and 0% of the municipality in which the resort lake is located speaks English as a first language.

When in Québec, our family was in daily contact with several members of Suzanne's family, who were able to speak very little English. Four of these family members either were, or currently are, schoolteachers. They knew from the outset about our research project, and greatly encouraged us in it: they all felt deeply about the importance of preserving French in North America. We have expressly solicited the informed opinions of Suzanne's family about our children's French speaking from the very beginning of our project to the writing of this book. During the summer after the girls' year in kindergarten (age 5;2) and the boy's year in second grade (age 7;2), the grandmother commented that during their first week in Canada, the girls hesitated often, and seemed to have great difficulty forming words in French. She also noted, however, that they had no trouble understanding her. She added that after a week or so, the girls had improved considerably in their ability to speak French. The grandmother noted no such hesitation on the boy's part. Until 1996 (when the twins were 9;2 and John was 11;2), they told us that the boy spoke better, and more fluently in French than the girls. This was in spite of the fact that the girls had already been in 18 months of school French immersion by this time, and John had only had six months of school French immersion in Louisiana.

The Québec family members also noted the presence of an American accent when the children spoke French in their early elementary years, but reported to us that their accents diminished as they grew older. All of the children's American English accents in French would eventually disappear completely (or seem to), but only in adolescence (more on adolescence in Chapter 8).

Regarding his efforts to rear his three children to be German-English bilinguals Saunders (1988: 51) made the observation that ...

> ... it is highly unlikely that the children will speak their home language as well as children in the linguistic homeland or as well as they speak the dominant language of the country in which they now live..

To us, Saunders' assessment simply meant that the children needed as much cultural and linguistic immersion in French Canada as possible – since our goal was to rear them to speak like natives.

Something that helped greatly in this regard was the French-speaking summer camp. When John was in first and third grades, we enrolled him in the residential camp program for one week and three weeks, respectively. During these two stays he was at the camp 24 hours per day, with no recourse to English. We noticed that on both occasions he picked up new vocabulary and Québec idioms that we could not teach him. Since we did not enroll the girls in the 24 hour summer camp program, John was exposed to much more French in Québec during our project's early stages than were the girls. Beginning when they were in the first grade, and for each summer thereafter, we did enroll the girls in the summer day camp program which consisted of three and a half hours in the morning, and one and a half hours of swimming lessons in the afternoon. These sessions, all in French, lasted for one month. The boy, too, attended the day camp when not enrolled in the 24 hour camp. Sinka (2000) documented the powerful effect that immersion in a summer camp dominated by the child's minority language can have on the child's propensity to speak that language. We cannot overestimate the contribution of this summer camp towards ultimately creating perfect bilinguals. This dimension of the project is analyzed more carefully in the chapter on adolescence.

In the summer of 1995 we began audiotaping family dinnertime conversations around our cottage table. Our tape recordings indicated that prior to each trip to Québec, the children's French speaking around our dinner table was at its lowest point of the year. In fact, during adolescence, our children had essentially stopped speaking any French around our Louisiana dinner table by the month of May. However, a pattern that repeated itself during each summer of our study, even during adolescence, was the children's almost complete abandonment of English while in Québec. For example, in 1995, during the first summer that I taped the children in Québec (aged 10;1 and 8;1), they eventually quit speaking any English around our Canadian dinner table. They could have very well spoken English had they so chosen, because as in Louisiana, we only taped when immediate family was present. This pattern would continue for the next six years of our taping. The 'norm' or expectation for the children while in Canada was to speak French. As an indication of just how powerful this norm was, I recorded the following on July 13, 1995, just after I joined up with the family following a brief 10-day visit to Louisiana:

> Yesterday both Valerie (8;2) and John (10;2), at two different times, asked me to speak French when I had inadvertently addressed them in English.

During this summer of 1995, when the children attended three weeks of Québec schooling (more on this in the next chapter), it seems that their vocabulary exploded. In addition to the input from their peers and teachers at the school, they had many Québécois friends around our cottage. My fieldnotes are replete with examples of the children either correcting my French mistakes, or teaching me new words I had never heard before. It seemed to me and others that their American accents, too, faded slowly over the course of the Québec sojourns. For example, after two months in Québec in 1995, the children's Québec relatives were commenting that they either detected no English accents when the children spoke French, or only a 'small' accent.

In fact, the children's French became so fluent and spontaneous after two months in Québec, that up until adolescence, they had trouble shifting back into English when returning to the U.S. At the first stop across the border in Plattsburg, New York in August 1995, John (10;3) said that he did not want to pay for the gas because he did not want to speak English. He said he was too shy. Moreover, the children would occasionally correct me for speaking English in the car on the way back to Louisiana.

Language Politics

From very early in our project, we carefully explained to the children the language issue in Québec in the broader context of Canada's linguistic and political history. As a family we carefully followed the political situation in Canada, like the fall 1995 referendum on Québec sovereignty. For two weeks leading up to the referendum, I was watching an hour of CBC TV news each evening (in French via satellite), about half of which was devoted to the critical issues associated with the referendum. The children often plopped down next to me on the sofa, and I would try to interpret the news for them. I explained about polling, and the reasons why some Québécois indicated that they were going to vote 'oui' and why others were going to vote 'non'. While watching a huge rally of 100,000 'nons' in Montreal on the news just days before the referendum, our children asked both my wife and myself the sticky, but obvious question of how we would vote if we could. Perhaps as a result of my social science training and orientation, not to mention my five years as a social studies teacher, I had always tried to project a certain neutrality to my children on the issue of Québec's independence, presenting to them both sides of the argument as best I could. When asked how I would vote I dodged the bullet, telling them that I did not know how I would vote, since I was not a Québécois, and could not understand the situation like they could. Internally, though, my feelings were more mixed, and part of me related to an ethnic minority fighting to preserve its language and culture. As all ethnographers know, it's very hard to live among a people and not 'go native' to some degree. Suzanne was less equivocal than me, and she told the children that she would probably vote 'oui' if she could. For her, the issue was more personal, and the debate swirling around the referendum drudged up memories for her of the history of English Canadian domination of the French-speaking province. The 'we love you, Québec' political slogan of the 'nons', which was orchestrated by the anti-sovereignty campaign to persuade Québécois that English Canada was truly on their side, irked Suzanne as manipulative and not genuine.

On the evening of the big referendum election, we watched the vote returns on TV in Louisiana with a small group of Québécois ex-patriots, which included the twins' French immersion teacher. The whole group consisted of 'oui's', and all were quite disappointed when the 'nons' squeaked out an extremely close victory of less than 1%. As a measure of my torn feelings, I found myself feeling disappointed that I couldn't pop the cork on the champagne I had bought in the event of a 'oui' win. The twins both told us they would have voted 'non', because when they go to Québec, they liked to tell their friends they're going to 'Canada'.

Our emphasizing to the children the language issue in Québec was done in part for informational and educational purposes, and in part to demonstrate to the children that the family was not alone in its efforts to preserve French speaking among a majority English-speaking population. Incidentally, and somewhat of a surprise to both Suzanne and myself, all three children have continually expressed dismay over the possibility of a political separation. As late as the summer of 2003, when they were aged 16;2, both twins felt that Québec would be better off as part of the Canadian federation, though they both had a more mature, nuanced opinion of the situation (like their father). During the summer of 2003 while working as counselors at the French-speaking summer camp, the twins had several friends who were avidly for Québec sovereignty. When discussing Québec independence on the way home from Canada after this particular summer vacation, Valerie (16;3) explained to me that while she still felt it was not in the best interest of the province or the country, she understood why some Québécois wanted to separate from Canada.

For the parents, these summertime trips to Canada were also linguistically refreshing, and beneficial. The mother's family noted on several occasions that Suzanne had incorporated many Anglicisms into her French speech, which were especially noticeable during the first days of a Canadian visit. We have both found that during each visit there were new French expressions we did not know, or had forgotten, and thus had need to learn or relearn each year. For example, in the summer of 2003 Suzanne was speaking on the phone to Valerie who was working at the summer camp as a counselor, and Valerie had mentioned that something was 'moche', meaning 'boring'. Suzanne asked Valerie three times to repeat the word, as she had never heard it. Exasperated, Valerie finally used the synonym 'platte' which is also widely used for the word 'boring'.

Both Suzanne and I found ourselves searching for words during the first few days of total French immersion in Canada when carrying on a fast-paced conversation with a native. Until 1995, I was not able to spend as much time in Canada as the rest of the family, often flying up weeks after everyone else. Upon my late arrival Suzanne was always struck by how much English I mixed with my French on the first few days of my stay, even though I was unaware that I was speaking anything but French. We believe that this mixing of English with French is indirect evidence that we were not speaking as much French at home in Louisiana as we thought we were before we began taping. After our systematic audiotaping of dinnertime conversations began in December 1994, we were able to empirically verify that the majority of our parental speech was indeed in French, but not all of it. Moreover, there were occasionally periods when the ratio was closer to 60% French/40% English (see Figure 4 on p. 168).

Pre-adolescence Fluency and Language Conflict

Upon the children's return to Louisiana in the fall of 1995, the twins entered their second semester of a school French-immersion program, this time in the neighboring Acadiana city of Lafayette: 50% of their academic day was now in French, compared to about 30% during the previous semester in a Cajun country school (more on this in Chapter 6). The program would never again be offered at John's grade level. When he first learned he would not be in the French immersion program he complained mightily about this. Still, as much as a setback to our project as this might have seemed, after two months immersed in French in Québec, and three weeks in an all-French-speaking elementary school, we felt that the family had reached another important milestone in our project. Our children ceased speaking English during this longest summer in Quebec to date. I recorded the following in my fieldnotes on August 29:

> ... at least in our family, I feel that we've crossed a threshold in terms of French speaking: we're more comfortable in French at this point than English. I don't know how long it'll last though.

For John, who was now in fifth grade, it lasted five months. He spoke predominantly in French around our dinner table through December, when he turned 10;8. John was still speaking to me in French in public during the first few months that fall, with absolutely no qualms. Once, when he was reading a book in English I asked him what it was about. He recounted the entire story to me in French. However, as the fall of 1995 wore on, and into the spring of 1996, John's French speaking in Louisiana fell off much faster than his sisters', who were still very enthusiastic about our family project.

This period of time marked the beginning of 'linguistic friction' in our family experiment. The twins would become truly indignant sometimes when John launched into an explanation of something in English. For example, I noted one day in December 1995 that the twins corrected John several times for speaking English, like, for instance, when he was describing playing school band music. He answered, 'Well how do you say "measure" and things like that in French?' I butted in and said he could say 'mesure', (French) if he wanted to. So he said about two sentences in French, but when he quoted his band teacher he switched back into English, and essentially stayed there for the remainder of whatever it was he was trying to say.

Indeed, just as John's enthusiasm for speaking French began to wane during pre-adolescence, the twins seemed to become ever more enthusiastic about our family project to only speak French at home. I recorded numerous incidences of Valerie, especially, demanding of her brother, and sometimes even her parents, to 'Parlez français!!' John grew increasingly belligerent of these demands. On one occasion I recorded John (age 10;8) firing back at Valerie, 'I have the right to speak any language I want to speak!' On several occasions John responded to Valerie's demands that he speak French by screaming back at her 'English! English! English!'

Valerie's nagging of John to speak French become so common, that John began anticipating her admonitions, and armed himself. He once looked up 'English' in the encyclopedia so that he would have a ready response for his sister the next time she demanded that he 'Parle français!' The next time she asked him, we were all in the car together. He responded calmly, in English, and with an exaggerated scholarly air, with a list of facts he had memorized about the English language from the encyclopedia article: 'English is spoken as a first language by over 400 million people worldwide, and is a second language to millions more; it is the language of commerce and air traffic control . . '. (age 10;8). This did not stop Valerie from asking John to speak French several more times on that very same day. At one point that evening, after she demanded that he once again 'Parle français!' he had enough. He launched into a lecture about his rights, and about how no one could force him to speak French, especially his sister. At that point I pulled him aside and whispered to him that he was right, he couldn't be forced to speak it by his sister, but that he was doing it to help preserve the language.

Our family language conflict grew increasingly violent. In January 1996, Valerie (8;8) was once so mad at John (10;8) for speaking English, that she threw a cushion at him while screaming 'Parle français!!!' On another occasion a few weeks later, I heard the girls scream so violently at John to 'Parle français!!!' that I feared it would come to blows.

The girls leaned on me to speak French as well. One day, I asked Valerie (8;8) to do something for me, and said she would – if I first promised to speak French. On another occasion, I was reading to the girls from a history book in English, and trying to clarify one of the concepts, when Valerie told me to 'Explique-le en français!' (Explain it in French). During the fall 1995 Valerie also sometimes corrected my French grammatical errors, like when I once mismatched a subject/verb agreement. I noted at least one occasion when Stephanie corrected my French pronunciation.

The girls' French speaking, though it decreased slightly during this third grade year (see Figure 1 on p. 166), remained very high throughout the fall, constituting more than 90% of the uttered words around our dinner table. Their French speaking did dip fairly significantly during the spring of 1996, though still constituted a slight majority of all the words they spoke on tape around our table during May 1996, when they turned 9;0. John's French speaking fell off dramatically in the spring of 1996, reaching almost zero French in May when he turned 11;0. Thus, we see a major reason for the language conflict in our house, with such large disparities between the language preferences of the twins as compared to their brother.

Vive les vacances! (Long Live Vacations!)

However, as evidence of the strong influence of the environment on all three children, but most especially John, after we returned to Québec in the summer of 1996 their English speaking fell off quickly. Ironically, two days after we arrived, the girls were still arguing with John to 'Parle français!!' Things got so hot between them I thought that Stephanie was going to physically assault John on one occasion. However, within weeks after the children were back in the French-speaking elementary school (where they attended the last three weeks of school), John was speaking more French than the girls. The girls (9;1) performed well in the Québec school, scoring first and second best on a social studies test, and validating the efficacy of their Louisiana school French immersion experience to teach French literacy. John went from speaking almost no French around our dinner table in May, to speaking almost no English around our Canadian dinner table in June, a pattern which continued for the next seven years.

I noted in my fieldnotes how the children did not confuse the gender of French nouns and adjectives as much as they had during our previous summer sojourn. I recorded an example of a sentence that Valerie (9;2) uttered under a crystal clear sky one evening after we had just watched the film *Tornado* (in French) at an outdoor drive-in theatre:

> 'Regarde la belle lune, ça veut dire le jour va être beau demain' [Look at the beautiful moon, that means the day will be nice tomorrow]. She got all of the genders of her articles and adjectives correct, like *'le'*, *'la'*, *'beau'* and *'belle'* ['le' and 'la' are the masculine and feminine forms of the

word 'the', and 'beau' and 'belle' are the masculine and feminine forms of the word 'beautiful'].

Upon our return to Louisiana in the fall of 1996, John's (11;4) shift back into English was almost immediate. By September his French speaking had fallen from more than 90% to less than 10% of his utterances. He was now in the seventh grade, and strongly identified with his decidedly all-English-speaking American peer group at school. He (11;10) commented to me that 'Speaking French [in his school] is not cool'. The twins, who returned to their French-immersion school program, continued to speak more French than English around our dinner table through January 1997, in spite of John's English speaking around the table.

In November 1996, when the girls were 9;6 and John was 11;6 we went to Disney World and the Kennedy Space Center in Florida. As an example of how comfortable the girls were in French, when we sat down to watch an IMAX film at the space center, both girls requested the headsets that translated the English narration into French! John, however, preferred to listen to the show in English.

Throughout the spring of 1997, the twins' French speaking steadily decreased from a majority of French spoken around our table in March, to only about 30% French by May, when they turned 10;0. Still, I observed that they spoke much spontaneous French with me and each other, without reservation – even in the presence of their non-French-speaking English teacher. In fact, I occasionally worried about what their English teacher thought of our French conversations around her when I would sometimes go to her classroom after school to pick up the girls. I rationalized to myself that their English teacher would not take offence since she was the other half of the girls' French immersion program.

Indeed, Valerie and Stephanie seemed to speak more often to each other in French than in English during this spring of their fourth grade year. I noted entire conversations between myself and either Valerie or Stephanie where they spoke only French with me, though I occasionally slipped up and spoke a word or two of English with them. Valerie, at least, apparently even dreamed in French. One day while helping me build a fence, Valerie (9;11) recounted to me one of her dreams (a nightmare, actually). She told me the whole thing in French. Then, when she said, 'Et j'ai dit à la madame dans mon rêve que j'ai essayé de trouver Pont Breaux' (and I told the lady in my dream that I tried to find Breaux Bridge) I asked her if she dreamed the dream in French. At first she said she didn't know, paused, and then answered, 'Je pense que oui'. (I think so.)

The twins also did not hesitate to correct my own French pronunciation. I noted, for example, that they (age 9;9) corrected my pronunciation of the French words 'jeu' (game) and 'jus' (juice). They also continued to encourage me to speak French. For example, one night around the dinner table, out of the clear blue sky, Stephanie (9;10) asked me, 'Pourquoi tu ne parles pas français, papa?' (Why don't you speak French, dad?) Such an admonition from John would have been unimaginable at this stage in his pre-adolescence. Nevertheless, I noted occasions when the twins would speak to John in French, and he would also answer in French.

John, who turned 12;0 in May of 1997, spoke exactly one recorded word of French on tape around our dinner table during this last month before the summer vacation.

When we returned to Québec for two months in the summer of 1997 when the twins were 10;1 and John was 12;1, a big concern of John from the outset was his English accent when speaking French, a concern we attributed in part to growing self-awareness associated with pre-adolescence. Dörnyei (2001) noted well the importance of self-confidence as a motivator to speaking a second language. Indeed, Clément and Kruidenier (1985) contend that self-confidence is the most important factor in motivating someone to speak a 'foreign' language. John's confidence in his spoken French, which was not technically a 'foreign' tongue to him, but one of two maternal tongues, was shaken for the first time in his life as we entered Québec during the summer of 1997 – and John entered adolescence. When we were considering re-enrolling the children in the Québécois elementary school (which we did not do), John was reticent because he was not sure he would 'fit in' with his accent. A week after arriving he told me he was going to ask a friend of one of his cousins if he had an accent, because he perceived that this boy would be more objective than his cousin who knew him so well. This new shy, self-consciousness on the part of our son pained us a little, but Suzanne and I reminded each other that being immersed in the French language and Québécois culture would help both diminish John's American accent, as well as ease his transition into a different social group.

Accent or not, in June 1997, the children's French speaking shot up to more than 90% of all uttered words around our Canadian dinner table. The children did attend the daytime French-speaking summer camp, but they did not return to the Québécois elementary school. Nor did they board at the summer camp. Neither was necessary to prompt their French speaking in our Canadian home.

The children attended the summer day camp during the month of July, three weeks of which sometimes involved activities that included reading and writing in French. The children had the same Québécoise counselor during this time, who completed our French survey (in Appendix 2) on each of the children. She did note that all three children could function *très bien'* (very well) in a French school at their level. However, she also noted that the girls not only wrote more grammatically correct French (Louisiana school immersion program?), but also that they had less of an English accent than John when they spoke French.

Both John's French comprehension and speech, however, were clearly better than mine by this time. One incident that summer highlights this fact. John was with me when I was having trouble trying to explain something very technical to a Québec flight instructor at the Jean LeSage International Airport in Québec City. Finally, John took over and clarified my point for the man. A look of understanding spread across the pilot's face. The instructor was apparently so impressed with John's French that the next time I met with the man, he inquired after John and commented on his excellent language proficiency.

However, upon our return to Louisiana in August 1997, when John entered seventh grade, his French speaking immediately plummeted to near zero within two months. His adolescent opposition continued as well, typified by a comment he made to his mother while we were eating pizza around the dinner table and Suzanne got up to get forks. John (12;6) called out to her, 'In America, we eat pizza with our hands!' (Québécois eat pizza with a knife and fork.) He did write a few letters in French, though he asked Stephanie to help him. As further evidence of John's ambivalence towards his biliteracy, at the end of the school year John (13;1) seemed happy to tell me that he scored the highest on a French exit exam at his middle school.

The twins, who were now solidly pre-adolescents (10;4) entering the fifth grade, also dramatically decreased their French speaking, going from roughly 95% of their dinnertime speech in August, to about only 25% in September. This was in spite of their return to a French immersion school program where all of their peers could speak French if they so chose – something we never observed the twins' classmates doing even one time outside of the classroom in the five and a half years the girls were in the program. McAndrew and Lamarre (1996) remarked a similar phenomenon among allophones (neither native French nor native English speakers) in Montreal's French language schools who also preferred English. I suspect similar social dynamics were operating in both instances.

I videotaped at least a half hour of Christmas morning interaction in 1997 when the twins were 10;7 and John was 12;7. There was much communication among all family members. Suzanne and I spoke some French, but the children spoke only English. The audiotapes corroborated the children's overwhelming preference for English in December, with only about a quarter of the girls' words being in French. However, less than 1% of John's dinnertime words were in French. John was expressing concern over his accent again in February 1998, while we were watching the Winter Olympics together and listening to a German speak accented English. John (12;9) turned to me and asked me if he spoke French with an accent as pronounced as the man. I, of course, said 'no'. I wanted to do everything possible to bolster his developing adolescent self-image. Still, as his father it hurt me to see my son's linguistic anguish.

Neither John (13;0) nor the twins (11;0) spoke one word of French on tape in May 1998. Though the twins' friends and classmates could all speak French, they only communicated in English when not being supervised by their native French-speaking teachers. Given that the twins were in a French immersion program, yet followed a linguistic pattern very similar to their brother at the same age, suggests that the effects of immersion for approximately three hours a day in classroom French in Louisiana did not extend beyond the classroom. Otherwise, they would have spoken more French then John at the same age. As we elaborate more in the chapter on adolescence, we have concluded that the children's peer environment during adolescence had a greater effect on their language choice than did either the school language programs or us (Caldas & Caron-Caldas, 2002). The children were exhibiting parallel monolingualism more than classic bilingualism.

Chapter 6
The School

Introduction

Now, I turn to focusing more specifically on how the children's formal schooling in English and French influenced their developing bilingualism and biliteracy. The children attended both public and non-public educational institutions in Louisiana. As noted previously, they also attended a French public elementary school in Québec for two three-week periods in 1995 and 1996. John attended only one semester of a partial French immersion program in the spring of his fourth grade year, whereas the twins attended five and a half years of school French immersion programs in Louisiana from the spring of their second grade year through the seventh grade. A central question addressed in this chapter is how the twins' school French immersion program influenced their developing French proficiency. In addition to test scores, grades, and standardized test results, this chapter includes results from the author created French Proficiency Survey administered to the three children's francophone teachers and counselors in both Louisiana and Québec over a four-year period. The children were administered a version of the same survey, and their results are compared with their teachers'.

Early Schooling

At 4;3 John entered a sectarian pre-school located on LSU's campus in the fall of 1989. Given that he was only speaking French at home following his return from Québec during this summer, we were sure that his pre-school teacher was aware of his bilingualism either because he told her or because French words occasionally slipped out during his classroom communications. During a parent–teacher conference the author attended in November, I casually mentioned John's French speaking at home as a sort of apology for any language problems John might have been having. His teacher was surprised – John had never mentioned his bilingualism. She said that John spoke English as well as any other child in the class.

At the end of John's pre-school year, when he turned 5;0, his teacher administered the Houghton Mifflin Reading Program Readiness to him. This test is used to determine a student's readiness for kindergarten. John scored above the readiness level in all 10 subtests. It seems that our speaking only French to him in the home was not negatively affecting his academic performance in English. John performed well in every academic subject and grade from that time forward to the present (at this writing he's a university sophomore who's doing well in his American school).

At this same time, when the girls turned 3;0, we took them for a speech screening test offered by our local school district. Both girls were individually screened by a speech pathologist who informed us that except for the /ʁ/ phoneme, the twins' speech was developing normally for their age. We speculated that the twins' constant exposure at home to the French uvular [ʁ] may have been the reason for their [ʁ] pronunciation in English, and thus would be an example of a bilingual cross-linguistic structure in the acquisition of phonology (Gut, 2000). Within months, however, this possible cross-linguistic structure in the twins' speech ceased, as Gut predicted such structures would in young bilingual children. The girls entered the same pre-school program as John did, and were as successful as he was. At the end of the school year, when they were 5;0, they also took the Houghton Mifflin Reading Program Readiness test. Valerie scored above the readiness level in all 10 subtests, while Stephanie scored above the readiness level in all but 1 subtest (sequencing), where she scored at the readiness level. This success is notable, given the twins' very late language development.

Early readiness for school has been identified as a predictor of later academic success (Butler *et al.*, 1985; Chall *et al.*, 1990; Steinberg, 1997). This could in part explain the future school success that the children would experience in both French and English.

Which Language to do Homework in?

An important bilingual issue related to the children's schooling in English was the need to help them with their homework. Though we tried very diligently to adhere to the one-language policy in our home, when it came time to help the children with homework given by their English-speaking teachers, we found it almost impossible not to switch to English. This included not only the more obvious areas like reading and English, but also social studies, science, and when they were in Catholic schools, religion as well. The following incident, when the twins were 7;5, gives a snapshot of what was an ongoing struggle:

I tried to do the girls' religious homework as much in French as possible, which made for an interesting session: half French and half English (all of the stuff in their catechism book is of course in English). I will continue to try to inject as much French as possible into this previously all-English domain.

Moreover, once we shifted into English to do the homework, it was not always so easy to shift immediately back into French. I recorded the following incident in my fieldnotes when Stephanie was 7;3. It seems to make this point well:

> After school yesterday, Suzanne went over homework with the kids. Of course, she has to do this in English. When homework was finished, however, she did not automatically switch back to French, but started giving orders to the kids in English. She wasn't happy with the way Stephanie was doing something, and told her so in English [evidence of the correction-in-English syndrome mentioned earlier]. Stephanie responded to her, a bit sarcastically, in the same tone of voice and rhythm, in English. It struck me as odd, and was obvious that Stephanie was self-conscious of the fact that she was addressing her mother in a different way. I immediately told Suzanne to 'Parle français!' As usual, she then said something quickly in French to Stephanie, as if this would counteract her use of English.

Indeed, the first English I heard from the twins after our return from Québec in this, their second grade year (1994), was when Valerie and Stephanie (age 7;4) were doing homework together. Interestingly, though, I noted that though they were doing the reading in English, they were discussing the reading among themselves almost entirely in French.

Cajun Country School French Immersion

It wasn't until we moved to Acadiana from the Baton Rouge area in 1994, when the children were in the fourth and second grades, respectively, that the French immersion schooling option was available to us. My first reaction to learning about this school program was very positive. Here was an opportunity for our children to be exposed at school as well as home to the minority language in which we were trying to rear them. Suzanne, however, who already had experience teaching in a similar program in Baton Rouge, was much less enthusiastic than I. In fact, at first she was adamantly opposed to the idea. She said that the material was presented at too elementary a level, and that our children would be bored in such a program. She said the emphasis of the program was more on teaching the students how to understand and speak French than on how to read and write it. She pointed out that our children could already understand and speak French. Moreover, she expressed concern about our children picking up the English accent of the other children in the classroom. Her latter concern would eventually seem to be validated.

Thus, we began the search for an appropriate school. We sought information from everyone we could about the local public schools, including the ones that had the French immersion programs. What we heard was not encouraging – pervasive low academic levels and discipline problems endemic to some high-poverty Louisiana schools. We visited four Catholic schools, inquiring at each one if they offered French during the instructional day. The only one that did offered French three days a week, but the tuition was beyond our means to pay. One offered French after school for a fee, but we did not need an after school program. We looked into other possible attractive non-public education options, and the tuitions were even steeper. Finally, Suzanne's argument against French immersion in questionable public schools won the day, and we decided to enroll our children in a local Catholic school that did not offer French. After all, we rationalized with a sigh, they had been enrolled in a very good Catholic school in Baton Rouge for the last two and a half years, and we were very happy with the quality of education they had received there. However, after writing the check for the hefty tuition, and three weeks of instruction later, we began to have serious doubts about our decision. We felt that the level of instruction was not up to what they had been exposed in Baton Rouge. If it is not already obvious to the reader, providing our children with a quality education, regardless the language of instruction, was (and still is) a driving concern throughout our children's lives.

At the same time we were having doubts about the Catholic school, we spoke with the native French-speaking teachers in our community's French immersion program, one of whom had her own children in the program. They made positive comments about the program, and even invited us to their schools to see for ourselves. We went, and brought the three children, who even sat in a class and participated. After the visit, the children told us they wanted French immersion. Throughout the coming Christmas holidays we debated what to do. I made a stronger case for French immersion, arguing that surely the children would learn some grammar and writing skills that we were not teaching them at home. Plus, I argued that the instruction appeared to be at least as good as what our children were now receiving in their Catholic school – and the public schools were free.

After much soul searching and hand wringing, we removed our children from the Catholic school, and took the 'plunge' into French immersion. In January 1995, when the twins were 7;8 and John was 9;8, we enrolled the children in programs in two different rural public schools where approximately two and a half hours of academic instruction per day was in French, an arrangement referred to as 'partial' school French immersion (Snow, 1990). John's fourth grade teacher was a native French-speaking Belgian, and the twins' French immersion teacher was a francophone Québécoise. The children's English teachers were natives of Acadiana, and both could speak some Cajun French.

A word about Louisiana's school French-immersion programs is in order. Not only are some subjects taught only in French, but Acadian (Cajun) culture and history are interwoven into the curriculum. For example, all children in the program are taught about the forced deportation of Acadians from Nova Scotia in the 1750s, and the students visit Acadian museums in the region that feature this theme. In other words, ethnicity is used as a tool of the program to help pass on the language. Indeed, the immersion programs could be classified as 'Franco-centric'. At least one French-immersion teacher in Lafayette punished children for speaking English in his class. The curriculum also emphasizes interaction between students and older members of the community who still speak French. The students in one school in Lafayette, for example, visited a local nursing home on a regular basis, where each student was paired with a French-speaking resident with whom they spent time in conversation – all in French. When Valerie and Stephanie were enrolled in the Lafayette French immersion program, they were paired with elderly Cajun women with whom they conversed in French. A general criticism of the program is that Cajun children are not being taught Cajun French, but dialects of French (e.g., from France) foreign to Louisiana.

John spent only one semester in a fourth grade French immersion program in a rural, grade 4-6, predominantly lower socioeconomic status (SES) school where a majority of the students were enrolled in the federally subsidized Free/reduced lunch program. Since only the academically able students were in the French immersion program, we rationalized that John, who had always been strong academically, would flourish. The other students certainly recognized John's capabilities, as he reported to us during his first week that another very good French speaker (whose mother was from France) asked him how he learned to speak French so well? John (9;7) answered 'Because my father says it's against the law in our house to speak English'. John was initially very enthusiastic about the program, saying he tried to speak with several of his fellow classmates in

French during recess. He said he even created a 'club for French speakers'. When I asked if his friends spoke French with him, John answered, 'sometimes, but they don't speak very well' (age 9;8).

While he did excel academically and was among the best students in his class, we had our doubts about how much French he was learning. Moreover, John's background was sufficiently different from his fellow classmates that he did not quite 'fit in'. Initially, John was always enthusiastically raising his hand in class with questions and answers. His Belgian French teacher really liked John's precociousness and fluency in French, believing he was a good example to the other students. She wrote that John was a 'breath of fresh air' in the class. But she also indicated that some students resented John's French speaking abilities. John's English teacher told us that she wished that John would ask fewer questions in class as she really didn't have time to answer them all. By the end of the semester, John had lost the academic enthusiasm that had typified his earlier school years. We reluctantly agreed once again that we could not leave him in an environment that did not seem to allow him to thrive academically. We did have to admit, however, that he probably spoke more French at home as a result of his being exposed to two and a half hours a day of French in school. Plus, he did learn the rudiments of French reading and writing for the first time. Thus, a foundation for future French literacy had been laid.

The twins, too, were doing very well academically in their country school's second grade French immersion program. The school began each day with the Pledge of Allegiance to the American flag – in French. Their school, like John's, was populated primarily by students from lower SES backgrounds, as a majority of the students were enrolled in the federal free/reduced price lunch program. It was our impression that the twins spoke the best French in their class. Their French teacher (from France) told us how surprised she was that Valerie knew expressions like 'feu d'artifice' (fireworks). Stephanie told us that several students in her class even wanted her to be their French teacher. Importantly, the twins' fluency in French was not necessarily an indicator of their language giftedness. Rather, their fluency was a result of their French-speaking environment at home since birth, and periodic societal French immersion in Québec.

Interestingly, more than nine years later the author met one of the Québécois immersion teachers who taught at this country school and remembered Valerie and Stephanie. She validated the linguistic influence of home and Québec at the time, commenting 'Oh yes, those were the two little girls who spoke like Québécois!' (A. Boivert, personal communication April 23, 2004).

As this spring 1995 semester wore on, we began to once again have nagging doubts about the quality of the children's education, both John's and the girls'. It was not the quality of the instruction that we questioned. The instruction was good. Rather, it was the quality of the children's peer environments that somewhat concerned us, a theme that we increasingly found ourselves reflecting upon, and eventually researching and writing about. The students at our children's two schools seemed to be fairly weak academically, as we had been informed beforehand. Given the impressionable age of our children, we felt that a stronger academic milieu was necessary, even if it would be all English speaking. As much as we wanted to rear children who were bilingual and biliterate, we felt it was even more important to rear children who had the strongest possible academic foundation, regardless the language.

Incidents like the following contributed to our growing concern. When John had completed a science project for his French immersion class, I asked him if he were going to write it up in French. He told me 'No, because no one else is'. I commenced lecturing him about how he was going to get from the program what he put into it. Still, knowing what I knew from my other research about the power of classmates to influence an individual's academics, I did not find John's reports from school very comforting. We did feel like the children learned to read and write some French as a consequence of being exposed to it in these country immersion classrooms. Moreover, we believed they were speaking much more French following this semester of French immersion in part because of their schooling. The other two major contributors, we were convinced, were the Cajun community into which we had just moved, and especially the satellite French Canadian television programming we were now constantly watching (more on this in the next chapter).

As a gauge of the children's overall academic functioning, after three months in their new French immersion programs, they took the California Achievement Test (in English, of course) in school. The twins were aged 8;10 and John was 10;8. All three children had composite scores above the 90th percentile. The children all finished this school year with a perfect 4.0 average, though we suspected that grading standards were lower than in their previous Baton Rouge private schools. So the combination of school French immersion, our prohibition against English in the home, our new Cajun community, and our encouragement to watch as much French television programming as the children wanted to, certainly did not seem to be hurting their English academics.

As for the French academics, we had their native French-speaking teachers complete the author-constructed French Proficiency Survey that was designed to measure the children's French competence (see Appendix 1 and 2 for the original French version of this survey, and its English translation). All three of our children's French immersion teachers circled the response on the questionnaire which said that our children were 'very capable' of functioning at their grade level in a francophone school. All three teachers did qualify this global assessment with additional comments that the children would still have to work hard to be successful in writing in French in a francophone school. We had all of their native French-speaking teachers over the next four years complete this identical survey on the children's French proficiency in their Louisiana schools as well as their Quebec school and summer camp. In this way, we were able to track their developing French proficiency. (See Table 10 on p. 179 for descriptive statistics of the survey.)

First Québec Schooling Experience

We were immediately able to test out their Louisiana French teachers' assessments that our children could function in a francophone school at their level after one semester of French immersion. Not only were they immediately immersed in French culture in Québec at the end of their Louisiana semester, but we enrolled the children in an all French-speaking elementary school for three weeks in June (the end of the school year is at least three weeks later in Québec than in Louisiana). We approached the principal the day after we arrived in Québec, and explained our family bilingual project to him. We told him that we did not want to be a bother to the teachers and increase their paperwork load, but only wanted him to allow our children to sit in their age appropriate classes and do everything that their Québécois peers were doing. He very kindly agreed to take our children, and immediately contacted the two teachers that would teach John and the twins. The teachers also gladly agreed to receive our children into their classrooms.

The only persons not gladly agreeing to our experiment were our two daughters. Valerie (7;1) was downright hostile to the idea, having repeated to us many times that she's 'on vacation' and doesn't want to go back to school. We cajoled and coaxed and persuaded, telling them how much fun school at the end of the year in Québec would be, when schools typically made many field trips. We also reminded the kids that the alternative was 'swatting mosquitoes' around our cottage for the first three weeks of June. We managed to drag the girls to the school (John went willingly), and after the first day, they felt better about the idea. It took two more days before they really warmed up to the idea of going to this new school. Within days all three children had assimilated very well into their respective peer groups, providing a classic example of the power of 'integrative motivation' (desire to communicate with friends who speak only the target language) to perform well in another language (Gardner & Lambert, 1972).

The elementary school is located in a very small Québec country community of only about 1000 residents. The school is so small that in the two years that our children attended, the first and second grades were combined into one class. Upon completing the sixth grade, the community children were bused to a secondary school about 15 miles away in a slightly larger community. The community is very insular, with the small population of students matriculating through all the grades together. Thus, it was amazing to me that our children, from the exotic 'far away' state of Louisiana, could so easily integrate into their respective peer groups. I knew these country Québécois children viewed Louisiana as something akin to the jungle in an Indiana Jones film, because I gave a volunteer lecture in the class John attended, and saw their wide-eyed wonder as I discussed Louisiana's poisonous snakes, spiders, and alligators.

The three children took and passed all their assignments and tests, which no doubt made them feel better about going to 'summer school'. The following entry shows how John's integration into a francophone peer group likely had much to do with his almost instantaneous switch from speaking predominantly English to speaking predominantly French around our dinner table within weeks.

> Suzanne and I stayed in the [school] parking lot after dropping him off for lunch, and watched him walk across the playground. Very quickly he (10;1) was surrounded by all 7 boys in his class, and was the center of attention for several minutes.

It did not hurt John's self-esteem that he scored a '100' on a spelling test of 100 French words in the same classroom as his French speaking peers. He studied very hard for this test, not wanting to be embarrassed around his new friends. Again, we see strong evidence of the power of the peer group on individual academic performance. The teacher had John's classmates give John a round of applause for his efforts. John's Québec school experience was building his linguistic self-confidence. During the three weeks he was in the school he did the assigned homework each night without too much complaint. One day he even gave the class a presentation comparing the American and Canadian dollars.

John told us he loved his Québec school much more than the French immersion program in Louisiana. Our sense was that the school was much calmer and more peaceful, with less roughhousing, violence, and student ridicule than we had observed in John's Louisiana school. Children at this Québec school even removed their street shoes before entering. The boys told John that the girls were chasing after him, and John was praised for his ability to play a version of gym hockey. In short, they liked him, and he liked them. When his three weeks of immersion came to an end, he informed us that he wanted to enroll in this school for an entire year! After the rough semester in his Louisiana country school, Suzanne and I were thrilled that our son was having so positive an experience in a Québec country school.

The girls completed all their classroom and homework assignments with apparent ease. Once, they brought home a stack of completed school assignments for us to sign. Just to make sure that the teacher had not read the questions to the girls or helped them with the answers, I quizzed them randomly on several questions. I asked them to read me the question and give me the answer. They had no difficulties at all. They had also checked out books from the school library and brought them home to read. Suzanne and I were both thrilled and amazed that they could read French so well!

When the children's three weeks of 'summer school' were over, all three indicated that they wanted to return next June and repeat the experience. Once again, we see the powerful effects of peer groups, which in this instance were all positive. Plus, the children were speaking more and better French, and had learned more about how to read and write the language. Their Canadian experience seemed to come much closer to what authentic school second language immersion is all about. Moreover, at least based on the twins' experience, their authentic language immersion in a Canadian school seemed far superior to attending a language immersion program with peers who are all learning the second language together, most only appearing to be 'extrinsically motivated' (Oxford & Shearin, 1994) by factors such as good grades. Our children's experiences suggest that for some students an 'immersion' program that actually requires the student to 'sink or swim', with native speakers, may be the best for learning to read and write another language – provided, of course, that they don't 'sink'. Importantly, we, the parents, provided much support and encouragement, which likely helped make the children's Québec 'school immersion' experience a success. Also, the children already spoke the language. But their reading and writing skills were very rudimentary compared to their Québec peers, and our children at this time would likely have been labeled 'limited English proficient' (LEP) had they demonstrated a comparable level of English proficiency in the United States.

The children's Québécois teachers completed surveys I created to measure the children's French proficiency, and all indicated that the children could function in a francophone school at their level, though in this first summer at the Québec school the girls' teacher indicated the twins might need some extra support in the first months of such an experience. The twins' second grade teacher in Québec also indicated that the twins did not read or write as well as a native French student of the same grade, an assessment that is not surprising. John's teacher indicated that he did tend to confuse the gender of French nouns, something also noted by a friend of the family regarding the girls' spoken French.

Suburban School French Immersion

Upon returning to Louisiana after the summer of the Québec school immersion experience, we transferred our children into the more affluent suburban Lafayette schools where Suzanne secured a position as a fourth grade French immersion teacher. The twins entered a French immersion program as third graders in Suzanne's suburban school, where the median fourth grade percentile ranking on the California Achievement Test was at the 77th percentile. The parish median percentile ranking for all fourth graders was at the 67th percentile. For comparison purposes, their previous Cajun country school district median percentile ranking for all fourth graders was only at the 40th percentile (Louisiana Department of Education, 1996).

The children's new suburban school offered even more French instruction than had their Cajun country school. The English portion of their instruction lasted only from 8:15 to 10:00, after which French instruction lasted the rest of the day, until 3:10. As in their Cajun immersion program, only native French speakers taught in these suburban immersion classes. There was no French immersion program available at John's grade level in Lafayette, and he was never again enrolled in such a program. Valerie and Stephanie once again appeared to be among the best French speakers in the program, as most of the other students were not being reared in bilingual households. As evidence of how well they were speaking French, later in the school year when their French teacher went on maternity leave and was replaced by another Québécois teacher who spoke very little English, Valerie and Stephanie were asked to translate conversations between the new substitute and their English teacher.

At this point, the twins (aged 8;4) continued speaking French spontaneously at home, and at school around their schoolmates (but not _to_ their classmates outside of the classroom). After a couple of weeks in the program I asked them if they were still speaking in French to each other at school, and they answered 'oui'. They added that at recess (récréation) people were turning their heads and staring at them when they spoke in French, commenting that they were speaking 'chinois' (Chinese) or some foreign language like that. They also said that they were not speaking French to their French immersion friends because their friends did not speak well enough.

Our sense was that the suburban program our twins were in, and particularly the students in the program, were as academically advanced as any programs or students in the parish. Many of the twins' peers were also in the district's gifted academic program. The twins' Québécois teacher was demanding, making the students write much in French, for which we were very grateful. The twins would occasionally write notes to us in French, unprompted, and stick the notes under our pillows. Research conducted a few years later confirmed that the students across the state who participated in the programs available in several parishes (districts) performed better academically than their non-immersion peers (Caldas & Boudreaux, 1999). Still, for the first time, I now began to have reservations at this point in my twins' academic development that they might not be getting enough English in school, and that this lack could ultimately be detrimental to their English literacy. I assuaged my concerns by reminding myself often that as two educators, Suzanne and I placed so much emphasis on academics in our household that this 'pressure' would somehow (though I was not sure how) translate into better grades.

Though John would never again be enrolled in French immersion, during the late winter of 1996 when he was in the fifth grade (age 10;9), he still read spontaneously in French. I recorded an instance of his taking a book from the 'Chair de Poule' series (*Goosebumps*) which Suzanne used in her own immersion class, and reading the entire book on his own. The book was 120 pages and written on at least a fifth grade level. So it no doubt helped in our efforts to encourage French literacy in our children that we had high interest books in French lying around. My 'sense' that just fostering a positive academic environment in the home would somehow rub off on the children once again seemed validated.

My faith in our project and our academic strategies was bolstered further at the end of the 1995-96 school year, when the children were aged 11;1 and 9;1. They once again all scored above the 90th percentile on the California Achievement Test and completed the year with straight 'A's. Though we were not exactly sure how our bilingual project was translating into strong academic performances, we could not ignore the various indicators of academic success. However, there was one indicator that worried me a bit. On our French teacher survey at the end of this school year, the girls' Québécoise French immersion teacher indicated that both Valerie and Stephanie spoke French with a pronounced [English] accent. I recalled one of Suzanne's original concerns about French immersion for our children, and wondered if she might not be right – that being exposed all day long to Americans speaking French with an English accent might be influencing the children's accents. Our concern in this area would continue to grow over the coming few years.

Second Québec School Experience

As the summer of 1996 approached, John was very excited about the prospect of returning to the Québec elementary school for three weeks and meeting his friends from the previous year. The twins were less excited about the idea of 'summer school', though at least they were not actively revolting against the idea, as they had done a year earlier. Immediately after arriving in Québec in early June, we approached the principal and once again received his permission to enroll our children in the school.

John was placed in the fifth grade class and the twins were put in the third grade class. As in the previous summer, they completed all the assignments and tests required of their Québécois classmates. Again, they performed well. For example, the girls took end of the year achievement tests, and on the section dealing with 'Les Sciences Humaines' (social sciences) Valerie had the highest score in the class, and Stephanie had the second highest score.

After the second three-week stint in the Québec elementary school, I had the children's teachers complete the same survey on the children's French capabilities as their previous year's Québec teachers had done (and which their Louisiana French teachers completed). This time, the teachers all gave the children (twins 9;1 and John, 11;1) higher marks in written, spoken, and oral comprehension, with the indication that all three children could function in a francophone school on their grade level. John's teacher wrote the comment that John's overall test results were comparable to the other students in his class. His teacher also indicated the presence of a moderate English accent when John spoke French. However, the twins' teachers noted a strong English accent in the girls' spoken French. So did we. Once again, we wondered if perhaps this might be a consequence of their Louisiana French immersion program. We were hoping that two months of societal French immersion would help erase vestiges of the English influence on their spoken French.

Summer Camp and French Literacy

The French-speaking summer camp that our children attended for much of their childhood and into adolescence also had an educational component that fostered the children's French literacy. Certain activities for the campers required reading and writing in French, and the children 'learned through doing'–à la John Dewey. Also, I was able to get feedback from camp counselors about their perceptions regarding our children's literacy compared to other children their ages.

For example, during an entire week in July 1997, when Valerie (10;2), Stephanie, and John (12;2) were the only children in her group, a camp counselor had them write a script and present a piece of theater to the public. Thus, the counselor had a pretty good idea how well they could read and write French. So, at the end of their day camp experience, I had the counselor fill out my standard questionnaire form on each of the three children's written, spoken, reading and oral French comprehension. Interestingly, she felt that the girls wrote more grammatically correct French than John. Perhaps this was the result of school French immersion? She also indicated that John had more of a pronounced English accent than did the twins. In the comments section of the questionnaire she wrote that John had '… plus de difficulté à se débrouiller en français' (had more difficulty getting along in French), though 'il fonctionne très bien'. (He functions very well). She indicated that his biggest problem was with the masculine and feminine. Her observations are interesting, because during this summer both their grandmother and aunt said that they thought John spoke more like a Québécois than the twins. These contradictory observations lend support to the notion that accents are often 'in the ear of the beholder'. The camp counselor's overall assessment was that all three children could function 'très bien' (very well) in a French school at their level.

Over the coming years, the children continued to attend this summer camp as either 'day campers', resident campers, and eventually counselors themselves. Five years after the camp counselor's above assessment, and just prior to their being hired as counselors, the twins attended a five-week resident counselor-training course at the camp when they were 15;2. They were able to perform all of the academic components of the course successfully. Out of the approximately 50 counselor trainees, Valerie was chosen as the outstanding trainee in a ceremony following the session. So we see that Valerie and Stephanie not only acquired a measure of French literacy very early (as early as the second grade), but were learning at a rate that allowed them to function at a practical level with their Québécois peer groups into their high school years.

Language Proficiency and Academic Placement

So, we see in the previous chapters that the children are fluent speakers of French and English, with dramatic fluctuations between French and English preference largely dependent on whether the children were in English-speaking Louisiana or French-speaking Canada. Overall, the children have performed well academically, having passed the Louisiana state criteria for placement into the 'Gifted' educational program. Each has had at least a 3.0 annual GPA on a 4-point scale during each year of the study. The children's measured IQ's as determined by independent, multiple, professional assessments, are all above the 90th percentile. Over the period of study, the children have consistently had composite scaled scores above the 85th percentile on school-administered national standardized-tests.

The children have never been administered a nationally normed French-test. However, we have accumulated a large body of evidence from many sources, including school district administered placement tests and SAT II's, which indicate that the children had become very literate in French by the time they reached high school. The evidence also indicates that the children probably do not function at the level of a native francophone student who only ever attended a francophone school. On the author-constructed French Proficiency survey, the children's several native French-speaking teachers in both Louisiana and Québec have all indicated that the children are literate in French. These same teachers have also indicated that the children could function well in a francophone school on their age level. As noted earlier, by the second grade the children were able to adequately perform every academic task performed by their francophone peers in the all-French-speaking Québec elementary school. Indeed, the three children commented to us that they found the curriculum easy.

At the end of the eighth grade, both girls (age 14;0) passed a state of Louisiana French placement test that qualified them for high school French IV, though only one girl actually enrolled. Valerie (age 14;3) has since told us that the class was 'too easy' for her. John (age 16;0) took a French proficiency test at the end of the tenth grade for the residential school for math, science, and the arts in Louisiana, and likewise placed into French IV, though he complained to us (age 16;3) that he found conjugating French verbs to be challenging. The three children regularly read novels in French simply for the pleasure of reading – with no parental prompting. Examples include 'Seigneur des Anneaux' ('Lord of the Rings' – John, summer 2001) and John Grisham's 'L'Associé' (The Partner' – Valerie, summer 1999). Upon returning to the U.S. from Québec in August 2001, Valerie made a photo scrapbook of a bicycle trip she took with a French-speaking summer camp. All of her captions were written in French. We had no part in this project. The three children regularly communicate with their Québec friends in both written letters and e-mail, always in French. They also write their Québécois relations in French. Once, when Valerie and I were traveling to Chicago for an academic conference, Valerie (9;11) sat down at our hotel room table and wrote one set of grandparents a postcard in English, and her French-speaking grandmother a postcard in French.

Finally, as a sort of capstone measure of the twin's overall literacy in French, as high school seniors both took the French SAT II, and both scored above the 83rd percentile.

In short, all the various evidence point to fairly strong French literacy on the part of the children, which is unforced, and seems entirely organic. Still, they probably do not write in French as fluently as native speakers attending all-French schools, who write in French on a daily basis. We do feel that a comment about the effect of the Louisiana French immersion program on the twins' French pronunciation is in order. We could not help but remark that for several years, until the twins were approximately 15;0, that they at times spoke French with what seemed fairly pronounced American English accents (also noted by several of their French teachers on the author-constructed proficiency survey, and Québécois relatives). We also noticed similar, even stronger American English accents among their French immersion friends, with whom we made an effort to speak French. Indeed, Suzanne taught in French to many of the twins' friends when they were in her fourth grade immersion class, where she could observe their speech behaviors on a daily basis. Not only did we notice the presence of an accent, but we also noted that the twins and their French immersion friends employed Anglicisms in their French that one would never see a native French-speaking child using. This included speaking French with English syntax, i.e., word order.

We were not the only researchers who noticed the use of Anglicisms among their children in the French immersion program, and who attributed these speech patterns to the other immersion classmates. The same phenomena was observed by another French-speaking couple who were rearing their children bilingually, and had also enrolled two of their three children in the immersion program. This family returned yearly to France for extended summer vacations. The mother is a native of France and a teacher in the French immersion program, and the father is a native French-speaking Cajun with a Ph.D. in francophone studies. Both parents are experts in the acquisition of French as a second language. What they noticed was that their two children in the immersion program were picking up incorrect French word order from their immersion classmates. For example, their children were translating word for word from English into French. Thus, they were uttering phrases like 'jaune voiture' (yellow car) instead of 'voiture jaune', and 'il a donné à moi', (he gave to me) instead of 'il m'a donné', and ' je cherche pour le livre' (I'm looking for the book) instead of 'Je cherche le livre' (D. Cheramie, personal communication, July 11, 2003). The Cheramies, like us, also noted the absence of such incorrect French language constructions among their older son, who, like John, was too old for the French immersion program. Once again, we see evidence for the strong influence of an individual's peers on the way he or she speaks. Still, the twins probably write more grammatically and syntactically correct French than does John, and this we attribute largely to their school French immersion programs.

Yet another very interesting example of the power of peers to influence accent was recounted by a native French language immersion expert and teacher who had only one of her two sons enrolled in a French immersion program in country Cajun schools just outside of the more cosmopolitan Lafayette (personal communication, N. Boudreaux, September 21, 2004). In fact, John was originally in the same Cajun country immersion classroom as this woman's son. She recounted that her older son, who never attended French immersion, spoke French with the accent of her native France, to which she returned regularly for summer and Christmas vacations. She believed that staying home with him and speaking only French to him for the first nine months of his life was an important factor in influencing his accent. However, her younger son who was enrolled in a French immersion program learned to speak French not like her, but like a Cajun, in both accent and syntax. She attributed his accent and syntax to being surrounded by Cajun children who didn't speak French with an American accent, like Valerie and Stephanie's peers. Rather, her son's Cajun classmates already spoke English with a Cajun accent. Thus, his peers' Cajun accents in English, the mother believed, transferred to her son's French who was being taught mostly by Belgians and Canadians! In other words, it was the younger son's immersion peers, and not his mother or francophone teachers who were shaping how he spoke French.

French Proficiency Surveys

In order to gauge the children's perceptions of their proficiency in French, I also asked them to complete a variation of the same French Proficiency Survey that I asked their French teachers to complete on them. They filled out the French version of my survey when they were 10;10

(twins) and 12;10 (John). Then, I asked the children to complete the same survey more than five years later when they were 16;1 and 18;1, respectively. During these same two administrations I also had the children complete the author-constructed Bilingual Self-perception Survey. The results from both administrations of this second survey are examined in more detail in Chapter 10, when a comparison is made between their early adolescent and late adolescent responses in order to gauge the changing perceptions of their bilingualism. Likewise, the results from the second administration of the child French Proficiency Survey are examined in Chapter 10, and compared with the children's answers on the first administration of this survey, to which I now turn.

Recall that each survey question was followed by a Likert scale with values ranging from '1', very inferior, to '5', very comparable. The French Proficiency Surveys were written in French, but translated into English in the appendices for this book's readers.

First, we look at how the children rated themselves on the French Proficiency Survey when they were 10;10 (twins) and 12;10 (John) respectively. We focus on the children's responses to three questions: general oral expression, general written expression, and ability to function at their level in a francophone school. Afterwards, we will examine more carefully the children's perceptions of the presence of an English accent when they speak French [Question #8]. (See Table 10 on p. 179 for descriptive statistics of French Proficiency Survey.)

The children, who were in grades five and seven, respectively, rated themselves high in overall general oral expression in French, with Stephanie giving herself the highest value of '5', believing she spoke comparably to a francophone child her age. Valerie and John both assigned themselves values of '4'. So, they did believe they spoke the language well. In the area of overall written expression in French, the values for John, '1' and Stephanie, '2', indicate they felt their writing was inferior when compared to an average francophone child. Valerie, on the other hand, assigned herself a value of '4', suggesting she compared her French writing ability quite favorably with other francophone children her age.

Did they think they could thrive in a totally francophone school? A value of '1' on this question indicated 'incapable' and a '5' indicated 'very capable'. John took the middle ground, assigning himself a value '3'. Both Stephanie and Valerie, however, were unequivocal in their belief in their abilities to do well in a francophone school, assigning themselves values of '5'. Thus, John's overall self-assessment of his ability to speak, write, and function in French were lower than his twin sisters' when he was 12;10. The twins' higher assessment of their abilities is likely a consequence of their already having been in a school French immersion program for three years when they completed the survey, and indeed their actual greater proficiency in reading and writing in French at this point in their school experience. We (the parents) have corrected the twins' French writing for both school projects and letter-writing to friends and relations in Québec, and offer our subjective but informed perception that their French literacy was not quite to the level of children their age who had only attended French schools. However, this did not necessarily mean that they could not have eventually flourished in a totally francophone school, but that they would have likely struggled in the beginning – like many LEP students initially do in the general population of American schools. Interestingly, though, recall that the twins actually made the comment that they found the Québec francophone school they attended easier than their American school.

As an overall global measure of French proficiency, we calculated an average for each child's rating on each question, by adding them together and dividing by the total number of survey questions (10). This is a valid approach, since each question was phrased such that the higher the Likert number, the greater the proficiency in some aspect of French. A perfect score would be 50 (10 × 5). John's overall average was 31, Stephanie's was 43, and Valerie's was 36. Thus, we see the children's overall assessment of their proficiency in French as they approached adolescence varies a good deal among themselves, but that John's self-assessment was significantly lower than his sisters' assessment of their abilities.

Comparison of Children's and Teachers' Perceptions of French Proficiency

Now, let's look at how the children's French teachers over the four years that I administered the survey viewed each child's French proficiency, and how their assessments compare with the children's own self-assessments. First, in the same way that I calculated a global rating for each child, I calculated a global teacher rating by first calculating the total number of Likert points assigned by each teacher on his/her survey. Next, I added together the total number of all teachers' ratings for each child, and divided by the total number of teachers (10 for each girl and 5 for John).

The overall teacher average for John was 36.6, for Stephanie it was 40.4, and for Valerie it was 40.6. Thus, we see that John's self-assessment rating of his own abilities was much lower than his teachers assigned to him (31 vs. 36.6), whereas Valerie's self-assessment was only slightly lower (36 vs. 40.6) and Stephanie's self-assessment was actually higher than her teachers' (43 vs. 40.4). Thus, we can perhaps speculate that John's French speaking was not being validated in his American middle school experience to the extent that his sisters' French speaking was more highly prized in their French immersion program. This difference in the value placed on French may account for his skewed (and inaccurate) perception of his true abilities–which in reality may not have been much different from his sisters at that time.

One question that was particularly intriguing to us was how the teachers rated the children in terms of an identifiable English accent when the children spoke French. The average teacher rating for John was a 3, for Valerie it was 3.4, and for Stephanie it was 3.3. However, another way to examine how the teachers responded to this question compared to the other survey questions was to determine if they were either more or less consistent in their responses. In other words, were the ratings the teachers assigned to this item more varied when compared to other items?

By generating a standard deviation for each item (a statistical measure of variability), we can answer this question. What we see is that the standard deviation for item 8, which asks how pronounced the child's English accent is when speaking French, is greater for each set of surveys completed on each child than any of the other items. In other words, their French teachers are less consistent in how they answer this question, some giving the children '1's' (a strong accent) while other teachers gave the same child a '5' (no accent). Thus, there is a great deal of subjectivity from teacher to teacher regarding what appears to be an English accent, with teachers in Québec more likely to indicate the presence of an English accent than others.

Can it be that having an 'accent' is perhaps more relative and subjective than is generally believed? Though the children almost surely did not speak exactly like native Québécois at the age when they first completed the French Proficiency Survey, and thus could be judged as having an accent by comparison with native speakers, could it be their accent was not just influenced by English? Could it be that their accents were, like most of us, influenced by many factors? In their cases, these factors are certainly Québécois French, but also Cajun French, French from France, and in John's case, French from Belgium (the native land of his only immersion teacher). To complicate matters further, there is also a French African American dialect prevalent in the Louisiana community of our residence at that time, referred to as 'Creole' (Brasseaux & Conrad, 1992). This dialect of Black French, and the English dialect spoken by these bilingual African Americans of St. Landry and St. Martin Parishes is unique enough to have been the subject of very specialized linguistic research (Dubois & Horvath, 2003).

Of course, I, their father, speak French tinged with an American English accent, and I cannot discount my influence on how my children learned to speak the language. In the end, then, it seems we all have accents. A major difference in the factors influencing John's and the twins' accents in French was that the twins were exposed to much more English accented French from their peers in their Louisiana school French immersion program than was John. We return to the issue of accents again in Chapter 10 when we examine how the children's perceptions of their bilingualism changed the next time we administered an identical survey more than five years later.

Chapter 7
Reading, Media, Hobbies and Games

Introduction

This chapter presents the study's findings with regard to the influence of media, hobbies, games, and reading at home on the children's developing bilingualism and biliteracy. The chapter pays particularly close attention to the influence of television and videocassette viewing on the children's propensity to speak French. Also examined are the influences of hobbies, such as computers, on the children's and parents' language preferences. The influence of parental reading to the children in both languages as toddlers and in early childhood is discussed first.

The Foundation: Reading

Being exposed to the printed word in the home has been identified as a strong positive predictor of vocabulary, acquisition of knowledge, motivation, and school success (Stanovich, 1986; Steinberg, 1997). Suzanne and I read French and English books to our children on a consistent basis from as early as when they were in diapers, a practice which is positively correlated to language ability and high scores on pre-school measures of reading readiness (Crain-Thoreson & Dale, 1992). Since Suzanne was teaching in a French immersion program when John was born, we had access to French reading material for children from the very beginning. When we read either French or English books to the children in infancy, we would put our fingers on the words we were reading so that they could begin associating the spoken with the written word. Thus, they had exposure to the French written word from almost as soon as we began reading it to them.

We were indiscriminate in our choice of English or French stories, and the children seemed equally happy hearing a story in either language. Not all bilingual families are as nonchalant as we were in our choice of language when reading stories to our children. For example, a child being reared in English and Japanese in Okita's (2002) study had problems understanding the Japanese stories read to him. Perhaps this is related to his father speaking no Japanese in the home.

Our reading sessions began when the children were toddlers, and were frequent, fun, and interactive experiences, allowing them to ask questions and comment on the material. One goal of our approach was to link academics and pleasure in the young children's psyches as early as possible (Schickendanz et al., 1990). We shared picture books and animated-type books with three-dimensional foldouts, making our reading sessions as entertaining as they were educational. The father can be a bit of a clown, and this may have increased the reading 'fun factor' for the children. The research base on reading to very young children shows that those children who are read to daily are greatly advanced in language comprehension and production compared to those children not exposed to this regimen (Valdez-Menchaca & Whitehurst, 1992; Whitehurst et al., 1994).

When John was three years old, we conducted a little experiment with him. We created flash cards containing both English and French words, which we showed him separately. He seemed to learn the words effortlessly, and quickly built a vocabulary of over 20 sight words in each language. It was a like a game for him. (We did not repeat this exercise with the twins at so early an age.) We believe that the children's early exposure to the written word in English and French, in the context of frequent and fun reading sessions, provided a strong foundation upon which the children's later English and French literacy skills would develop and flourish. However, since the children started schooling exclusively in English, and had no formal French instruction until they were 9;8 and 7;8, respectively (when they entered a French immersion program), the first language they began to read in was English.

The children began reading French for pleasure following their first semester in a formal school French immersion program (discussed in the previous chapter). All three began reading French comic books in Québec during the summer of 1995 at ages 10;1 (John) and 8;1 (twins). Most of these comic books were 'Betty and Veronica', 'Archie', and 'Jughead' comics translated from the original English into French. At first, either Suzanne or I read the comic books to the children. However, we expected them to follow along with us frame by frame. I often checked them, too, to see if they knew where I was in the story. They always knew. So at least from the ages of 10;1 and 8;1, respectively, the children could sight read French. I have to credit their first semester in a formal school French immersion program in the previous spring for giving all three children the jump-start they needed to begin spontaneously reading in French.

Soon after, the children were also reading on their own in French in Louisiana. In fact, I have to attribute American TV (discussed below) for probably giving John the inspiration for reading at least one book in French. During the early spring of 1996 John (age 10;9) read a book translated into French from the series Goosebumps – which the children had started watching regularly on English-speaking TV.

By the summer of 1996, when the children were 11;1 and 9;1, respectively, I recorded that they were reading something in French in their beds in our Québec cottage almost every night. I bought special lights for each of their small beds so they could read after their siblings went to sleep without bothering anyone. Prior to my installing these lights, there was constant complaining from those who wanted sleep about those who wanted to read. Secretly, we were delighted that they had such a strong desire to read. Of course, the children loved reading comics in English as well, and would eventually begin each day reading the newspaper comics in Louisiana while eating breakfast. The children's early ability to read in two languages led to interesting language mixing incidents. For example, one day Valerie (9;11) wanted to share with me a comic strip from our local Louisiana newspaper that she thought was particularly funny. She read the comic strip to me entirely in French – though it was written in English.

It was during the summer of 1997, when the children were aged 12;1 and 10;1, respectively, that their passion for reading any kind of comic books became all-consuming. We fed their hunger by buying literally dozens of French comic books for them, which they devoured, reading them each many times for hours on end. They often completed a quarter-inch thick comic book in one sitting. Since 10 months elapsed between each summer's comic book reading fest, the children would start over again each year and re-read their stacks. Importantly, we never had to suggest that they pick one up. It was almost reflexive on their part to reach for one. In fact, a few months later in Louisiana, I once observed Valerie (10;6) reading a 'Yassin' comic book – in French – for her *English* reading assignment. As I was working on a draft of this book chapter one morning in July 2003, Valerie (16;2) woke up, sat down at the kitchen table, picked up the Québec City French daily *Le Soleil*, and went right to the comics.

Until the children were about aged 14 or 15, we also attended weekly mass at a chapel around our lake in Québec. I made it a point to always hand them the missal, which was in French. I noted that the children were able to follow along with the readings from as early as when the twins were 8;2. Valerie often sang along with the French hymns as well, reading the lyrics from her missal. Her grandmother, who was ever complimenting them on their bilingualism, was so impressed with Valerie's ability to sing along using the missal, that she gave her a candy after the mass for her accomplishment.

As alluded to in earlier chapters, in spite of our best efforts to surround the children with French speaking in Louisiana, including reading and speaking French in the home, the children's exposure to either written or spoken French represented only a relatively small part of the children's day for much of their early childhood. Thus, we realized very early in the project the need for the children to be exposed to additional French media in Louisiana to help balance the powerful English influences that surrounded them.

Vive la télévision française! (Long Live French Television!)

In our efforts to expose the children to French-speaking media, we sought opportunities from very early in the project to expose the children to French-speaking videocassettes and television. Both of these media would become very important tools in our language arsenal, with television becoming perhaps the more important of the two.

Television has become a major cultural force since its initiation in the early 1950s. The U.S. Census Bureau (2004) predicted that the average American adult would watch 32 hours of television per week during 2004. There has been much debate over the effects of spending so much time in electronic communion with the 'flickering blue parent'. Some have argued that time spent focused on the small screen vitiates school performance, since this time could be more profitably spent reading or engaging in other developmentally useful activities (Potter, 1987; Hornik, 1981). Other opponents of TV contend that television not only uses up time that could be better spent, but also cultivates mental habits, like laziness, that are inconsistent with success in school (Scott, 1956; Hornik, 1978, 1981), and creates an intellectually passive and uncritical culture within its audience (Postman, 1985). Some detractors go so far as to condemn TV for exacerbating most of society's ills, intellectual and moral (Medved, 1992).

On the other hand, television's proponents (yes, there actually are some) answer these charges by pointing out that TV brings information to viewers that they would otherwise miss. No other medium of communication, they argue, can bring households the visual and audible world with such richness of detail (Bianculli, 1992; Briller & Miller, 1984; Davies, 1989). Other research suggests that the value of television – whether positive or negative – depends on the social context as well as the needs of a particular situation (Caldas & Bankston, 1999a). We decided that the social context of our family project, and the need to further the bilinguality and biliteracy of our children, did indeed call for TV – French television, that is. We sided with Bianculli's (1992) logic that the television medium can indeed open up children's eyes to other worlds and possibilities, especially when the only alternative cultures are their local and national (USA) ones. Our local Louisiana media did not offer 24-hour French television programming, so when we found a source that did, we literally seized it. We would be hard pressed to overestimate the effect that both French-speaking videocassette films and TV have had on our children's French speaking, comprehension, and even literacy abilities.

Though we had been showing French videocassettes to our children from almost infancy (more on this below), we still felt that French TV had the potential to be an even more important influence on the children's language development. We had been exploring the possibility of buying an expensive parabolic antenna early in our children's lives. After pouring over the want ads when we resided in anglophone Louisiana, we finally offered $500 to buy a second-hand unit from someone trying to sell theirs. Fortunately, our offer was refused. The television gods were watching over us, and unexpectedly smiled down on us when we bought our house not much later in Acadiana in 1994 when the children were 9;4 and 7;4, respectively. The Acadian style house (yes, even the architecture gods smiled upon us) came with a parabolic satellite antenna capable of receiving Québécois and French stations. We were literally beside ourselves with joy over our new tool. On August 30, right after we signed for our new house, I recorded one of the reasons why in my fieldnotes:

> Suzanne made the comment the other day that she thinks that due to the antenna, we are now over the hump in terms of ensuring that French will remain the dominant language of our family. I hope so. I must admit, the two of us have slipped up occasionally lately, when talking business [related to buying the house]. However whenever I notice we've switched to English, I immediately switch back to French and implore Suzanne to 'Parle Français!'

So, as is hinted at in the above entry, we were clearly in battle mode with the purchase of our new house, its French TV capability, and our impending move to francophone Louisiana (the educational battle was discussed in the previous chapter).

We seized this golden opportunity to further the goals of our project. We tuned the satellite TV to a French Canadian station, and largely left it tuned to Québec stations for at least the next two years. In fact, we even refused to hook up our aerial antenna to receive local programming for a full year. Beginning in about November 1994 when John was 9;7 and the twins were 7;7, we began receiving essentially all of our TV entertainment and news from Québec, and to a lesser extent, from TV5 in France, which was beamed down from the same satellite.

At this formative point in our children's development, rather than pry our children away from the screen like many concerned parents who wanted their young ones engaged in more 'meaningful activities', we smiled down contentedly on ours as they huddled before the flickering screen which fed them non-stop, rapid-fire French in vivid sound and color. It was not long before we began to see the benefits of our strategy. The following is but one example: about six months after we hooked up the satellite antenna, I was waiting for the morning school bus with Stephanie (7;11), when she used a new French word she apparently learned a couple of nights earlier when we watched the French version of the film *Karate Kid* together. She referred to a 'party' as a 'boom' in French, just like a young adolescent in the film (Québécois don't normally use this word).

Once we had access to French language programming, our one command about television watching was that it had to be FRENCH-speaking TV–not American. Apparently the children got my message, and adhered to the rule, at least for approximately eighteen months to two years. In the beginning, our rule was taken quite seriously. For example, our children loved watching cartoons on Saturday morning, and had done so since they were toddlers. On one Saturday morning not long after we began receiving French-speaking programming, as I walked by the living room I overheard John (9;8) say, 'Goody, they've got cartoons!' But then one of the girls (7;8) said, 'But they're in English. Dad won't let us watch cartoons in English'. The other girl said, 'Go ask him'. One of the twins came to me and asked, 'Dad, can we watch English cartoons?' I told her no. When I passed in front of the TV a few minutes later, the three were seated and watching French cartoons they had found on a Québec station.

Even more than two years later, the children were still very conscientious of our NO-ENGLISH TV rule. Once, I walked into the living room on a Saturday morning and apparently surprised the children who were watching cartoons on TV. Stephanie (9;11) abruptly turned around and blurted out defensively 'C'est en français!' (It's in French!) before I even had a chance to say anything. She was afraid I was going to turn off the TV.

Indeed, the children were watching so much French TV programming that I began to be concerned that perhaps they were watching too much. They had memorized the commercials, and even had their favorites, which were usually the glitzy Canadian beer commercials. They grew so attached to some programs that I could hardly pull them away from the set. For instance, one of their favorite weekly programs was 'Moi, et L'autre' (Me and the Other), a Québécois sitcom with such fast paced idiomatic Québec dialogue that I would venture to say even an individual from France would have had trouble completely understanding the discourse. I know I did. One evening in particular when our satellite reception was very marginal, the children (10;9 and 8;9) were glued to the set watching 'Moi, et L'autre'. The noisy static from the set was grating on my nerves, and I approached the TV to turn it off. The children protested so vehemently that I capitulated and let them finish watching the show they loved so much.

Another occasional concern Suzanne and I had with Québec and French television programming was that it tended to be more sexually explicit than American TV (hard to believe, but true). For example, references to alternative sexuality, like lesbianism and sadomasochism, seemed more common. There was also much more explicit nudity. Language too, seemed to be rougher. We lived in a very conservative part of Louisiana, where at least in theory, some subjects were simply off limits. Like all children, mine no doubt internalized to some extent these conservative community standards. My wife and I both found ourselves grimacing uncomfortably at times at some of the sexually explicit images and dialogue spewing forth from the francophone programming. Suzanne would sometimes make a face, pull me aside, and say something like, 'Steve, do you think we should let the kids see this show?' Not that we were raising our children to be prudes. Indeed, I always felt that our fairly extensive traveling probably contributed to our children being more open minded than some of their peers who rarely, if ever, left the state. However, they still lived in Louisiana most of the time, and had learned, like everyone else, what the local norms were. And the norms regarding sexuality tended to be very traditional.

For about two years, during which time the children ranged in age from approximately 9;8 to 11:8 (John) and 7;8 to 9;8 (twins) our media schedule was as follows: In the evening, we watched French-Canadian television, and on Saturday mornings, the children watched French cartoons. On Saturdays, our radio was often tuned to KRVS, my university's public radio station that featured Creole-French Zydeco music. On Sundays we tuned to the same station for a day of French Cajun music, where the D.J. spoke predominantly in French. On both Saturday and Sunday evenings we watched feature-length films on either Québec or French TV stations.

It was not until the spring of 1996, after a year and a half in our new home, that the children began to watch English TV programming on a regular basis – though still less than French TV programming. I felt like their increased English TV watching was related to their increase in English speaking at about the same time (see Figure 1 on p. 166 for trend), and we began trying to reassert some semblance of control over the set. However, once the 'English TV genie' was out of the bottle, it was very difficult – indeed, impossible – to put it back in. Like an addiction, the children developed a quick affinity for certain American TV programs. One of these was 'The Simpsons'. One Sunday evening, when the children were 10;9 and 8;9, they had just begun to watch 'The Simpsons' when I walked into the living room. I quickly sized up the situation, then declared that they had a choice: they could either turn off the set, or watch 'Les Beaux Dimanches' (Beautiful Sundays), a weekly Québec program that featured a film. Following some crying and pouting, we reached a compromise: we would all watch the film *Patton* (in English) which I had checked out of the library. I rationalized that at least *Patton* was a bit of a history lesson. Our formerly 'divine right of parental control' over the TV was slipping ... and Suzanne and I both knew it.

As if to emphasize our growing impotence, a month latter, when I turned off the TV at 18:30 in the evening right after an English program, John (10;10) started complaining. He contended that if he didn't watch the sitcom 'Fresh Prince of Belaire', which was on next, then he couldn't talk about it at school the next day with his friends, and would feel 'left out'. He swore all his friends watched it. Ouch. What was a parent to do? We were so concerned about their English TV watching, that when the set malfunctioned a month later, I decided that I was in no hurry to fix it and it stayed 'broke' for a few weeks. No TV, Suzanne and I rationalized, was better than English TV – even if it meant they would miss Québec programming.

Though our children were grumbling with increasing frequency at our TV censorship, most of the programming they watched was still in French through the end of 1997 when they were 12;7 and 10;7 – even though we had hooked up our rabbit ear antennas and began receiving local Lafayette programming in early 1997. Thus, for almost three years the children were exposed to more French than English TV. A typical day of television programming in January 1997, even with the growing resistance to our control over the TV set, looked like the following (recorded on January 20):

11:30-12:30:   Les Belles Histoires des Pays d'en Haut (French sitcom from Québec)
15:00-15:30:   La band à Frankie (French cartoons from Québec)
17:00-18:00:   CBC Nouvelles (French news from Québec)

18:00-18:20: Channel 10 News (English news from Lafayette, Louisiana)
18:30-19:00: La Petite Vie (French sitcom from Québec)
19:00-20:00: Quatre et demie (French sitcom for adolescents from Québec)

One of the biggest disappointments in our bilingual project occurred later in 1997 when the Canadian TV stations we had been receiving for three years went digital, and our analogue equipment could no longer receive their signals. At first we were mystified as to why all we could see was a blank gray screen when we tuned in our usual channels. After numerous telephone calls and e-mail requests to the Canadian stations, we eventually pieced together the problem, and after even more research discovered that it could cost us up to $2000 (at that time) to have a digital system installed and re-gain Canadian programming. As committed as we were to the project, we just could not justify so enormous an expense, and faced up to the sobering reality that any future TV in Louisiana would be in English. However, the timing could have been worse: we felt that we had exposed our children to French TV during the very formative period just prior to adolescence, when they were still receptive to our control of this major source of entertainment. As adolescents, they would not be so pliant.

To sum up, for 31 months the Louisiana home television set was tuned primarily to French-speaking stations in France and Canada, via satellite dish. This capability was lost in August 1997 when the children were 12;3 and 10;3, and, perhaps not coincidentally, corresponded with a subsequent decrease in recorded spoken French by the children in the home (see Figure 1 on p. 166). There were, however, other factors, like pre-adolescence and their American peer environments, which also depressed the children's French speaking in the home at about this time (more on these factors in the next chapter).

During summertime vacations in Québec, when the children were at home in our cottage, we did not discourage television viewing either. They spent much of their free time in our house watching their favorite television programs in French (or reading, which we discussed earlier). However, we had a household rule against listening to the one Québec English station our TV could receive. This rule was adhered to rigidly and naturally, and I cannot recall even one instance where an entire anglophone program was ever watched from beginning to end.

Videocassettes

While still in anglophone Louisiana, and before we acquired francophone TV programming via satellite, we decided that the children needed additional exposure to French media apart from family communications. Thus, we began the slow process, which continued for more than 10 years, of building a library of high-interest French-speaking videocassettes. In addition to purchasing cassettes, we rented and checked out from the library a steady stream of French videocassettes (which the Lafayette Public Library stocked for francophone citizens). The children would ultimately watch many of their favorite cassettes as many as 10, 15, or more times.

Our first VHS acquisitions, while still in anglophone Louisiana, included all 25 episodes of the Canadian series 'Téléfrançais' which the children liked very much, and which we played very often, likely more than 15 times apiece. 'Téléfrançais' was a high interest educational program that taught spoken, written, and French comprehension in a very subtle and entertaining fashion. It could be compared loosely to a sort of Sesame Street for older, pre-adolescent children. We also began acquiring the French versions of several feature-length films, including *The Little Mermaid* (*La Petite Sirène*), *Star Wars* (*La Guerre des Etoiles*), *Beauty and the Beast* (*La Belle et La Bête*), and *Snow White* (*Blanche Neige*) that the children also watched so many times over the years that we lost count. We eventually acquired a library of 63 individual full-length VHS cassettes containing French films and programming.

It is important to point out that like exposure to French TV programming, we provided our children access to these videocassettes at what was probably the opportune time in their development. They were still young enough where they loved to watch the same film again and again, and repetition is a tried and true technique for learning a second language. Repetition is simply multiple input, and the more input there is the more likely there is to be the corresponding output (Baddley, 1986; Cowan, 1995). The interests of adolescents differ somewhat (as we note in Chapters 8-10), and they are less likely to get the same pleasure from repetitive film watching. Moreover, an adolescent's peer group takes on increasingly greater importance, and is more likely to take a young person out of his or her domicile and away from the TV (Berndt, 1979; Prado, 1958) – for better or worse.

Good examples of the influence of repetitive French film watching were some expressions John learned from the translated film *Ritchie Rich*. When John was 10;4, he surprised me by saying , 'C'est génial papa'. [That's cool, dad]. John had learned the expression from the *Richie Rich* film that he had watched three times to that point. I knew he had not learned the expression in Québec, because Québécois rarely used this expression, preferring to say 'cool' instead of 'genial'. More than a year later, after John (11;10) had seen *Ritchie Rich* in French at least 10 or more times, he surprised me again. I was working on our lawn mower and called to John to 'cherche-moi les outils dans la boite-là, le set du box'. (Get me my tools there in the 'set du box' [socket set]). John answered me 'Tu veux dire les clés à douille'. (You mean 'les clés à douille'.) I asked him in French where he learned that sockets were called 'les clés à douille'. He told me from the film *Ritchie Rich*.

French videocassettes not only helped the children's French comprehension and vocabulary, but also their French literacy. During the summer of 1998, the girls and I had asked Suzanne how to say 'step mother' in French, but at the time she said she wasn't quite sure, since it could be more than one expression. A month later in Louisiana, when Valerie and Stephanie (age 8;3) were watching the videocassette *Blanche Neige* (*Snow White*) in French, Valerie suddenly called out to me in my office, 'Papa, on sait qu'est-ce que c'est 'stepmother' en français. C'est "marâtre".' (Dad, we know what 'stepmother' is in French. It's 'marâtre'.) So, I asked the twins 'Comment savez-vous ça?' (How do you know that?) They answered that they saw 'marâtre' written at the beginning of the film. I was curious, so I went into the living room and re-wound the film, replaying the first part that shows an open book with a paragraph explaining about Snow White and the wicked stepmother queen. Indeed, there were the words 'la reine marâtre' (the stepmother queen). I asked Valerie how she knew that 'marâtre' meant 'stepmother'. She answered that in the English version of the film (which we also had) 'stepmother the queen' was written in the same place. This incident demonstrates several important facts. For one, it showed the girls' acute curiosity to learn French. Secondly, it showed that they could read the script in French, recognize an unknown word, and link this word with what they had previously read in English. It also showed the importance of repetition. They had seen both English and French versions of *Snow White* many times, and had time to notice details such as 'reine marâtre' and make the connection with what they had seen in English.

Watching French-speaking films at the cinema, too, played a role, albeit a more minor one, in the stream of French entertainment the children received. The only times we could watch French-speaking films at a movie theater were when we visited Québec. But even here we applied the 'French-only' rule. In many Québec City theaters, there are often two salons for each film: one offering the English version, where applicable, and one offering the translated French version of the same film. Thus, there was ground for conflict. One day John (11;2) and I drove to Québec City to see the film 'Independence Day'. It was being shown in both French and English at the theater we went to, so we had the choice of which one to see. John wanted to see the English version, since one of his favorite American actors, Will Smith (of 'Fresh Prince of Belaire' fame), starred as a U.S. Marine fighter pilot in the film. I had to agree with him that the original version would probably be better, since it would have the actual voices of the American actors, with all of their idioms and expressions. However, I decided (to myself) it would be best for his French to see the French version, since I knew he would be glued to the screen for two hours trying not to miss a word – and thereby perhaps picking up some new expressions. So I made my solemn pronouncement. Of course, he didn't like my decision. So I pointed out to him that the English version started a half hour later, and I didn't want to be out too late that night. So, he acquiesced and we saw the French version. He still laughed at Will Smith's cocky comments in French, noting that they were funny even in the translation.

Hobbies: The Trojan Horses

Even though we felt very good about having French television in Acadiana and a growing library of French videocassettes, there were several English Trojan Horses that entered the equation, and it was not just English schooling and American peers, though these were probably the most important. Hobbies are very specific activities that have very specific terminology. This is particularly true of technology related areas. The following fieldnote entries make the point, beginning when John was 9;7:

> Last night, I loaded Word Perfect 6.0 on my computer, with John at my side. As we talked about the new software and its capabilities, I was conscious that almost all of our communication was in English. It's unfortunate, but almost all of the technical language of computers is in English.

A week later the enemy re-appeared:

> Again, while working with John on the computer, I found myself explaining computer related technology to him in English. There are so many English words (hard drive, tape backup, curser, load, etc.) which I don't know in French, that apparently it's just easier to speak in English than switch back and forth in both languages.

And yet again one month later when John was 9;8:

> Again, I noted that when I spoke with him about the computer both last night and the night before, I spoke more English than French. There are so many technical English words, like 'modem', 'hard-drive', 'baud', 'parity', 'disk-drive', 'bytes', 'logon', 'password', 'on-line' that I either don't know the French equivalents for, or don't have French equivalents, or have bad French equivalents, that it is so much easier to say these terms in English, which apparently triggers a switch to English. I try to speak in French sometimes, but am conscious that it is much more difficult, and end up switching back to English.

John would become increasingly enamored with computers, taking a university course in Louisiana when he was 11;8, and eventually building several of his own computers from individual components. In fact, he would eventually choose computer science as his university major. In listening to the audiotapes while recording the number of French and English words that we heard him speak, Suzanne and I were struck by how John would invariably shift into English when talking about computers. Eventually, I gave up trying to speak French when discussing technology-related issues with John. I suppose it was of some consolation to learn that the French, too, had the same penchant for using English words when there existed French equivalents (Dolbec, 2003). Fast forwarding a bit, in a phone conversation I had with John while he studied computer science at a distant university (age 19;7), we only spoke French – right up to the moment he began telling me about his new laptop. From that point on we spoke English.

Three additional hobbies that John and I would pursue together, entirely in English, were coin collecting, stamp collecting, and building/flying airplanes. I had the same concern as with computers, that whenever we would talk about coins, stamps, or airplanes, we tended to do it in English. I found that even discussing financial matters with John, like stocks, was easier for me in English, even though if I paused and reflected about what I needed to say, I could have explained myself in French. Indeed, I did at times do my best. For example, when John was 9;4, I asked him to read a short article in the Baton Rouge newspaper about the smallest coin ever minted in the U.S. (he was enthusiastically into collecting coins at that time). After he read some of the article, he exclaimed to me in English 'The smallest American coin was a gold dollar!' I immediately responded to him in French, 'Vraiment, ça c'est interesant!' (Really, that's interesting!). His very next sentence to me was in French. So I knew the importance of persevering – something that simply made me feel even guiltier when I was not being so vigilant.

And we were not always so vigilant. Even after being immersed in nine weeks of French while in Canada during the summer of 1996, we were not back in Louisiana for two weeks when John (11;3) and I were speaking about coins and computers in English again. It was so obvious a shift back into English that Stephanie was the one who pointed out our 'language deviancy' to us.

Adolescence conspired with another hobby, aviation, to almost completely snuff out French speaking between John and myself – at least when talking about our new passion. In the spring semester of 1997, when John was 11;9, we both enrolled in a private pilot class together at my university. All of the reading materials were, of course, in English. Thus, together we learned all of the terminology together in English, much of it for the first time. In many cases I could not have used the French equivalent even if I wanted to, since I simply did not know it. So, whenever we talked about anything related to flying, we almost invariably had to speak English. It was also during this spring that John essentially stopped speaking any French around our Louisiana dinner table for any reason (see Figure 1 on p. 166). Given his advanced pre-adolescence and increasingly early adolescent attitudes, we began to realize the futility of even pointing this out to him.

There were some heartening episodes in Louisiana in the area of pastimes. When John was 9;7 he told me that he taught our new Cajun neighbors the French word for computer: *'ordinateur'*. The neighbors were apparently quite serious about learning the word, because when the twins returned from a visit with the neighbors a couple of weeks later, they told us that the mother kept asking them again and again how to say 'computer' in French, because she just could not remember the word.

The children also liked to play a few French educational computer games including 'Mission Math' (Math Blaster), and 'Circus'. At times I even had to fight to get them off these games so I could do work on my computer. The children also knew several words and expressions in French that they had to later learn in English. For example, one day in August 1996 right after we returned to Louisiana from our Québec summer vacation, Stephanie (9;3) asked me if I knew how to do a certain swimming stroke, using the French word for the stroke. I had never heard of it, and told her so. When she demonstrated the stroke to me, I realized that it was the sidestroke, and told her the English term. She had never heard it before. On another occasion when I was explaining to Valerie (9;10) all of the sites to visit around Los Angles, I mentioned Malibu, where the TV show *Baywatch* was filmed. She corrected me in French, and said, 'Tu veux dire, Alerte à Malibu'. (You mean *'Alerte à Malibu'*.) At that point it occurred to me that she may have never seen the TV show in English, but watched a translated version of it daily on Québec TV during the summer. In French, the title is not 'Baywatch', but 'Alerte à Malibu'. Still, on balance, English tended to dominate in the realm of the children's extracurricular hobbies and activities.

Games

Like most children, ours have always loved playing games. Game playing presented its own challenges to our project. For example, Valerie and Stephanie were speaking almost only in French for almost three months after we returned to Louisiana from Québec in 1994. The two areas where I first noted them speaking English to each other were doing homework–and playing games together (age 7;5). One of the games was a card game with English words written on the cards, and the other was a board game invented by John, and written entirely in English. Both instances of the girls speaking English contrasted so sharply to their pattern of speaking mostly French that I felt compelled to immediately make fieldnote entries of what I had observed.

I used the children's interest in games as a springboard to teach correct French grammar usage. I devised a very simple game to play with the children around the table during their first sojourn in the Québec elementary school when they were 10;1 (John) and 8;1 (the twins). The game involved calling out a noun, and then asking the children whether the word was masculine or feminine. Then, I asked which articles ('le', 'la', 'de la', or 'du') preceded which nouns. They very much liked the challenge of competing with each other to see who could get it right. Once, Valerie adamantly insisted I was wrong, and challenged me on a gender question. She whipped out the French-English dictionary (Robert's) and successfully looked up 'poivre' (pepper) to identify its gender. I was wrong and all the kids were right about its being masculine, and not feminine. This encouraged even more interest in playing the game and 'outsmarting' *papa*.

The Library

We found that visiting the local library in Québec was very helpful in promoting our children's French reading skills. During the summer of 1995 when the children were 10;2 and 8;2, respectively, we began the practice of going to the local public library in the village not far from our cottage as often as we could. For several summers, this meant making the trip as often as two to three times per week. The children would check out books they found interesting, and read them in our residence at night, weekends, or when the weather was too inclement to go outside. For two summers, in 1995 and 1996, we also enrolled all three children in the reading contests sponsored by the library, which gave awards to those students who read the most. During the first summer, I had to bribe John to participate in the contest, offering him '50 cents American' (the US dollar was stronger than the Canadian dollar during the entirety of our project) for each book he read. The librarian would give a test on each book read, and if the child passed the test, a 'star' would be placed next to the child's name on a publicly displayed bulletin board. It proved quite an incentive.

All three children read many books that first summer, in addition to Suzanne's reading a few of the harder books to them. John won an award when he was 10;2 for the large number of books he either read (or had read to him). Both Valerie and Stephanie, who enthusiastically participated in the local library contest, read the maximum number of books that could be read for the competition. We found many of the books challenging, which in the twins' category in the second year of the competition were written on as high as an 11year old's level (when they were still 9;2). Valerie was the first to read 11 books in the second year's competition. Valerie and Stephanie finished ahead of most of their Québec peers during their second summer contest.

The children did not just check out and read books that counted toward the contests, but checked out other books simply because they wanted to. They loved the comic-type books, and read many 'Tin-Tin' (Belgian) and Peanuts (translated) books. The children not only checked out books they liked from the library, but music audiocassettes as well. For example, John (10;1) checked out an audiocassette of French rap.

In sum, the most important media that fostered the development of the children's French reading, writing, speaking, and comprehension skills were French television, videocassettes, and reading material. Our systematic indiscriminate reading of English and French stories to the children beginning when they were toddlers laid the early foundation upon which their later French proficiency developed. While we still had the authority to do so, keeping the TV set tuned to French programming and forbidding the viewing of English programming seemed to foster the acquisition of French vocabulary. Following only one semester of school French immersion, simply providing ready access to high-interest French reading material, whether at home or in a library, seemed all that was necessary to ensure that the children spontaneously read in French.

Chapter 8
The Psychology of Pre- and Early Adolescent Bilingualism

Introduction

This chapter attempts to understand and explain the effects of the children's pre- and early adolescent development on their biliteracy and bilingualism. A main focus of this chapter is how and why the language preferences of these three bilinguals shift from childhood into early adolescence, in both of their linguistic societal contexts. Comparing their shifting language preferences over this period of time helps better illuminate the interaction of social context, emerging identity issues, and language choice. Research indicates that females tend to enter puberty as much as two years earlier than do males (Berk, 1996; Malina, 1990), so the two-year difference between John and the twins does not necessarily represent a two-year gap developmentally, and indeed, may be no gap at all.

Adolescence and Bilingualism

Most of the research on child bilingualism to date has focused on the acquisition of language by young children, with little or no follow-up on the language usage of those bilingual children once they enter adolescence. Exceptions include Saunders (1988), though his study stops with his oldest child reaching age 13. Steinberg defines early adolescence as occurring approximately between the ages of 11 and 14 (Steinberg, 1993), and comprising the middle school years.

Individuals face increasing external pressure as they enter pre-adolescence and early adolescence to behaviorally conform to their peer groups, and disengage from their family (Eckert, 1989). These normative pressures range from academic achievement (Caldas & Bankston, 1999b; Bankston & Caldas, 2002) to speech behavior (Eckert, 1989; Heller, 1999). Language is very closely associated with class, nation, culture, and ethnicity, all components of a person's self-identity (Fishman, 1985a; Caldas & Caron-Caldas, 1999). A key identifying characteristic of adolescence, in particular, is the individual's struggle to come to terms with the very personal issue of who they are (Erikson, 1968), and how they 'fit in' in their various social contexts (Eckert, 1989; Ferdman, 1990; Rotheram-Borus, 1989).

We would expect, therefore, that bilingual adolescents would use language in ways that validate their developing self-images. We would also expect that bilingual adolescents immersed in a monolingual culture would have additional identity pressures, as they reconcile conflicting societal messages about what it means to be a part of one – and more likely two – larger societies (Katz, 1996; McKay & Wong, 1996). Also, bilingual adolescents have the added task of assimilating into their developing identities the dimension of 'bilingual person', a complexity that many of their peers do not have. Identity development issues are even more complicated in the United States where a bilingual-bicultural adolescent is likely to be confronted by an apathetic peer group with little interest in exploring their ethnic roots (Phinney, 1993).

In the United States in particular, there exists tremendous pressure to conform to the linguistic norm of speaking English (Caldas, 1998). Some researchers go so far as to link this pressure with a sort of American colonialism (Macedo, 2000), though Tomiyama (2000) contends that in Japanese society as well there is unusually strong pressure to conform linguistically. However, few societies – especially Japan – have the diversity of the U.S., where even in the large Hispanic-American community, where literally tens of millions of individuals speak the U.S'.s second most spoken language, adolescents feel pressure to speak English (Galindo, 1995). Indeed, most second generation Hispanics prefer to speak English, and by the third generation most Hispanic Americans are no longer even able to speak Spanish (Portes & Schauffler, 1994, 1996). How much more, then, must bilingual adolescents in America's much smaller linguistic communities feel social pressure to conform to the country's 'English standard'?

Bilingual Preference

The twin girls were aged 13.8 (eighth grade), and their older brother was aged 15.8 (tenth grade) in December 2000, when the last family audio recording was made. Thus, the twins' changing bilingual preference over the period of their school French immersion experience – which spans pre, early and middle adolescence – can be examined for trends, as well as compared with their brother's bilingual preference when he was the same age. Additionally, for John, the effect of early and late adolescence on language choice can be analyzed.

In earlier research Suzanne and I clarified the concept of 'bilingual preference', demonstrating that a bilingual's preference for either of his or her two languages is essentially context sensitive (Caldas & Caron-Caldas, 2000) – and is clearly distinct from language proficiency. I elaborate more on the technicalities of this measure in Chapter 11. We operationalized a measure of this construct that we called the Bilingual Preference Ratio, or BPR. We showed that through ages 10;8 (twins) and 12;8 (John), the context with the greatest influence on the children's propensity to speak either English or French in our bilingual home was the linguistic community within which they were immersed. We showed how simply living in either language community strongly influenced the language used in the household among the family members who all have the ability to communicate fluently in either French or English. Even though the children had greater measured proficiency in English – i.e. superior mastery of its syntax, grammar, and other language skills due to much more exposure to English – they still preferred to speak French among themselves and with us, their parents, when in French-speaking Québec.

As noted in Chapter 5, part of the family strategy early in our bilingual project was to foster pride (and diminish the possibility that the children might be ashamed of their French) by linking the French minority language to both parents' French ancestry: Louisiana's French heritage, and Québec's strong identification with the language (see Thomson, 1995, for discussion of self-identity and French in Québec). In essence, through discussions 'in-French' with our children, we were purposefully trying to 'construct' our family identity as French-Canadian-American. However, though we believe this 'heritage' strategy was initially successful in promoting home French-speaking in Louisiana when the children were preadolescent, this approach not only seemed increasingly less effective as the children moved into adolescence, but ultimately counter-productive, as they strove to 'demarcate' a linguistic space separate from their parents, and more in-line with their American peer groups.

The next three chapters focus on early, middle, and late adolescence as developmental stages that influenced the children's shifting language preferences in the home, in both the U.S. and Québec. The chapters explore possible answers to the following questions:

- Were the children more or less likely to speak either of their two languages, as they progress through early adolescence, when in either predominantly English or French speaking environments?
- Did the previously identified French-speaking gap between John and his younger twin sisters (which was attributed to the twin's

early experiences in a school French immersion) either diverge or converge as the children move into and through early adolescence?
- Is there a relationship between the amount of time the children have spent in the U.S., and their preference for speaking French in Québec and English in Louisiana?
- Is there a relationship between adolescence, the amount of French spoken by the parents' in Québec, and the children's preference for French-speaking in Québec?
- Given the twins' unique long-term experience in a school French immersion program, does their preference for speaking French as they move into early adolescence differ from their brother's preference for speaking French at the same age?

And finally,

- What are the indicators of linguistic identity achievement in the children?

The Louisiana Context in Adolescence

As seen in earlier chapters, through roughly age 10;5 the children were not hesitant to speak French in Louisiana around anglophones. The following observation, recorded one school day when John was in the fourth grade, captures his indifference to speaking French around his English-speaking peers:

> I [the father] pointedly spoke with him in French as I dropped him off [at school], asking him to do something for me. He responded to me in French, in full hearing of several of his comrades. He apparently is not ashamed to speak French in front of his peers (aged 9;7).

During a visit to the American grandparents' house for Christmas when the children were aged 10;8 and 8;8, all three children spoke with us (the parents) in French around their numerous English-speaking cousins. They had no inhibitions whatsoever.

During the first two years that we lived in francophone Louisiana (1995 and 1996), when the children were in the second through fifth grades, all three children were speaking more French than English around our dinner table, as can be seen in Figure 1 on p. 166.

Our efforts to link our family bilingualism with the French heritage of Louisiana seemed to be successful. We were largely able to control the media in our home to the extent of only watching mostly French Québec and French TV for almost three years. However, as the children moved toward early-adolescence, things began to change. For one, though we lived in a rural francophone area of the state, the children attended suburban schools in the moderately sized nearby city of urban/suburban Lafayette. We were eventually not able to perpetuate the connection between our family and our Cajun community as our children aged. In spite of our early success linking our family bilingualism to Louisiana's Cajun heritage, the children ultimately did not seem to identify at all with this aspect of their Franco-American roots. For example John, who during the summer of 2003 began working at an all-Cajun restaurant in our virtually all-Cajun Louisiana community, came home after the first day (age 18;1) and told us that he had trouble understanding the English of the Cajun workers there. He said that they understood him because they watch American TV and have heard his kind of accent before. Recall that nine years earlier when we first moved to this same Cajun community, he had begun to speak English with a Cajun accent. No more. He now made a clear distinction between himself and Cajuns. He also complained that when he spoke French with some of the black francophone workers, they did not understand him (more on that in the next chapter).

Cajun 'Country' Culture

Perhaps the children's diminishing lack of identification with Cajun culture as they moved into adolescence was due in part to the perceived archaic nature of much Louisiana French, and/or the rustic quality of Cajun culture and music. Though we lived in a rural Louisiana Cajun community for 10 years of our family project, the children's Louisiana peer groups were in suburban Lafayette, where they attended large Lafayette elementary, middle, and high schools. Their circles of friends were largely the sons and daughters of professionals who were almost completely oriented toward American pop culture and music. One of the more fascinating aspects of Lafayette, which is the self-proclaimed 'Hub City' of French Louisiana, is the noticeable lack of the strong, distinct Cajun accent that characterizes the speech of citizens in its surrounding rural parishes. I spent nine years and hundreds of hours as a university student-teacher observer in high school classrooms all over Lafayette as well as the Cajun communities that surround the 'Hub City'. I noticed a stark contrast in how teenagers in Lafayette's most affluent high schools spoke compared to the mostly Cajun schools in outlying rural areas. In many ways, the speech of the Lafayette students was hardly distinguishable from the teenage speech one might hear on television programs set in southern California.

One reason for Lafayette's decidedly more cosmopolitan flavor is the influence of the university and the oil industry, both of which bring thousands of relatively affluent and well-educated outsiders to Lafayette from all over the U.S., and indeed the international community. The city of Lafayette had a 2000 population of approximately 110,000 (U.S. Census, 2000). Economically, Lafayette Parish (county), with a total population of approximately 190,000 in 2000 (U.S. Census, 2000) is the strongest parish in south-central Louisiana, and one of the financially and educationally most advanced in the state of Louisiana. The 1999 median household income was $36,518 per year, compared to the state median of $32,566 (U.S. Census, 2000). The 2000 U.S. Census also indicated that the parish had a lower average poverty rate than the state (15.7% as opposed to 19.6%). Educationally, a higher percentage of parish residents possessed a bachelor's degree or higher (25.5%), a rate roughly equivalent to the national average (25.6%), and much higher than the state average of 18.7%. Racially, 73.4% of the parish population identified themselves as whites and 23.8% of the population identified themselves as black in the 2000 census.

Interestingly, 18.3% of the population of Lafayette parish indicated that they spoke a language other than English at home in 2000, double the statewide average of only 9.2%. Given that only 2.5% of the population was foreign born, and only 1.7% of the population indicated that they were of Hispanic origin, we can safely conclude that the vast majority of those who spoke a language other than English were speaking French. However, one was much more likely to hear French spoken in public places in one of the surrounding rural Cajun communities than in Lafayette.

Once, when talking with my graduate education students about the distinction between Cajuns in Lafayette and Cajuns in the hinterland, one 'country' student of Cajun ancestry (in her thirties, fall 2002) shared that when she was younger, country folk would remark about someone moving to Lafayette that 'they were moving to the city to get themselves a brick house'. Another Cajun student commented that Cajuns in Lafayette were ashamed that their Cajun accents would mark them as 'from the country' so they tried to modify how they spoke. When our family first moved to Acadiana in 1994, and I was still making a big deal out of the fact that many in Acadiana spoke French, we went shopping one day in Lafayette. With the children in tow as we made our way through the city's Sam's wholesale store, I spoke to three different salespeople in French. (I identified French speakers by their strong Cajun accents when they spoke English, and rarely guessed wrong.) One of the saleswoman with whom I was speaking French asked me if I were surprised that she spoke French. I answered 'no', because I knew that many people in Lafayette spoke French. She answered me that many people 'could' speak French – but 'wouldn't'.

As for the children, ultimately I could not even convince them to go to festivals featuring Cajun or Zydeco (Black Creole) music. Suzanne and I, on the other hand, had grown quite fond of these musical styles, and had even taken dancing lessons so that we could 'cut a rug' (or at least stir up some dust) at the many local Cajun music festivals. As teenagers, our children much preferred a rock concert, especially if they could sit with their friends. All their American music CDs were alternative, classic, or punk rock, Broadway musicals, 1950s crooner music – anything but Cajun or country.

In the same way that the children seemed to develop a bias against Cajun music, it is also true that there seemed to be a bias amongst some more traditional Cajuns against pop music – even if it were sung in French. For example, in speaking with a Cajun farmer one day, I mentioned that Zachary Richard, a very famous Cajun 'pop' singer from a town not 20 miles from where we were standing, had performed in a Québec music festival that summer. The Cajun farmer grimaced, and made a face – commenting that Zachary Richard was 'too wild' for his tastes. This farmer's negative sentiment was not isolated. It was (and is) very rare to ever hear a Zachary Richard song played on traditional Cajun radio stations, though he continues to be very popular in Québec and France.

Early Adolescence and John's Language Shift

The children's peer groups in both the U.S. and Québec have been largely constituted of suburban children from advantaged socioeconomic status (SES) backgrounds, for whom school-success is at least reasonably important. The twins' Louisiana social group throughout much of the period of this study has been suburban Lafayette, fellow French-immersion students known as 'Frenchies' – a peer group which, like Eckert's (1989) 'Jocks' or Foley's (1990) 'socially prominent' – accepts the hegemony of the school. The twins attended Lafayette schools from age 8;3 to age 16;1. Most of their 'Frenchie' friends were also in the academic 'gifted' program. Apart from their common, and somewhat isolated experience in immersion classes, an identifying characteristic of this close-knit group is not that they speak French together, but that their family backgrounds are predominantly white, middle and upper-middle class. Common parental occupations include attorneys, teachers, engineers, business owners, and professors. John never associated with the 'Frenchies', but did associate almost exclusively with the children of professional parents both in Québec and in Louisiana. Thus, there would be no reason for the children to associate either of their two languages with a 'disadvantaged' class, in the way that Spanish-speakers in Foley's (1990) study of high-schoolers in a Texas border town were looked down on by Anglo students, or some other Franco-Americans tend to negatively view their own French speaking (Rioux, 1994). This later group includes Cajuns in Louisiana, and Acadians in New Brunswick, Canada.

John's French speaking in Louisiana began to fall off two years before his sisters', which, as I noted in an earlier chapter, was the source of a good deal of linguistic family friction. The decrease began during the fall of 1995 when he was in the fifth grade, and continued to slide into the spring of 1996 (see Figure 1 on p. 166). During the next year – 1996 – when John turned 11 years of age, and the girls turned nine, John's French speaking around the family table in Louisiana plummeted. His twin sisters' French speaking, however, actually increased slightly, and constituted a large majority of their speech around our dinner table. Importantly, the twins were still in a French immersion program. The following suggests their strong feelings toward speaking French at home at this time:

> ... when John (11;8) said something in English, she (Valerie, aged 9;8) screamed at him, '*Parle français, espèce d'embécile!*' [speak French you idiot] It was so vehement that Suzanne and I exchanged looks of wonderment.

This could be a good example of establishing 'social identity' through adopting a strong 'stance', which Ochs defines as a social act which is in part a display of an affective attitude toward language (Ochs & Schieffelin, 1989; Ochs, 1993). Valerie still viewed the family context in francophone terms, and insisted on maintaining the status quo with which she so strongly identified.

However, John not only ceased receiving any formal French instruction of any kind in his Louisiana school during 1996, but it was obvious that he was exhibiting the 'signs' of early adolescence. During this time we noted John's increasing awareness of and attention to his peers. For example, he developed his first 'crush' during the 95-96 school year. Though he was speaking much more English, he was still not hostile to speaking French in Louisiana as he approached his eleventh birthday, a sentiment captured in the following fieldnote entry:

From time to time John complains about the fact that the girls have French immersion and he does not ... (aged 10;8)

He once even asked Suzanne to give him 10 French spelling words a day to learn. Still, he began to be more and more aware of his unique bilingual status – and he was not always comfortable with it. For example, when John (10;11) and I were discussing the upcoming sleepover for his eleventh birthday, he said, 'Dad, don't embarrass me by speaking French to me'. He went on to add, 'And don't make a big deal of it if I change the channel to an English-speaking station'.

We noticed an abrupt change in John's attitude to French speaking in Louisiana within a month of our return to the state in the summer of 1996. One incident toward the end of August was ominous. We were at the university bookstore together, and I was chatting in French with a Cajun worker there that I spoke with each time I went. Each of us addressed John (11;3) in French a couple of times, but he always answered in English, not seeming the least interested in demonstrating how well he spoke French. Then, on the way home he commented that he wished he lived in a certain Lafayette subdivision where all his friends lived. I mentioned offhandedly that if we bought a new house we would not be able to keep our cottage in Canada. He answered that he would rather have his friends than a cottage in Québec. This comment foreshadowed a major linguistic shift.

During the spring of 1997 and the latter half of his sixth grade year, John's Louisiana French speaking fell off even further, hitting zero in May (see Figure 1). Regarding the perception of his own bilingualism, John made a telling comment to me that spring when I asked him if he spoke French with one of his French-English *bilingual* friends. He responded that, 'It's not cool to speak French in school!'

On another occasion, when John was 11;10, he commented, ' ... if you speak French outside of school, your friends will think you're a nerd because they don't know how to speak French. If everyone speaks English', he continued, 'why would anyone want to speak French?'

An event which highlighted the increasing importance which John's middle school peer group was taking on for him occurred during the end-of-the-year sixth grade award ceremonies in May 1997 when John was 12;1. I was seated in the bleachers with the parents, and John was on the floor with the rest of the sixth grade. When the ceremony was over, I went down to see John who was among his classmates seated around him. I spoke to him only in French, and he sort of grunted in return, not answering me in French. He didn't seem to want to talk, and I only spoke with him for a moment, and then left. When I picked him up at school that

Psychology of Pre- and Early Adolescent Bilingualism 115

afternoon, he mentioned to me that after I left, his classmates gathered around him and 'made fun of him' (though I suspected he was greatly exaggerating) and asked him 'a bunch of questions', like 'does your dad always speak to you in French?' and 'Do you speak French?' He recounted all of this in a tone that suggested he wished I hadn't spoken to him in French.

Whereas situations like this might not be surprising in most U.S. schools, in John's middle school most students were of French descent, have relatives (usually grandparents) who speak French, and take French as an elective, as he did as a seventh grader. Significantly, another researcher recorded a similar comment made by a Chicano bilingual adolescent in Austin, who said it was 'uncool' to use Spanish with his *bilingual* friends (Galindo, 1995). This brings to mind Foley's (1990) observation that 'Schools were [sic] middle-class bureaucratic organizations dedicated to stripping kids of their ethnic identity . . '. (p. 161). The incident also lends credence to Phinney's (1993) belief that Caucasian American adolescents in particular are not driven to understand their ethnic roots.

Another interesting event occurred in our car on the way to our Québec summer vacation just days after the honors ceremony. The children were picking on each other and calling each other names in the car's backseat when Stephanie (10;1) started harassing John for not speaking enough French. John fired back at both his sisters, calling them 'bilingual nerds' – as if *he* were not bilingual!

Several months later in the fall, when John (12;6) was in the seventh grade, he referred to the girls as 'goody-goody immersion students' who didn't know about the 'real world'. I had the feeling he was sending the message that his middle school environment was a lot rougher than what the girls were experiencing in the cloistered French immersion world of their elementary school, and that he was therefore somehow 'tougher' because of it. Ironically, he was enrolled for a one-hour French class during the seventh grade. Its influence apparently did not extend beyond the classroom – if that far.

A little more than a month after the 'good-goody immersion student' comment, when John was 12;8, I noted a decidedly much more hostile attitude towards my speaking French to him around his peers, who had assumed even greater importance to John. His 'reconfigured social identity' (Ochs, 1993: 298) most definitely did not include French speaking in Louisiana:

> ... when I went to John's middle school to pick him up after band practice, I ran into him with a group of his friends. When I addressed

him in French, he said, kind of under his breath, 'No, Dad!' I again addressed him in French and he said, more forcefully, 'Dad, No!' When I did it a third time, he said almost in desperation, 'Shut up Dad!' The message was clear: he didn't want me speaking French to him around his friends. [OK, maybe I unnecessarily provoked him.]

Few, if any of John's friends identified strongly with the French-speaking Cajun culture like earlier generations had. None, in fact, as best I could determine, were able to speak Cajun French fluently. There were still those students who had learned to hunt and fish, owned four-wheelers, collected guns, and had extended-family craw-fish boils and devotedly attended weekly mass. However, they seemed to have a somewhat diluted version of the much more authentic Cajun culture one could still find in the countryside surrounding Lafayette. Even in the countryside, though, one would be very hard pressed to find a fluent French-speaking 13-year-old. And if one did, my experience suggested that he or she would more than likely be a Creole of African American decent than a Caucasian.

On a couple of other occasions during this fall of 1997, John expressed embarrassment when we spoke to him in French within earshot of his schoolmates. It was clear he wanted to fit in, and not just in how he spoke. In the domain of clothes, even though there was no formal uniform at his large public middle school of 800 students, I remarked on how similarly most of the students dressed. They wore the same name-brand baggy khaki pants with cargo pockets, the same casual Doc Martin boots, and a T-shirt with a logo. Eckert (1989) noted well the powerful symbology of clothes for peer group identification. Music, also, was an important rallying point of identification between John and his group of school friends, though decidedly *not* Cajun music (they preferred alternative rock). When talking about clothes and music, John once commented to me that the white country students attending school outside of Lafayette tended to dress more like the blacks and listen to rap music. In any event, French language, culture, and identity were clearly not on the radar screen of any adolescents John knew, or even knew of – outside of Québec. Interestingly, John commented to me that Québécois teenagers were also dressing like American blacks and listening to rap music.

When we told John there was a possibility the family could move to a francophone country on a Fulbright Scholarship, he asked us if any English was spoken there. When I told him 'not much', his response was an insouciant: 'Uh, uh, I ain't going if they don't speak English' (12;7).

As resistant to French as John was becoming at this time, I still occasionally noted cross-linguistic structures in his English. A week after protesting against the idea of living in a country where English was not spoken, I asked him if the light was still on in his room. He answered, 'No, I *closed* the light in my room'. 'Closed' in French ('fermer') also means 'to turn off'. 'Open' in French ('ouvrir') also means 'to turn on'. Everyone in the family occasionally used 'close' to mean 'turn off', and 'open' to mean 'turn on'. These expressions had become part of the family vernacular. Another switch everyone in the family made all the time was in reference to the yellow seat along our house's bay window. It was simply known as 'le banc jaune' (the yellow bench). I would dare to say that no one ever referred to it in English. An example of the twins code mixing occurred one evening a week after John 'closed' his light, when both girls were speaking with their mother. Within two minutes of each other both girls (10;7) used the word 'explicate' to mean 'explain'. They said something like, 'He needs to *explicate* what he means'. In French, 'to explain' is '*expliquer*'. Yet another example occurred two months later when Valerie (10;9), speaking English, said 'sensible' to mean 'sensitive'. In French 'sensible' means 'sensitive'. Ironically, though John would occasionally use a cross-linguistic structure as a teenager in Louisiana, he teased his sisters for doing the same thing, blaming it on their French immersion program.

In 1997, the twins' collective Louisiana French speaking took a slight, much less precipitous dip than their brother's (from a yearly BPR of 0.86 to 0.74, see both Figures 1 and 2), though French still constituted the majority of the words spoken around the dinner table. Ominously, during the fall of 1997, when they were in the fifth grade, they were speaking more English than French during supper. John had actually been speaking much more French around our dinner table two years earlier when he was the same age as the twins were in the fall of 1997. This discrepancy could be explained by John's negative influence on the girls' preferences for speaking French. The twins were now poised on the edge of adolescence, and their BPR for this calendar year can be used as a baseline against which to compare future BPR shifts with changes their brother experienced following his tenth birthday.

John's Shift is Complete

In 1998, John entered the eighth grade – and his teenage years. There was no doubt for us that his American middle school peer group had become for him an all-absorbing, important social institution to which he 'needed' to fit-in at all levels, including music, dress – and speech. Such an instantaneous and total identification with the peer group beginning in the middle school years was documented in Eckert's (1989) ethnographic study, who described the sudden affiliation with one's social category in school taking place 'overnight' (p. 76). His school was monolingual English – with 'bilingualism' comprising no component of any student social categories. Moreover, John's attitude – or lack of one – toward bilingualism carried over to the linguistic context of the home, where he was far from the hearing and scrutiny of his classmates. In the year 1998, his French speaking around the table in Louisiana essentially ended (see Figures 1 and 2 for the downward trend.).

Entire months went by without John saying one word on tape in French around our table. When the twins once admonished John to *'Parle français!'* John (13:3) retorted, 'English! English! English!' He was obviously being peevish. However, his outburst could also be interpreted as aggressively participating in the social construction of his 'identity', taking a 'stance' and affirming the monolingual dimension of his social group by 'contradicting another person' (Ochs, 1993: 288). Ochs (1993) may well have captured the essence of John's linguistic posturing when she asked rhetorically, '… is it that some speakers more than others are struggling to change social expectations concerning particular identities through systematically altering their social acts and stances?' (p. 298). John was establishing a social space separate from adults (his parents), who he knew wanted him to speak French. Adolescence involves disengagement from the family (Eckert, 1989; Hill & Holmbeck, 1986; Steinberg & Silverberg, 1986), and for John, not speaking French was one way of 'denying parental domination of personal behavior' (Eckert, 1989: 70).

The Twins' Early Adolescent Language Shift

The twins' French speaking fell-off dramatically too, even though they were still in a French immersion program, and even though almost all their peers were functionally bilingual girls and boys enrolled in the French-intensive program. The twins' French speaking decreased from a majority of their dinnertime conversation in 1997 to almost zero by May of 1998 at the end of the fifth grade when they turned 11. In fact, this decrease in French speaking marked the steepest decline among any family members in the Louisiana context in a one-year period (see Figures 1 and 2). The twins' massive shift in language preference around our dinner table corresponds with John's large decrease in French speaking two years earlier – when he was approximately the same chronological age as they were in May 1998, i.e. 11;0.

That Valerie and Stephanie's decrease in French speaking was more precipitous than John's may also be explained in part by John's English-speaking presence around the table in 1998. When John's French speaking fell off dramatically at roughly the same time of the year in 1996, the twins were still speaking mostly French around our table. Now, however, John was seated next to them at the table and spouting off almost continuously in English. English input at our table, therefore, was dramatically up. Moreover, not only was he not speaking French, he was quite possibly infecting his sisters with his negative sentiment toward French speaking in the monolingual Louisiana context. In other words, John may likely have contributed to a home atmosphere that was more conducive to English than French – in spite of our efforts to the contrary (more on the parents below). It did not help that he at times even teased his sisters for speaking French, or mixing French with their English (13;0).

However, the following fieldnote entry suggests that the school French-immersion program was perhaps no more immune from English-speaking pressures than was our home environment:

> When discussing with Stephanie (10;10) how much French she spoke with her French immersion classmates during their French P.E. class she answered, 'We don't speak French that much at P.E. because our [Québécois] teacher doesn't make us like our other [French immersion] teacher does.

When I pressed for a reason why the French immersion students did not speak more French without being coerced, Stephanie answered, 'Because it's not cool'. Again, I sensed the influence of her brother on her peevish response.

The pressure to speak English in their supposedly monolingual French-immersion program mirrors closely what Heller (1999) observed in her study of an ostensibly monolingual French school in Toronto. She discovered that 'the peer culture has implanted English' (p. 140) as the informal language of communication in a school environment she typified as imbued with 'fictive monolingualism' (p. 19). English has even become the common school language among some 'allophones' in Montreal's French Language schools, though more research is still needed to determine how prevalent this practice has become (McAndrew & Lamarre, 1996).

Though I never observed the French immersion students communicating to each other in French outside of the classroom, two months after Stephanie said it wasn't 'cool' to speak French, she did confess something very interesting and telling to me. She (11;0) said that immersion students sometimes speak French around other students just 'to get on their nerves' and show them how they can talk about them right to their faces without the non-immersion students understanding. While admittedly not very polite, it does make the point that the 'Frenchies' were indeed a very tight group of students with their own group identity.

Though the girls had almost stopped speaking French around the dinner table beginning in January of 1998 at age 10;8, I still noted entire conversations between myself and one or the other of the twins taking place entirely in French during this spring of their fifth grade year. Perhaps when the girls were beyond John's conversational presence, they unconsciously felt freer to speak in French. After all, he was teasing them for speaking French on a fairly frequent basis during this period of time, and it was apparently having a depressing effect on their French speaking. As noted earlier, he also teased them for mixing French with their English. Once, Valerie commented that 'Mrs. [So-and-so] is *enceinte* [pregnant]' to which John retorted, 'Would you have said that if you were around someone other than mom?'

Cyberspace apparently offered to John enough of the privacy he needed away from the eyes of his friends to communicate in French. When I sent him an e-mail message in French a week prior to his thirteenth birthday, he responded to me with an e-mail he wrote entirely in French. The accuracy of the French communiqué was not perfect, but then neither were the e-mail messages being sent in English between John and his coterie of friends, who had their own abbreviated code for electronically communicating with each other (yet more evidence of their desire to exclude pesky, prying grownups from their lives).

I now turn to the question of whether this same pattern of increasing English speaking in the home with the progression of adolescence was also taking place around the dinner table in French-speaking Québec. That is, was the children's increasing preference for English, which seems to be a consequence of their powerful adolescent peer environments in the United States, also influencing their family communications in Québec?

The Québec Language Context in Adolescence

As noted earlier, during this same six-year period from 1994 through 2000 that we systematically audiotaped dinnertime conversations, the five family members spent approximately two months each summer in the very heart of French-speaking Québec. This practice continued through the writing of this book, though we had ceased systematically taping family conversations due to the virtual impossibility of getting all five family members around our Québec dinner table at the same time. Indeed, John stayed in Louisiana during the summer of 2003, and one girl spent part of the summer of 2004 in Germany whilst the other spent part of this summer in New York City. As already noted, in Québec, except among themselves or with Suzanne and me, the children had no recourse to English. However, just as in Louisiana, the children had the free choice of speaking either French or English around our cottage dinner table. We were acutely interested in knowing which language they chose in this francophone environment.

As can be seen in Figure 3 on p. 167, during the first summer in 1995, when John was 10:2 and the twins were 8;2, the vast majority of the children's words around the dinner table in Québec were in French.

John and the twins had a greater preference for speaking French in Québec than they exhibited in our home in francophone Louisiana during this same calendar year. This greater propensity for speaking French in Canada is not unexpected, since their days were filled with French, and it would be logical to expect that when speaking of the day's activities around the table they would resort to the language within which these activities were conducted – French. Also, as discussed in Chapter 6, they attended a French-speaking elementary school near the home for the final three weeks of the academic school year in both June 1995 and June 1996. However, the sheer magnitude of their preference for French is notable, since, after all, they could have spoken English if they so chose. Everyone around the dinner table in Québec was capable of speaking English, and we were far from the scrutiny of native Québécois.

After the return to Louisiana in the fall of 1995, John's French speaking remained high through December. Then, John's French speaking around our Louisiana dinner table began to plummet in the spring of 1996, reaching almost zero French speaking by May 1996, when he turned 11;0. He was at the doorstep of early adolescence (Steinberg, 1993). However, during the next summer of 1996 in Québec, John's and the twins' French speaking shot up again. In fact, though 1996 marks the year that John's French speaking fell off most steeply in Louisiana – never to recover – his French speaking in Québec actually increased over the previous summer's level around the Québec family dinner table. It is important to note that once again the three children attended an all French-speaking school for the first three weeks of June. Thus, the children were immersed in peer groups that could only speak French.

John loved his Québec school experience. He did well academically (again, a tribute to the one semester of Louisiana French immersion), and seemed to be very much taken with his Québécois peers, who reciprocated their friendship. What we see with John, then, as he moved into early adolescence, is a trend toward much greater English speaking in Louisiana, but also greater French speaking in Québec. In fact, there was little room for him to increase his French speaking in Québec in 1996, as he was approaching 100% of uttered words in French around our dinner table.

The Accent Issue

John first began expressing concern about the presence of an American accent when he spoke French at about the age of 11;10. Up to this point, he spoke French relatively un-self-consciously. The issue reared its head one day when speaking with John about the possibility of returning to the Québec elementary school in June for a third year in a row (which went through grade 6). He seemed to like the idea. However, he said he was self-conscious about his accent in French. Within days of our arrival in Québec three months later, after he had begun hanging out with friends, John (12;1) asked Suzanne and me if he had an accent when he spoke French. It pained us to see him so uncomfortable and embarrassed with the way he spoke French. We told him he didn't have an accent, though we knew he probably did. Apparently he did not believe our reassurances to the contrary, because he said he was going to ask a boy he had just met who was a friend of two of his Québécois cousins. He reasoned that the new friend could be more objective about his accent since he did not know John. Here, we see a good example of the self-consciousness of early adolescence typified by the exaggerated belief of the young teen that he or she is the center of everyone else's attention (Elkind & Bowen, 1979). Just two years earlier John appeared completely un-self-conscious about how others viewed his accent, and indeed, he was probably unaware whether he had one or not.

Within a very short time after arriving in Québec during this summer of 1997, the children were speaking almost only French around the family dinner table. This is notable, since in this year John's French speaking around our dinner table in Louisiana continued its very steep plummet, reaching zero in May. His French speaking in Québec, however, remained very high, constituting the large majority of words he spoke around our Québec dinner table. The twins' collective French speaking actually increased to the point where they spoke not one recorded English word.

Earlier, it was shown how the twins' French speaking fell off dramatically in the fall of 1997, when they entered the fifth grade, exactly as had their brother's French speaking two years earlier. In the spring of 1998, John (approaching age 13) and his sisters (approaching age 11) were speaking almost no French around our Louisiana dinner table. Moreover, immediately upon crossing the border into Québec in early June 1998, John

(13;1) confided nervously to me at a rest area that he didn't want to speak French. He said he didn't want everyone to hear his accent. He seemed even more distraught at the prospect of having to speak French than he had the year before when he expressed concerned about his accent. However not 10 minutes later, Valerie (11;1), who was apparently suffering none of her brother's linguistic angst, made the following comment at a rest area just inside the border: 'Maintenant on va parler français tout le temps!' [Now we're going to speak French all the time!]

Her comment represented the mind-set that had taken place every previous summer with all three children. This summer, though, it did not take place immediately with John.

The audiotape results from the summer of 1998 must be interpreted with caution. The cassette we used was defective, though we did not realize this until after our return to Louisiana. Thus, we only have two recorded sessions of dinnertime conversation from around our Canadian dinner table. The first was made five days after our arrival in June, and the second was made four days later.[1] Whereas most of the words the twins uttered during this taping were in French (BPR of 0.79), most of John's words were in English (BRR of 0.27).[2] The audiotaped results were corroborated by my fieldnote observations that the children seemed to be speaking more English within the first two weeks of arriving in Québec than they had in the previous two years. In fact, their English speaking was so obvious that on several occasions I caught Suzanne's eye and silently mouthed the word 'English'. We were a bit disheartened, but were hoping that as soon as they started interacting with Québécois, their French speaking at our cottage would increase.

In both 1995 and 1996 the children had attended a Québec elementary school almost from the day we arrived in Canada. This no doubt greatly influenced their preference for French in those elementary years, as they were immersed in their respective peer groups, with continuous French input. The next year, in 1997 at age 10;1, the twins were still in the 'John, parle français!' (John, speak French!) mode. However, as already noted, in the months preceding this summer of 1998 stay, the twins had begun to increasingly side with their brother on the family 'language issue'. Valerie was no longer throwing cushions at her brother and threatening to assault him for speaking English. Moreover, for the first three weeks of this summer vacation the children stayed in and around our cottage, since most of their Québec friends and cousins were still in school. Therefore, they were reinforcing each other's English speaking. Given these conditions, then, it is almost a marvel that the children – especially the girls – spoke as much French around our dinner table as they did. Perhaps this mind-set was the effect of years of summertime conditioning, epitomized by Valerie's proclamation in French at the border that 'Now we're going to speak French all the time'.

Based on a study of our tape recordings from previous summers, we noted that there was somewhat of a residual effect of American English on family communications within the first weeks of arriving in Canada. With this in mind, the magnitude of the children's French speaking in 1998 seems all the more impressive. After only a week and a half in a French-speaking environment, John was at least speaking some French (up from zero French in May). The majority of the twins' words around our dinner table were in French not even two weeks after leaving their American peer environments, whereas in the month of May the twins spoke only 10 French words in the whole month. Clearly, any 'forgetting' associated with 10 months absence from uttering French (for John), and five months of any significant French speaking by the twins, was very temporary indeed, a characteristic of language attrition also noted by other researchers as well (Cohen, 1989; Tomiyama, 2000).

No doubt, had the tape not malfunctioned, we would have recorded much more French speaking by all three children later in the month and certainly into July. Beginning in July, Valerie and Stephanie spent the majority of each day at the summer day camp totally immersed in French. The twins even put on a play during their last week (with their counselor) which they jointly wrote – all in French.

John went on a two-week bicycling expedition during July with a group of his all-French-speaking camp buddies. When John (13;3) returned from the expedition near the end of July, we only heard him speak French on his first day back. He spent the last two weeks we were in Québec with a group of his friends who also lived around the lake. He had essentially stopped speaking English. In fact, when one of the girls spoke English in our cottage, John, clearly aggravated, admonished her to *'Parle français!'* (Speak French!) Both girls immediately taunted him with chants of 'English! English! English!' What a difference two months can make. This same scenario played itself out the next day as well! It was the mirror image of what had been happening in Louisiana, when John and his sisters' French speaking began to diverge two and a half years earlier. The big difference this time was that the girls immediately reverted to speaking French after teasing their brother a little bit – no doubt taking the opportunity to get back at him for all his jabbing at them about being 'immersion goodie-goodies', 'bilingual nerds', etc.

All my evidence this summer, including tapes and fieldnotes, indicated that the majority of the girls' speech was in French, as it had been in every previous summer spent in Canada. The children were using many new expressions in French I had never heard before, and I had to often eat humble pie and ask them to explain something they had said. Indeed, all three children were so obviously fluent in French that I felt a little guilty asking their various camp counselors to complete our survey soliciting their input about the children's French competency. For example, our survey question that asked about the children's ability to understand the teacher seemed completely ridiculous. However, for the sake of consistency I did not want to modify the survey, and distributed it to their camp counselors at the end of the summer.

Quick Shift Back

Within a month of our return to Louisiana in August of 1998, all three children had shifted back to speaking almost only English around our dinner table. Indeed, John (13;4) did not speak even one recorded word of French at suppertime in September. There was no 'residual effect' this year for John. The girls (11;4) spoke only marginally more French than John in September, though still less than 1% of all recorded words. September 1998 marked the quickest reversal from speaking mostly French to speaking mostly English of all three children at the same time. John, who entered the eighth grade of his large middle school, continued to 'hang out' with the same large group of peers with whom he had been associating since at least the sixth grade.

The twins, who were now in the sixth grade, transferred from their elementary school to John's middle school, where they continued in the French immersion program. They were taking three French immersion classes: French, Science, and Social Studies, all taught only in French. They had French Canadian teachers for their French immersion classes. During the rest of the school day they were matriculating from class to class like the rest of their middle school classmates, and for the first time in three and a half years were sitting in classrooms with non-immersion students. Still, their friendship network was largely constituted of French immersion students – 'Frenchies' – with whom they had been going to school since the third grade. For the first time since they were in the second grade, they were riding the same bus as John in the morning, where they were able to watch John close-up in interactions with his peers. A few years later, Stephanie (16;0) even confided in me that during this school year John and his friends all slouched down together the same way in their bus seats, with headphones on, listening to their punk rock music.

I still observed episodes in September of only French speaking between the girls when they did their French homework together. I also noted the girls at times speaking only in French with their mother. There were other times that fall when the girls spoke mostly in French with me, like a time I noted when Valerie called me at work and our entire conversation was in French. So it is quite likely that John's presence at the dinner table suppressed the twins' propensity for speaking French in this familial venue, which would account for the twins' low BPRs this fall.

The three children were, however, writing their Québécois friends in French during this autumn. John (13;5) asked Valerie (11;5) to proofread a letter he had written in French to a Québécois friend, a sort of validation of the efficacy of the twin's French immersion school experience. I took advantage of this opportunity to ask John if he thought Valerie could write in French better than he could. He answered 'yes'.

As the fall waned, the girls were speaking less and less French until there was simply nothing to write in my fieldnotes related to French speaking. Now squarely in early to mid-early adolescence, they had followed in their brother's footsteps of two years earlier, when his French speaking took a similar precipitous dip in the sixth grade. Our tape recordings validated what we were observing. From September 1998 through May 1999, the children – in sixth and eighth grades – had, for all practical purposes, stopped speaking French around our dinner table in Louisiana. This shift to all-English occurred in spite of the fact that we, the parents, were speaking mostly in French (see Figure 4 on p. 168). Our influence was rapidly waning into insignificance.

Early Adolescent Identity Construction

The family is a very dynamic unit, and language usage within this unit is influenced by a myriad of factors, many of which are hard to isolate and quantify. Still, given the trends, which were very similar for John and the girls when adjusted for age differences (more on this issue in Chapter 11), we have to conclude that entrance into adolescence – when there was the increasing influence of, and identification with the external, American peer environments – coincides perfectly with a drop in French-speaking. A defining characteristic of adolescence is the child's search for, and construction of, identity apart from their parents. For John and the twins, *who* they emulated was increasingly a function of whom they 'hung out with' at school – and not the parents. Their Louisiana friends were all English-speaking Americans for whom bilingualism did not appear to be valued. Moreover, even if those friends were learning their studies in the

French language, as was the case of the twins' bilingual peers, English was overwhelmingly the preferred language of communication apart from academic classroom activities. On a deeper level, the children were socially constructing identities for themselves, at times quite aggressively, which were essentially monolingual – while in Louisiana.

But why, as early adolescents, did the children carry over English from the school to the home environment, when they were far from the scrutiny of their American peers? For one, young teenagers often feel like they are 'on stage', a phenomena referred to as the *imaginary audience* (Elkind & Bowen, 1979). This 'imaginary audience' tends to make adolescents very self-conscious of their behavior (Hudson & Gray, 1986). As Pierce (1995) points out, an individual's language choice is closely associated with who they are and how they relate to the larger social world. As the children moved into adolescence, their sense of who they were in the social world of Louisiana – even when around the family dinner table – was inextricably bound up with what it means to be American. And most Americans in their world, with the exception of some Cajuns (with whom they did not identify), spoke only English.

At this point in their identity development, they did not seem to view themselves, nor did they desire for their Louisiana friends to view them, as bicultural-bilingual individuals – a non-valued status in their social world. This is a point that they emphatically pointed out to us on numerous occasions. We had NEVER seen them speaking French with their bilingual Louisiana peers. Not even once. Not even a 'bonjour' or 'au revoir'. However, Pierce also points out that our struggle with identity is context-sensitive, and constantly changing across time and space. Rampton (1995) likewise noted that 'individuals form complicated and often contradictory patterns of solidarity and opposition across a range of category memberships' (p. 8). This notion is borne out in the children's abrupt shift in language preference when immersed in French-speaking Québec – where their self-identification likewise shifts from that of monolingual English-speaking American – to French-speaking American – Québécois.

However, they did not see themselves as exactly 'Québécois'. For one, the Québécois educators who had worked with the children in school and summer camp indicated (on author-constructed surveys) varying degrees of the presence of accented French – something which was kindly pointed out to the children, and of which they were aware during early to midadolescence. Thus, they could not keep their bilingualism a secret in Quebec, as they could, and did, in the United States. However, this slightly uneven balance of 'linguistic power' (if having an accent is perceived as somehow inferior) in the children's communications with native Québécois seems to have had no negative consequences for their apparently confident developing self-images during early adolescence, complex though these self-identities were. Indeed, research has found that accented speech is often associated with social attractiveness (Giles & Powesland, 1975), and the children's Québécois peers told them that they liked their accents.

Ochs (1993) noted that individuals are capable of constructing multiple, compatible identities, which may blend into unique forms which have no label. What we see during this period of early adolescence is the beginning of the children's building their two national identities. The next chapter follows this social psychological 'construction project' through middle adolescence.

Notes

1. In an earlier publication (Caldas & Caron-Caldas, 2002) we only reported results from the second recording. We have since recalculated this summer's BPR from both recordings.
2. We miscalculated John's Québec 1998 BPR from the second June recording in an earlier publication, erroneously reported it as 0.83 (Caldas & Caron-Caldas, 2002). We apologize for this error. It should have been 0.46. It was caused by entering 671 French words for John into our equation instead of 67.

Chapter 9
The Psychology of Middle Adolescent Bilingualism

Introduction

This chapter follows the children's shifting language preferences as they move into and through mid-adolescence. Steinberg (1993) defines middle adolescence as occurring between the ages of approximately 14 and 18, and comprising the high school years. This period was characterized by the children's demarcating clean, well-defined spaces within which they spoke their two languages – English in Louisiana and French in Québec. It was during this period of time that John appears to have lost all vestiges of his American English accent when he spoke Québec French, and the twins' French language proficiency markedly improved, both largely the result of francophone peer influences.

Throughout this period our familial bonds remained warm and strong, though our household did not lack in the excitement – and even occasional fireworks – found in most families with several energetic adolescents. Indeed, there is evidence that links strong attachments between parents and children with strong peer attachments (Armsden & Greenberg, 1987), and vice versa (Fisher, 1990). The children's strong peer attachments during middle-adolescence, which were important for their healthy identity development, almost certainly squelched their French speaking in Louisiana – and perfected it in Quebec. Toward the end of this period, as the children worked out bilinguistic identity issues, there appeared once again occasional instances of spontaneous French speaking in anglophone milieus.

Summertime Changes

The summer of 1999 marked several significant changes and advances in our bilingual project. John had just turned 14 years of age and had graduated from middle school (eighth grade). The twins had just turned 12 a month before leaving for our annual summer societal French immersion experience in Québec, and had completed the sixth grade. During this summer, we deviated from our previous vacation routines in a couple of ways that had linguistically significant consequences. In June, Valerie (12;1) and I only spent one week in Québec before leaving on a three-week European trip. Most of our trip was spent in French-speaking environments: France, French-speaking Belgium, and French-speaking Switzerland. During the trip I made a concerted effort to speak as much French as possible with Valerie. Given our sojourn through countries where we had to speak French with the local population, I felt confident that our level of French speaking was relatively high. I knew, however, with just a twinge of guilt, that we were also speaking English with each other. I just didn't know exactly how much English since I didn't audiotape any of our discussions.

However, upon our return to Québec, Suzanne was quite ready to give me some idea of the magnitude of our language deviancy. My wife expressed shock at the amount of English that both Valerie (12;2) and I were speaking in our cottage. I was disappointed in myself. Still, on a positive note, Valerie was reading adult level novels in French during this summer, entirely of her own accord. For example, on our European trip she read the entire translated John Grisham novel, *L'Associé* (*The Partner*) as easily as if it had been in English. She seemed to have no particular preference for either French or English written material.

Peer Influence and Accent Loss

Perhaps the most linguistically important event during this summer vacation of 1999 was John's (14;2 to 14;3) being hired to work full time at the French-speaking summer camp where he had only ever been a camper in the past. In late June, he moved into a hut with 10 other teenaged Québécois boys who also worked at the camp. The group in his hut, who were called 'Les Ratons' (literally 'young rats'), formed a team who worked exclusively in the camp kitchen together doing the food preparation, serving, cleaning, and all other food-related services. When not working together, Les Ratons, hung out together, playing football, wrestling, and in general just horsing around during any down time. John was completely immersed in Québécois adolescent peer culture and language for five weeks – with no recourse to English. For John's French speaking, these five weeks were perhaps the most important five weeks in his life.

I spoke with John on several occasions in July on either the phone, or at the camp itself during one of his infrequent breaks. He never, as best I could tell, spoke any English during our conversations. This was not necessarily unusual, as in previous summers he usually spoke little if any English in July. However, what struck both Suzanne and me was *how* he spoke French: his French seemed to us to be accentless 'Québécois', to the extent of using Québec Gallicized expressions borrowed from American English – but spoken with a Québec accent. We were absolutely amazed at his fluency. I recorded the following in my fieldnotes on July 2, 1999:

> We went to see John (14;2) at his 'hut' the day after we returned, and I talked with him about his new job. Without any doubt, I'm sure he didn't say even one word in English during our roughly half hour conversation. He spoke fluently and in a very heavy Quebec dialect/ accent. I noted that even when he used the word 'cool', it was in the heavily accented way that Québec youth say it. We talked with him on the phone a few days later, and once again, no English.

Research has noted that males, in particular, are more likely than females to prefer local, non-standard word pronunciations (Trudgill, 2001). From roughly this point forward, John would always, as best we could tell, speak the more non-standard Québécois French than would either of his sisters.

'Shhhh, papa, don't speak English'

John seemed very taken with his new group of friends, and told us several times that he loved what he was doing. He recounted with laughter the numerous pranks Les Ratons played on each other. They often stayed up until midnight or later, only to have to rise at 6:30 in the morning to open the kitchen. Their workdays did not normally end until 8:30 at night, with their completion of a thorough cleaning of the large kitchen and dinning area following the evening meal. Even with workdays of 12 hours or more, and a habitual lack of sleep, John told us he would awake every morning looking forward to all the fun he was going to have at camp during the day.

This total immersion in a tight group of his French-speaking peers had a much more profound influence on John's French than anything we could have done at this point in his linguistic development. Indeed, we have concluded that his peers accomplished what we, his parents, were not able to do. The following incident, which occurred at the camp this summer, underscores John's linguistic transformation, and the influence of the Québec peer culture with which he so totally identified.

During one of my visits with him, he and I walked into Les Ratons' cramped and unkempt living quarters. I thought we were alone. While we were chatting, and without realizing I had done so, I unconsciously shifted from French to English while talking to John (14;2). Suddenly uncomfortable, John stopped me as he pointed to a closed door in their hut. Then he said in a hushed tone, 'Shhhh , Papa, parle pas d'anglais. Il y a quelq'un dans cette chambre-la' ('Shhhh, papa, don't speak English. There's someone in that room there'.) What made his aversion to English all the more interesting was that several of John's co-workers were bilingual, and able to speak English. Nevertheless, French was the language of choice between these boys, and John wanted to fit in.

The language politics of music

It is well established that the dialects of adolescents are much more influenced by their peers than their parents, and also that summertime peer relationships have a profound effect on developing self-identities (Eckert, 1989). This would help explain John's strong orientation to the Québec language and youth culture. He even started listening to Québec alternative rock, having been introduced to several rock groups by his fellow Ratons. Once, he insisted that I listen to the 'political' lyrics (in French) of one of these rock groups. Perhaps tellingly, the verses John had me listen to by the group 'Grimskunk' in their song 'Lâchez Vos Drapeaux' (drop your flags) made fun of both the Québec separatists and the Québec federalists. They were: ...

> Les anglais sont venus massacrer les indiens
> Les français sont venus massacrer les indiens
> Mon pays, ce n'est pas un pays, c'est la terre
> De quel droit osez-vous la refaire
> En nous imposant lignes et frontières ...
> Lâchez vos drapeaux, la terre est à vous
> Lâchez vos drapeaux et la terre est à nous
> J'me calice de vous, politique de fou (from the album 'Fieldtrip', 1998)
>
> (The English came to massacre the indians
> The French came to massacre the indians
> My country, it's not a country, it's the earth
> What right have you to remake it
> by imposing lines and borders ...
> Drop your flags, the land is yours
> Drop your flags and the land is ours
> Screw you, politics of fools) [translation by the author]

Though he did not appear to be a 'sovereignist' (or 'separatist', depending upon your political viewpoint), John did tell me that most of his friends in Québec were for a Québec independent from Canada.

On two occasions during this summer, while John was on break and visiting our cottage (when I would dutifully tape our dinnertime conversations), I had apparently slipped into English again. I noted earlier how John had admonished us, his parents, to speak only English to him in Louisiana (in public, at least). However, in Québec, we see a flip-flopping attitude (or the same attitude with the other language in a different milieu). The very next time John returned to the family from the summer camp, on July 11, I recorded the following in my fieldnotes:

> Yesterday, on two separate occasions, John asked me something in French, and I apparently responded in English, and he chided me. He asked me, 'Pourquoi tu ne réponds pas en français?' [Why don't you answer in French?]

I noted with some shame that during that particular summer I seemed to be speaking more English than anyone else in the family. I, obviously, was not being a very good role model. However, in John's case this did not seem to matter – evidence once again for the greater influence of peers than parents on an adolescent's speech.

It was by the end of this summer vacation of 1999, when John was aged 14;3, that he appeared to have completely lost any vestiges of his American accent when he spoke French. He never again complained of having an accent when speaking French, like he had done in the previous two years. When he completed our French self-perception survey four years later at aged 18;1 (discussed in the next chapter), he indicated that he believed he had no accent when he spoke French. He went on to comment on our survey that when he was around Québécois, 'most people don't know that I'm not Québécois the first time they meet me'. During this summer of our project, the vast majority of the children's words recorded at dinnertime were in French.

'Crossing Over'

So, as the children moved through mid-adolescence, we see an increasing identification with Québécois peer culture. Part of the reason that the children grew increasingly confident and comfortable in Québec throughout their adolescence is likely a function of the high esteem with which English is almost universally held there. Even though they avoided speaking it, all of their acquaintances knew they were Americans. English is the 'language of popular culture' throughout the world (Heller, 1999: 149), and Québec is no exception. Québécois youth pepper their speech with English pop-cultural words and expressions, and Québécois adolescents who linguistically 'cross over' into English are perceived as 'cool'.

Indeed, English words and expressions so permeate Québec youth culture that it appears the usage of many English words and expressions are the more preferred not just because they're more 'cool', but because using the French word is simply unthinkable. The author was speaking in French with a 15-year-old Québécois nephew in the summer of 2004 about music, and noted his use of the word 'speaker' instead of the French equivalent 'haut-parleur'. When I asked the Montréal native why he didn't use the French word, his answer suggested he wasn't completely sure that the word 'speaker' wasn't French. He said it was the only word he and his friends used to describe this piece of musical hardware.

In the first decade of the 21st century Québec adolescents were saying 'chilé' [sic] in the same sense as their American counterparts say 'chill out'. They were also saying 'Moi too' ('me too') and 'Full-cool' ('really cool'), 'Je vais caller' (I'm going to call) and 'Il est "yo"' (He's 'yo', or 'cool'). Using these expressions is somewhat analogous to the use of Creole among Anglo adolescents in England, who 'linked it with being ... cool', (Rampton, 1995: 47). Mixing in English expressions with French is even more pronounced among francophone adolescents in New Brunswick who 'throw out' Anglicisms 'to be a part of the group' (Boudreau, 1996: 144, translated from French).

Though throughout much of this study the children had what appeared to us and others as an identifiable American English accent when they spoke French, during middle adolescence they never indicated that francophone Québécois thought less of them for either their accent, or their anglophone status. This is not the experience of many immigrants to the United States, who sense a lower value placed not only on their native tongue (Macedo, 2000), but also on their accented English (McKay & Wong, 1996). Indeed, in a California study by Giles *et al.* (1995), Anglo-accented speakers were perceived as 'superior' to Hispanic-accented speakers.

The perception which the French-speaking Québécois have of English and English speakers has been conditioned by many factors: a history of dominance and oppression by their English-speaking countrymen on the one hand (Heller, 1999), and warm, generally favorable relations with their giant southern neighbor and world superpower, the United States, on the other. In both instances, English has been in a dominant, if not prestigious position. Not only are English speakers not viewed in an inferior light, most Québécois believe it is important to speak at least some English. Consequently, at a very personal level, this likely translated into positive feelings between the children and other Québécois, for whom French-English bilingualism is held in particularly high esteem in a country in which 'there is increased value attached to French-English bilingualism' (Heller, 1999: 50). Moreover, Americans learning fluent Québécois French is a sufficiently rare occurrence that it sends a strong signal of respect for and identification with a traditionally oppressed people and language. This is somewhat akin to Anglo English adolescents who 'cross over' and try to speak Punjabi with Bangladeshi youth in England (Rampton, 1995), who have responded, 'these [English boys] ... are one of us' (p. 44), and learners of Welsh as a second language who immensely please native Welsh speakers interested in the survival of their language (Trosset, 1986). That the children are Louisianans has also undoubtedly contributed to their warm reception by native Québécois, most of whom are aware of Louisiana's 'exotic' French heritage. Of course, it did not hurt that the children's mother was Québécoise. In rather stark contrast, there were no equivalent factors among the children's adolescent peer groups in Louisiana that encouraged bilingualism.

No Residual Effect

Back in Louisiana during the fall of 1999, when the twins entered the seventh grade and John entered the ninth grade – high school – the children uttered not one recorded word of French around our dinner table. Indeed, they spoke no French around our dinner table immediately upon our return to the Bayou State in August. In the past, August was usually the month in Louisiana that the children spoke the most French. We attributed this to the 'residual effect' of having been immersed in French in Québec only days or weeks earlier.

There was no 'residual French effect' whatsoever this August. The girls' officially measured BPR of 0.002 this fall was marginally smaller than even John's minuscule 0.003, and represented significantly less French-speaking than John manifested two years earlier when he was the twins' age (12;4). This is striking, since in 1999 the girls were still in a French immersion program where three of their academic classes were taught in French, and their peer group and close friends were still all children enrolled in the French immersion program, and who were all able to speak in French – if they so desired. However, there was clearly much pressure in this 'Frenchies' peer group to only speak English. Moreover, this absence of any French on the part of the children was in spite of the fact that on average we (the parents) were speaking more French than English around the dinner table. Once again, we see non-existent parental influence on our children's language preferences, yet incredibly powerful peer influences.

The transformation back to mono-linguistic Americans was abrupt and complete. Moreover, it was not without its ironic moments. One morning in September 1999, I dropped the twins off at their middle school, where they were taking French immersion French, Social Studies and Science courses – all taught only in French by francophones. As they climbed from the car I was reading aloud the French phrase written on a new, large sign in front of the school proudly proclaiming that the French immersion program was housed here (the program had just been moved to this particular middle school as a result of a federal desegregation order). Stephanie (12;4) said, 'Shhhhhh!!!' – she didn't want me reading the sign aloud in French around her French immersion peers!

Recall that neither Suzanne nor I ever noted even one instance when the 'Frenchies' spoke French among themselves in relaxed conversation. Based on our observations, there seemed to be little desire among the twin's French-immersion friends to speak French among themselves outside of the classroom. When I would greet one of the immersion students in French, they would often politely respond in French, but then usually almost immediately shifted back into English. One incident makes this point. On a cool October evening that autumn I drove the twins to a football game where we were to sit by one of their French immersion classmates whose father was coaching one of the two rival teams. I recorded the following incident right after we entered the high school stadium:

> We saw Danielle [the twins' French-immersion friend] at the top of the bleachers, and made our way up to her. As I was getting ready to say 'hi' to her, Stephanie (aged 12;5) grabbed my arm and hissed 'Don't speak French to her'. But I said *'Bonjour, comment ça va?'* [Hello, how's it going.] anyway, and she [the friend] answered something like *'ça va bien'*. [It's going fine.] In any event, I didn't hear a word of French between the three girls during the game, though I did speak to Valerie (next to me) in French probably about half the time (though she always answered in English).

Somewhat ironically, one of the very few instances I noted of an adolescent in Louisiana speaking to either me or one of my children in French was an eighth grade boy in John's middle school who *was not* in the French immersion program. The boy was being reared bilingually by native French-speaking parents – the mother was from France, and the father was a Cajun (the Ph.D. in Francophone Studies mentioned earlier). I occasionally gave the eighth grader a ride home after school, and often spoke to him in French. In the car he always spoke French to both John (who was in the seventh grade at the time) and me. However when I asked John (12;10) if he ever spoke in French to his bilingual friend on the school grounds, he answered, 'no', because the others would think he and the boy were weird. He added that none of the bilingual children spoke French outside of class.

'Weird Language Crap'

When John was in the ninth grade, the few times I noticed him speaking French in the fall of 1999 were when he was speaking about something that happened in Québec earlier during that eventful summer with Les Ratons. However, these instances of French speaking were slips triggered by recalling events that had taken place entirely in a francophone context. He would always immediately shift back into English. Though John's transformation back into English was immediate and complete, he commented to me that he really liked the required novel in his English class (*Les Misérables*, translated from French into English) because 'I can read French, and every other word is in French' (age 14;4). So he was gradually moving beyond the defiant 'anti-everything French' stage he had been exhibiting in early adolescence in the seventh and eighth grades.

Nevertheless, during his ninth grade year John still occasionally exhibited negative sentiments toward his bilingualism. One of these displays occurred when he was studying for an English test that involved conjugating verbs and pronouns. I tried to show John how to do this using what he had learned in French. But he stopped me fast, not wanting to hear anything in French, and vowing never to take another foreign language class if he could avoid it. A couple of days later while discussing his English class, he complained how hard the study of English was for him in general, compared to his other classmates who seemed to get some of the grammatical rules, etc., quicker than he did. He concluded by exclaiming, 'I blame it on being bilingual'. I asked why, and he answered, 'I have twice as much stuff in my head as everyone else. I have to remember twice as much as everyone else. Jeeez, it isn't fair!' (age 14;4). He expressed frustration with language on another occasion as he was trying to help Suzanne in the French version of the spreadsheet Microsoft Excel. After a few minutes of fruitless pecking at the keys, he yelled out 'I can't deal with this weird language crap!' (Ironically, though he did not realize it at the time, this 'weird language crap' would exempt him from four semesters of a foreign language at his university.)

About this same time, Valerie (12;4), now a seventh grader, complained to me that being taught classes in French immersion, like social studies, was going to hurt her ACT (college entrance) test scores, because she was not being taught the terms in English like they would appear on the test. Indeed, Suzanne and I shared some of her concern. For example, I had actively observed Valerie and Stephanie's language usage while studying their homework together over a two-day period in September 1999. I remarked that when they were studying for courses in English, they spoke English, but as soon as they shifted to a course administered in French (i.e., Science or Social Studies) they immediately shifted into French, and mostly stayed in French while discussing that subject. One night early in their seventh grade year, they were reviewing the great European explorers for social studies, and referred to the Portuguese Henry the Navigator as *'Henri le Navigateur'* and his explorations of *'le côte d'Afrique, en cherchant une route vers les épices de l'est'* [the African coast, in searching for a route to the spices of the east] (12;4). I was tempted to ask them if they knew how to say these things in English, and actually found myself wondering if they would be able to recognize this material on a standardized test in English. So, I apparently had the same apprehension as Valerie.

We (the parents) were still speaking more French than English around our table during this fall of 1999, but it was apparently not increasing our children's preference for French – not even a minuscule amount. Once in October, the girls were explaining to me in English what their various teachers were teaching. In discussing one of their French teachers (who taught them social studies) they quoted something that he said to the class, repeating the quote in English. I asked if he had said it in English or French, and they said it was in French. What a change from a few years earlier when they would recount in French what a teacher had said to them in English!

No Peers, No Language Influence

In December 1999 when John was 14;8 and the twins were 12;8 we had the good fortune to spend two weeks at our Québec lake cottage to celebrate the arrival of the year 2000. Though we had some interaction with Suzanne's family, we spent most of our time together as a family unit sequestered in our snow-bound cottage on the frozen lake. We also made two tape recordings during this period. More than 90% of John's utterances were in English, whereas almost 99% of the twin's recorded words were in English. It appeared that with no Québécois peer group influence, English prevailed. A few years earlier, just being in Québec triggered an increase in French speaking. No longer: geographic proximity did not seem to matter any more. What mattered were friends.

During the spring of 2000, essentially all communication by the children around the Louisiana dinner table was in English, though over half of the words uttered by Suzanne and I were in French. We seemed to have increasingly less linguistic influence on our children, if that were possible. Indeed, in the entire year 2000, John spoke an average of only 4.5 French words throughout the entire school year in Louisiana, whereas the twins' combined total average was only 4. It is possible for even a monolingual English speaker to utter an occasional French word, especially in Louisiana. Thus, it is safe to say that in Louisiana, the children's French essentially stopped. The children no longer responded to us in French. Neither was there any expectation that they would. We realized that it would have been fruitless to even suggest that they speak French, as we knew that our 'encouragement' would be met with adolescent opposition.

However, as has been demonstrated, the inverse was occurring during the summer months in Québec, where French speaking was the norm. Moreover, we had a developing sense that the family project was a success: the children were bilingual, and spoke French where they deemed it appropriate, as part of their 'reconfigured social identities' (Ochs, 1993: 298). It so happened that for them Louisiana was, somewhat ironically, not the appropriate venue – their socially constructed views of themselves as Louisianans did not include speaking French. Not at this point in their adolescence, anyway.

Summer of 2000

In the summer of 2000, the patterns were the same – with John, anyway. During this summer, it was Stephanie who traveled with me to Europe during three weeks of the summer, including two weeks in France, French-speaking Belgium, and French-speaking Switzerland. John once again worked full time at the local all-French-speaking summer camp. Thus, we could not tape the family's conversation in June 2000, and could only record two sessions in July. Valerie was not present for either of the tapings, as she was also at the summer camp full time. Given the evolving logistical concerns, it was clear that this would be the last summer that we could record our family's dinnertime conversations in Québec.

Still, even with the recording limitations, the results were telling. John's recorded French speaking was as high as it had ever been. As during the previous summer, John returned home from his job at the summer camp speaking what struck his mother, all his Québécois relatives, and me as fluent, unaccented Québec French. We exchanged surprised glances with each other several times during our brief hours together with John, absolutely amazed at his fluency, and his use of the local vernacular. Indeed, he used French expressions even Suzanne had never heard.

Stephanie, who had had the least exposure to French (among her francophone peers) that summer, spoke slightly less French than English around our Québec dinner table – and much less French than John. Suzanne and I noticed that she had, what seemed to us, a decidedly more 'French' than 'Québec' accent – in stark opposition to her brother. We attributed Stephanie's accent to her exposure to the French spoken in Europe. Stephanie had very much liked Europe – its fashion, internationalism, and the suave way she perceived that the French there was spoken. I suspected that she associated the accent, especially in France, with being cosmopolitan and cultivated. When we picked up Valerie after a three-week stay at the French-speaking camp, we actively noted that she spoke no English with us during the rest of our stay in Québec, and that her French was rapid-fire fluent. She did, though, seem to have what sounded to us like a slight American English accent.

No French

The shift back to all English in August 2000 was absolute and complete – the children uttered not one word of recorded French around our dinner table during August (there was no 'residual effect') or any other month that autumn. For fun (and not research) I shot a brief, less than 10 minute videotape in September when the twins were 13;4 and John was 15;4. There was not one word of French uttered by the cameraman (me), John, or the twins. Since the vast majority of the words I uttered on audiotape that September around our dinner table was in French (BPR=0.98), this discrepancy between videotape and audiotape could suggest that the French I uttered around the dinner table was more contrived (and less organic) than I had originally imagined.

We returned to our cottage in Québec for two weeks in December 2000 under the identical, frozen, snowed-in conditions of December 1999. Indeed, there were three major snowstorms during this short vacation, so we were even more isolated than the previous year. One of our most common 'family activities' was digging out our snowbound car. Our isolation kind of reminded us of the film *The Shining*. Anyway, we again made audiotapes. This time, our children, aged 15;8 and 13;8 uttered not even one word in French. So, as if further confirmation was needed, just physically being in the geographical locale of Québec was no longer enough to trigger the children's French speaking in the home, as it had been before they were adolescents. It took immersion in their Québécois peer groups to accomplish this feat. And, as had been the case for approximately the previous three years, parental French speaking, which constituted the majority of words Suzanne and I spoke around our Québec dinner table that cold December, had zero influence on our children's language preferences. Indeed, it was even possible that our French speaking was triggering the children's adolescent opposition, and thus their preference for English.

We suspended our systematic audiotaping after December 2000 when John was 15;8 and the twins were 13;8. At this point we decided there seemed no good reason to make recordings of conversations that in Louisiana were all in English. We sensed that an important phase in our family project had come to an end. Our children spoke French and English fluently, but they had demarcated spaces where either the one or the other language was appropriate for them. At this point in their adolescent development, French was essentially a language only to be used in a French-speaking environment with French-speaking friends, and English was only to be spoken in an English dominant environment like south Louisiana. The children had decided not to converse with us, their parents, in French, in the privacy of our home, if the home were in an English-speaking milieu. We knew at this point that any suggestion to the contrary would be counter-productive, and useless. Oddly, there seemed a certain tragic logic to John's (11;10) sixth grade pronouncement that 'If everyone speaks English ... why would anyone want to speak French?' Not only did we have a 'sense' that parental language choice had no influence on our children's language preferences at this point in their adolescence, this fact was empirically validated by an analysis of our taped dinnertime conversations, which is examined next.

No Parental Language Influence

To determine how much French Suzanne and I were speaking around our dinner table, I calculated the ratio of French to English spoken by both of us from January 1997 through December 2000 – the date of the last audiotape. Over this four-year timeframe the children ranged in age from 12;8 and 10;8, to 15;8 and 13;8, respectively. This timeframe corresponds fairly closely to the early adolescent period of the twins, and to John's middle adolescence (Steinberg, 1993). Figure 4 on p. 168 shows the average

BPR's for both parents in Louisiana and Québec over this four-year time frame, and Figure 1 shows the fluctuating BPRs for all family members.

As can be seen in Figure 4, there is overall much less divergence between the parents' Louisiana and Québec French speaking. In other words, our French speaking does not fall off nearly as precipitously as does the children's when in Louisiana, though it does decrease somewhat. In 1997, the large majority of the words spoken by both Suzanne and me around our dinner table were in French. However, in this same year, John's Louisiana French speaking had essentially ceased. In Québec that year, we, like the children, spoke essentially only French around the dinner table during our summertime sojourn in the Canadian province.

In 1998, the large majority of the parental dinnertime speech in Louisiana was again in French, in stark contrast to the children who all spoke almost no French. However, once in Québec, all the family members' French speaking once again rose in unison. Back in Louisiana in 1999, the mother's and father's French speaking fell off somewhat, but took nowhere near the tumble which the children's French speaking did, as it fell to near zero. However, in keeping with the pattern, once back in the French-speaking environment of Québec in the summer of 1999, the parents' and children's French speaking converged yet again. During the year 2000 in Louisiana, while Suzanne and I spoke mostly French at the dinner table, the children only spoke English. However, back in Québec in the summer of 2000, the children's French speaking increases dramatically, as it had in every previous year.

In short, what we see is the children's fairly sharp divergence from the predominantly French-speaking parents in Louisiana, where John and his sisters increasingly prefer to speak English, but then convergence once the family is immersed in French-speaking Canada. Since the parental level of French-speaking while in Québec is fairly constant over the period, we cannot say that one of the reasons the children maintain the high level of Québec French speaking is due to *increasing* parental French speaking over this period. We must look beyond parental influence to explain why French speaking is falling off in Louisiana, but not in Québec.

Could part of the explanation for the sharp divergence between the parents' and children's French speaking in Louisiana be due to the children reinforcing each other's English speaking? For example, could it have been that John initiated a conversation in English, say, about something that transpired in his Louisiana school, and the girls responded in English, setting up a cycle of conversation that was self-perpetuating? In other words, if John had initiated the same conversation in French, would it have been more likely that his siblings would have responded in French?

Since so much of the children's conversation in Louisiana during middle adolescence was in English, it is hard to answer this question with any degree of precision without re-listening to many hours of tapes for the occasional French word – an arduous proposition indeed since there were almost no French words. However, since the parents spoke so much French in Louisiana, often in discussions with the children, as we tabulated word counts by listening to the tapes we were able to consciously make note of whether or not the children ever responded in French, since such a response would have been so surprising.

We were literally shocked by what we heard. The rule – rather than the exception – was that entire conversations transpired between the parents and the children during which time either the father or mother spoke only French, and the children responded only in English. Since the parents' Louisiana French speaking did not fall off drastically over the three years for which we have tabulated data, as it did for the children, the pattern becomes increasingly striking as first John, than his sisters, moved into early and mid-adolescence. We therefore have to rule out 'linguistic family atmosphere' around the table in Louisiana as a primary determinant of the children's increasing propensity to speak English in Louisiana. A better explanation is that the children's increasing preference for English in the home is the result of peer influences outside of the home. Eckert (1989: 12), describes well the all-pervasive nature of this social force:

> In secondary school, where the social structure of the student cohort dominates virtually all aspects of life in the institution, choices in all domains are restricted not so clearly by adult judgment as by peer social boundaries.

French-speaking was not within these Louisiana peer-defined boundaries.

Lord of the Rings

As was our custom, we returned to Québec for two months in June and July 2001. Once again, John lived and worked full time at the French-speaking summer camp. We dropped by the camp to talk with John (16;2) just outside the camp kitchen where he now supervised a staff of teenaged kitchen help. We chatted with him for perhaps 10 minutes just out of earshot of his colleagues. I did not hear even one word in English, except maybe if you count 'steam cooker' – which was apparently only referred to by its English name, and pronounced with a Québec accent. Also this summer, John, whose only formal French instruction was a half-year of

French immersion in fourth grade and one year in an hour-long French course in the seventh grade, was reading Tolkien's *Lord of the Rings* trilogy in French. So, our goal for John to achieve some measure of French literacy was achieved. However, John's ability to read, and to a lesser extent write in French also has to be attributed to non-school, as well as formal academic, environmental influences. These home influences on his French literacy would include exposure to written French material and a family norm that greatly encouraged French literacy.

Summertime English

We noted that Valerie and Stephanie (14;1) seemed to be speaking a lot more English around our Québec residence in June 2001 than had ever been the case in any previous summer. I noted, for example, that one day when I went cycling with the twins, Suzanne, and an aunt who did not speak English, I spoke with the girls almost exclusively in English. The aunt also noticed, and politely pointed this out to us. That the twins would speak English so uninhibitedly around a francophone in Québec is yet further evidence that they did not perceive an 'anti-English speaking norm' in Québec in the same way that they perceived an 'anti-any foreign language speaking norm' in Louisiana.

In July, however, the twins took a two-week bicycle trip in New Brunswick with about 15 mostly French-speaking campers. Upon their return, we noted much more French-speaking. Once again, in the absence of French linguistic peer pressure – regardless the venue – the children resorted to English. This language pattern was not observed before early adolescence.

End in Sight

Immediately upon the family's return to Louisiana in August 2001, the children essentially stopped speaking French – with a few rare, notable exceptions. It was these exceptions, however, which presaged the emergence of more mature bilinguistic identities in the children. When Valerie (14;3) began explaining to us in the car something that happened on her bike trip in New Brunswick, she immediately shifted into French, and for perhaps three to five minutes uttered not even one word in English. Suzanne and I both looked at each other in happy acknowledgment of her shift into French. Moreover, she spoke very fast. At about this same time when Valerie began taking French IV in ninth grade (14;3) she told us she wanted to get out because it was too easy for her. In fact, she said rather immodestly 'there's nothing left for me to learn. I've learned it all already'. In August she put together a scrapbook of her two-week summer bicycle expedition around New Brunswick with her French-speaking camp mates. As we mentioned earlier, she chose, with no prompting from us (as if we had any influence at this point anyway) to write all of the captions in French.

At this time John (16;4) did not exhibit the same degree of confidence in his French literacy skills as his sisters did. He was attending a residential school in Louisiana for advanced students, and e-mailed us that his French teacher did not like the way he conjugated [those ever pesky] verbs. Still, he was apparently able to keep all this 'stuff' in his head, because on the French placement assessment that landed him in this same teacher's class, he had scored the highest possible grade. At this time John had also begun wearing 'Québec' T-shirts, some emblazoned with the Québec flag, to his American high school. I offhandedly asked him if he was speaking any French with a fellow bilingual student who was also a French national, and with whom he was doing a project. To my surprise (and secret delight), John answered 'yes, a little'. When I shared this tid-bit with Suzanne, she too was ecstatic that John was finally speaking French again in Louisiana. These incidents suggested an evolving and maturing bilinguistic self-confidence that we had not seen since early adolescence. The end was now in sight.

Approaching Fluency

During the summer of 2002 John (17;2) lived and worked at the camp for most of the summer, and the girls (15;2) attended a full-time, five-week, live-in counselor-training program at the all-French-speaking camp. After their training session, they then worked at the camp for another two weeks as residents. As in the previous three years, John spoke Québec French with others and with us with no noticeable American English accent that either Suzanne or I could detect. It seemed that the twins' French speaking acquired a fluency it never had before during this summer, though it also seemed that both girls may have had a slight American English accent when they spoke Québec French. However, we noticed they used Québécois idioms that we never heard in the past. There was no hesitation in their speech either. Upon returning from Québec, Stephanie (15;3) stated that her goal next year at the French summer camp was to learn to speak unaccented French. Both Stephanie and Valerie expressed admiration for a fellow camper who had a francophone mother and Korean father. They said that he spoke perfectly unaccented French and English, which is what they were striving for (again, evidence for the strong influence of adolescent peers). Thus, as with John, we were beginning to see the emergence of a maturing bilinguistic identity in the twins. In the next chapter, we examine the children's maturing 'bilingual identities' in more detail.

Chapter 10
Emerging Bilinguistic Identities

Introduction

This chapter focuses on the emerging bilinguistic identities of the children in middle and late adolescence; a period marked by greater linguistic self-confidence and diminished self-consciousness regarding language choice. Steinberg (1993) identifies late adolescence as the period beginning at approximately 18 years of age. John turned 18 in May of 2003, and left Louisiana in the fall to attend an out-of-state university. The twins turned 16 in May 2003, worked full time at the French-speaking summer camp as counselors in the summer of 2003, and left home to attend a residential school for advanced students in the fall of 2003. This chapter includes an analysis and comparison of both the pre- and late adolescent bilingual self-perceptions of the children captured on the author-constructed Bilingual Self-perception Survey.

A New Phase

Beginning some time around the summer of 2001, when the children were 16;3 (John) and 14;3 (twins), our project was entering yet another phase, as our children were all past early adolescence, and indeed, John was moving toward late adolescence (sometimes called 'youth') (Berk, 1996; Steinberg, 1993). Importantly, adolescence is by definition a period of change and identity construction, with older adolescents less susceptible to the rigid peer cultures which peak in influence in the eighth and ninth grades (Eckert, 1989). In the autumn of 2001 the twins were in the ninth grade and John was a high school junior.

During this period, there were an increasing number of indicators that the children's use of French and English, and their identification with American and Québécois culture, were evolving in ways that were quite different from what we had thus far observed and recorded. There was a hint of the coming changes during the summer of 2001, when John (16;3) returned from seven weeks of work in the all-French-speaking camp. As expected, he spoke no English for days after his return to the family at our

Québec cottage, but quickly – and smoothly – shifted into English upon return to the U.S. and contact with his American peers. However, such were the bonds with his Québec friends, among whom he seemed to be very well accepted and liked, that he was considering the possibility of completing his secondary education in Québec, and perhaps even attending university there.

His plans suggested very strong, positive ties with the language and culture, and the possibility of a life trajectory, personal identity, and language usage that could be radically different from a life lived in the U.S. John's evolving attitude during this summer contrasted sharply with his negative response nearly four years earlier to the possibility of moving to a francophone country. Recall that his response had been an insouciant, 'Uh, uh, I ain't going if they don't speak English' (12;7). On the Bilingual Self-perception Survey that he completed at age 18;1 (discussed in more detail below), he indicated that he felt he was more popular in Québec than in the United States.

Decreasing Linguistic Self-consciousness

With seemingly fairly healthy self-images and self-confidence in the kinds of individuals they were becoming, there appeared once again occasional – though at first still rare – spontaneous French communication with the children in public places in Louisiana. One such incident took place when I was at a cellular telephone store with Stephanie (14;4), and told her something in French that I did not want the salesman to understand. In what seemed remarkable to me at the time, she answered me completely in French, and with none of the reticence or self-consciousness I would have expected the year before.

On another occasion, Suzanne and I took the twins on a brief visit to Mexico during our Christmas break in 2002. Our plan was to go shopping in the outdoor markets of the border town, Juarez, we visited. Prior to crossing the border, Suzanne suggested to all of us that while in Mexico, we speak only French, to distinguish us from 'wealthier' American tourists. This strategy would ostensibly allow us to dicker down prices even farther than Americans could negotiate them. The girls (15;8) not only did not protest, and happily went along with the plan (they loved shopping), but they actually chided ME for MY English speaking on several occasions. The girls had not demanded that I 'Parle français!' for approximately five years at that point. Suzanne and I were both greatly heartened.

The twins confidently spoke French in Mexico without self-consciousness. Additionally, they tried their best to speak Spanish with the various vendors, though their command of the language was very limited (they knew a few words and phrases learned in Spanish I at their high school). Since I knew a bit more Spanish from my college years (before a certain Québécoise changed my life course), my status as a father was temporarily enhanced. So, here we see an example of the twins' diminishing self-consciousness while speaking not only French, but their much more limited Spanish in a public, non-francophone milieu. We also see a corresponding increase in self-confidence in the twins' developing sense of who they were becoming linguistically.

A year later the twins decided to take a very difficult advanced Spanish immersion class in the eleventh grade, and then re-enrolled in this same class as high school seniors. Valerie enrolled in a German class as well during both her junior and seniors years. She was expressing much interest in learning other languages. Both girls said that they wanted to become tri-lingual following their 2003 summer camp counselor experience in Québec when they had met fellow campers who were not only bilingual French and English speakers, but German and Russian speakers as well. Indeed, after spending three weeks living with a German family during the summer of 2004, and taking Spanish and German as a senior, Valerie was well on her way to becoming quadralingual.

Increasing Linguistic Self-confidence

As for John, a very telling experience that underscores his increasing linguistic self-confidence occurred when he (17;1) called us from his American girlfriend's house just before we left as a family for Québec. At this point, it had been nine months since his last societal immersion in Québec. This made it all the more remarkable that his entire conversation with Suzanne was in French in the presence of this English-speaking friend. This would have been unimaginable just a year earlier. Yet another example of John's increasingly confident self-image as a bilingual occurred seven months later in the hallway of his American high school in a three way discussion between John (17;8), and his Belgian calculus teacher, and me. She was a native French speaker, so I initiated the conversation with her in French. She then spoke only French with us, and John spoke with both of us in French – in the middle of the high school corridor. At roughly this same time John was seriously considering attending McGill University in Montreal – because 'Montreal is a bilingual city'. What a stark contrast with his attitude of five years earlier.

Both John's and the twins' growing linguistic self-confidence, and perhaps even pride in their bilingualism, were increasingly manifesting themselves as they moved toward late adolescence and beyond the peak period of concern over the 'imaginary audience' which is more typical of early adolescence (Enright *et al.*, 1979; Lapsley *et al.*, 1988). The children's increasingly positive view of themselves as bilinguals who were not ashamed to reveal this dimension of their personality to others is one mark of a person who is identity-achieved (Adams *et al.*, 1987). As compared to their early adolescence which seemed to be more characterized by parallel monolingualism, or a sort of linguistic schizophrenia, by middle to late adolescence the children seemed to be successfully unifying their two cultural/linguistic halves into a healthy and coherent whole.

Society Stronger than Will

When we crossed the Canadian border during the summer of 2003, Suzanne made the comment that we should all speak French. (John stayed in Louisiana to work during this summer.) Apparently, we had not been speaking much French during the three-day car trip. The girls did not protest, and proceeded to utter a few words in French, but within minutes were only speaking English again. After a week in Québec, I audiotaped the conversation of the family. The girls, who were 16;1 at this time, were packing their bags in preparation to go to work at the French-speaking summer camp as counselors. They uttered no French during the audiotaping, though Suzanne and I very conscientiously and intentionally spoke only French.

The girls then entered the summer camp as live-in counselors for the first time in their lives, with groups of French-speaking Québécois children under their charge 24 hours a day. The girls called us just three and a half days after their first day of work. We spoke with both girls on the phone. Valerie uttered a couple of sentences in English at first, but otherwise spoke only French for 10 minutes. Stephanie spoke for another ten minutes – and uttered not one word of English. What neither I nor even the twins' volition was capable of doing (recall their fledgling efforts to speak French when crossing the US-Canadian border), a monolingual French environment accomplished effortlessly in just days. After three weeks in camp the girls made a short, three-day trip with us to Boston. During the entire trip, they spoke only English. To us, it seemed entirely natural, even though Suzanne and I spoke French at least some of the time. We were in the U.S., and we encountered no other French speakers.

Beyond Peers

So we saw earlier that during their adolescent years the children essentially stopped speaking French around the dinner table in Louisiana for months right up to the eve of our summer vacation. Then, once amongst their peers in Canada, they would stop speaking English with us. This pattern, when considered in combination with parental language preferences, provides strong evidence for the overwhelming influence of the French-speaking environment and peer groups – and lack of a corresponding English-speaking *peer* environment – on the children's language usage in Québec. This shift also suggests the relatively weak to non-existent influence of us – the parents – on our children's language preferences while they were adolescents. However, as the children moved past the 'imaginary audience' of early adolescence, we once again began to see spontaneous French speaking in situations that defied peer influence.

We made the summer 2003 yearly pilgrimage to Québec, *sans* John. He decided to spend the summer working at a Cajun restaurant in Louisiana, where, he jokingly agreed with me, he might learn some Cajun. As a testament to how confident *we* were in his French-speaking ability, we had no reticence about his missing the annual cultural and linguistic 'French shower'. Such a position would have been unthinkable in earlier years, when we knew our summer trips to Québec were vitally critical toward John's becoming bilingual and biliterate. As noted earlier, the primary reason for purchasing our summer cottage was to provide a base in Québec where our children would be immersed in French culture and language. As an indication of his linguistic maturity, just before we left the Bayou State in early June, John told me he had spoken French with two black workers at the restaurant, one a teenager and the other an elderly gentleman, who both spoke Creole. It had been at least six years since I had noted John's speaking French with a native Louisianan.

Our decision not to coerce John to follow us to Canada was in a sense validated during the summer when I once phoned John (18;2) from Québec. He answered the phone 'bonjour' (apparently recognizing it was me from caller ID), and did not utter even one single English word during 10 minutes of conversation. John was at a friend's house and speaking in the presence of several of his peers. I thought perhaps he was 'showing off' his bilingualism, which would have been in a sense a positive development, indicating greater self-confidence in his bilingualism. However, later in the summer the same scenario repeated itself, though this time John was alone when we talked. Again, he spoke no English. The two episodes taken together indicated an even more positive development: both increasing linguistic self-confidence and a certain linguistic spontaneity to speak French in Louisiana that had been absent in the Louisiana context for about six years, since early adolescence.

A week after the first phone conversation with John, when Stephanie came home from camp for a short break, she called her brother in Louisiana, who answered his cell phone while in a shopping center. I was on the other line. The two spoke to each other only in French the whole time. I had not witnessed John speaking French with his sisters when he was in the Louisiana context, and after so long an absence from Québec, in about six years. He had moved beyond much of the peer influence that had dictated his early adolescent linguistic behavior.

Bilingual Self-perceptions

So, as the children moved toward late adolescence, we see a weakening influence of their American monolingual peer groups on their propensity to speak French in a monolingual English environment. We also see the apparently healthy assimilation of their bilingualism into their developing identities. This evolution in the children's perceptions of their bilingualism is captured in the 'French Proficiency Survey' and 'Bilingual Self-perception Survey' that I created and administered to the children first when they were ages 12;10 (John) and 10;10 (twins), and then five and a quarter years later when they were 18;1 and 16;1, respectively. I slightly modified the wording of the French Proficiency Survey, which I had their French teachers complete, to address the questions to the children and not the teachers (see Appendix 3 for original French version or Appendix 4 for the English translation). In the 'Bilingual Self-perception Survey' I included seven open-ended questions that solicited more detail about how the children viewed their bilingualism in both their Louisiana and Québec contexts (see Appendix 5).

Pre- and early adolescent bilingual self-perceptions

The purpose of surveying the children was to solicit their views on their bilingualism in a structured, yet relaxed and non-threatening way. For both administrations, I asked the children to complete the two surveys on their own, emphasizing the importance of complete honesty. The children did not collaborate on their answers. I was particularly interested in getting at the question of how the children viewed themselves culturally and linguistically, in the context of their two languages and nationalities. This, I believed, would also indirectly reflect how the children perceived the predominant linguistic norms extent in the U.S. and Québec, both in

Emerging Bilinguistic Identities

early and later adolescence. The children's responses during pre- and early adolescence are presented first. Then, I compare their early adolescent responses to their mid-to-late adolescent responses of more than five years later. The differences are telling.

Question 1 solicited how the children felt being bilingual compared to their American friends who spoke only English. John's response at 12;10 when he was in the seventh grade hints at his reluctance to broadcast to his schoolmates his mastery of two languages, implying the lack of importance bilingualism had as a status-enhancer among the students at his middle-school. He answered that being bilingual he felt: 'Normal, most of my friends don't even know'.

The twins' responses when they were 10;10 and in the fifth grade suggest that they still weren't feeling the strong middle school peer pressure to conform like their brother. Their responses may also suggest the different atmosphere that a French immersion program created in their (former) elementary school. Stephanie answered: 'It felt cool in one way ... 'cause the teacher would ask me how to say words in French'. However, Stephanie also admitted that being bilingual 'felt bizarre because sometimes I would have some wrong grammar, coming from my mother who was a French immersion teacher who spoke English wrongly . . '.

Valerie echoed Stephanie's positive sentiments about being bilingual around her American friends when she answered: 'I feel special in a way because I know more than them [her monolingual classmates]'.

She was also somewhat ambivalent, as she added: 'I mix my English words with French and I feel embarrassed . . '. concluding on an upbeat note that ... 'except for that [her mixing of words] I feel smart'.

Question 2 solicited information on how the children felt about being bilingual around their monolingual French-speaking friends in Québec. Here, they were all unanimous about their sense of having an accent and not speaking like their friends. John's answer was curt and to the point about how he felt being bilingual in Québec: 'Weird, because I sound different'.

Stephanie, too, said she felt 'weird' because: '... when I speak in French I have a great accent. I don't hear it, but they do, so it makes it even more embarrassing'.

Valerie was the most positive, answering Question 2: 'I feel different and smarter at the same time', adding that, 'sometimes I feel dumb because I have a little accent [though] I usually feel smarter'.

Thus, all three children were cognizant of not speaking exactly like a Québécois, something that was politely pointed out to them at various times during their early adolescence by some of their Québec teachers and friends. We can conclude that in spite of some occasional grammatical mistakes, they were clearly more comfortable in English at this time. The children's responses were consistent with their ratings on Edelman's Measure of Bilingualism (Edelman, 1969) based on 20 months of administering the index to them when the twins ranged in age from 9;9 to 11;0, and John ranged in age from 11;9 to 13;0. Edelman's is a measure of language dominance in the three domains of home, neighborhood, and school. The coefficients suggested they were indeed English dominant (see Chapter 11 for more elaboration on the Edelman results). However, on the Bilingual Preference Ratio, which measures language preference (as distinct from language dominance), only John had a preference for speaking English in the home at the time the first survey was administered.

Question 3 queried the children about how they felt when their parents spoke French to them around their English-speaking friends. This question attempted to probe deeper into how they felt in situations where their bilingualism was thrust before their American peers, and they were presented with an opportunity to demonstrate it.

John's response to this question leaves little doubt that he felt bilingualism was not a desired characteristic among his American middle school peer group. He said he felt '... humiliated, because none of their parents talk to them in another language'.

There is every reason to believe his answer was sincere, too. As noted in the previous chapter, on several occasions when we addressed John in French around his American middle school classmates, he implored us under his breath to 'Please speak English!' or 'Stop it! Stop it! Stop it!' His embarrassment was obvious, and clearly not contrived.

Stephanie, too, wrote that ... 'it feels real embarrassing', elaborating that... 'Sometimes I even answer [my parents] in English in stores and stuff, so it's less embarrassing'. She did concede, though, that ... 'sometimes it's cool to speak two languages'.

Valerie provided a more in-depth, but no less negative assessment of having one's parents speak a foreign language in the presence of American friends:

> I feel embarrassed and kind of stupid at the same time because all my friends are starring at me like if I was a nerd or some alien. Most of them don't have French parents and it makes me different. Children these days don't accept kids who are different, so that is what makes it hard.

It is important to note that this assessment is from one whose American friends (though not their friends' parents) mostly spoke French, at least in their French immersion classrooms. Indeed, at the time, both girls told us that all of their friends at school were in the French immersion program. It makes one wonder how Valerie would feel if, for example, the foreign language her parents spoke was more exotic to Louisiana, like Russian or Hindi.

Question 4 is the reciprocal of Question 3, soliciting the children's feelings when their parents spoke English to them around their French-speaking friends in Québec. John's response is interesting. He said he felt ... 'Normal, at least they [friends] know I'm not a weirdo who can't talk'.

When he was asked later to clarify this statement, he said that he meant that at least his French-speaking friends would realize that the reason he had an accent is because his native language is English. So, we see once again reference to having an accent.

Stephanie had a somewhat similar response to her parents speaking English to her in Québec when she was in the fifth grade, writing that ... 'It wouldn't feel as bad as if I was around my American friends . . '.

Valerie had a different perspective on her parents speaking English in the presence of her Québécois friends:

> I would be really, highly embarrassed because it would make me different and all my friends would think, 'Oh, well she has a big accent and her parents don't even speak French to her!'

We do see, however, that for all three children, fitting in with their Québec peer group at this time was very important, though it seems that fitting in with their American peer group, with whom they went to school, was perhaps even more so.

Though we see that the children were in general not very pleased to broadcast their bilingual status to their friends in either the U.S. or Canada, they were still apparently quite happy to be bilingual. Question 6 asks them if they felt fortunate to speak two languages, and why. John answered: 'Yes, because I can understand tourists and they don't know I hear everything they say'.

Stephanie, too, felt fortunate, writing: 'Yes, I do, because I can speak French and English. French to my friends in Canada and English to my friends in America'.

Valerie responded in a similar fashion to Stephanie, elaborating somewhat by adding: 'It makes me look and be smart, and people think highly of me'.

This is the third instance that Valerie associated being 'smart' with being bilingual. Thus, the children felt torn between wanting to be a part of their peer groups on the one hand, where they perceived that bilingualism was not necessarily valued, but happy nonetheless to have the somewhat unusual ability to communicate in two different languages.

Having established that the children did recognize the value of bilingualism as pre- and early adolescents, Question 6 probed the children about whether they felt they were perfectly bilingual or not, and if not, why not.

John answered 'no' because he said he had an accent in French and not in English. Valerie also answered 'no' she didn't feel *perfectly* (emphasis hers) bilingual because she didn't know how to write as well in French, and she didn't have 'right' grammar in French. Stephanie, alone among the three, believed she was perfectly bilingual at this time – even though she felt she spoke French with an accent. Therefore, she apparently did not believe an accent disqualified one from being perfectly bilingual, whereas her two siblings did. Importantly, then, we see that the perceived weaker language among the children at this time was French. Once again, while this perception was somewhat substantiated by each child's average index on Edelman's Contextualized Measure of Degree of Bilingualism, it was not borne out by the Bilingual Preference Ratio, which indicated that the twin girls actually preferred to speak French at home during the fifth grade.

Establishing that John and Valerie felt more dominant in English, and that even Stephanie, though she felt perfectly bilingual, perceived that she had an accent in French, Question 7 asks the children how they might feel differently around their Québec friends if they spoke exactly like a Québécois. John responded that he would have felt more 'comfortable'. Stephanie, too, indicated she would have liked it and would have felt less embarrassed. She added that she'd probably have had more friends. Valerie also wrote that she would have felt 'good, because I would be more like them'. The children's answers to this question simply underscored their strong feelings that though they valued their bilingualism, they valued at least as strongly being accepted by their peer groups – and they believed their peers made personal judgments based on how someone spoke.

So we see that the issue of having an accent arose often with the children during the first administration of the survey. Early adolescence is a time of acute self-consciousness, and it corresponds to the children's new sensitivity about their accents. Questions 8 and 9 asked the children to indicate on a scale of 1–5 how strong a detectable accent they felt they had first when they spoke English (Question 8), then when they spoke French (Question 9). All three children indicated a value of '5' for Question 8, indicating that they believed they had no detectable French accent when they spoke English. Their answers, however, varied for Question 9. John circled a value of '2' for the degree of English accent present when he spoke French, indicating that John believed he had a moderately strong English accent when he spoke French at age 12;10. Stephanie, on the other hand, indicated a value of '4', which indicates that she believed she had only a small English accent when she spoke French at age 10;10. Valerie circled a value of '3' which is the exact middle of the scale, suggesting she believed she had a moderate English accent when she spoke French.

Comparison of early and late adolescent bilingual self-perceptions

I re-administered the same French Proficiency Survey and Bilingual Self-perception Survey to the children five and a quarter years later when they were 16;1 (twins) and 18;1 (John), ages which correspond with late-middle to early-late adolescence (Steinberg, 1993). They were given precisely the same directions to complete the surveys on their own without collaborating with each other on their answers. They were not shown their responses to the first administration of the surveys five years earlier until after they had completed both surveys.

The results are starkly different from the first administration. In the second administration of the French Proficiency Survey, John rated himself as overall much more proficient in French than he did five years earlier, giving himself a total of 41/50 compared to 31/50 when he was aged 12;10. The twins both rated themselves about as proficient as they had rated themselves five years earlier. Valerie rated herself as 37/50 compared to 36/50 when she was 10;10, and Stephanie rated herself as 41/50 compared to 43/50 five years earlier. Indeed, John gave himself an overall higher rating than one of his sisters (Valerie), though five years earlier he gave himself a substantively lower rating than both of the twins. His four years of French language immersion in the French-speaking camp no doubt contributed much to his enhanced French proficiency, as well as his awareness of his improved abilities.

In the second French Proficiency Survey, John also indicated that he now believed he had no accent when he spoke French (Question 8), in stark contrast to his belief that he had a quite noticeable accent five years earlier, even more noticeable than his sisters at the time. On both the first and second surveys Valerie and Stephanie indicated the same degree of the presence of an English accent when they spoke French ('3' for Valerie and '4' for Stephanie).

Some of the children's responses on the Bilingual Self-perception Surveys are also striking from the first to the second administrations, indicating just how much their perception of themselves as bilinguals evolved from early to later adolescence. In response to Question 1, John indicated that being bilingual was 'definitely an ability' compared to other monolingual Americans, though he added that he believed his English suffered as a result of speaking two languages. (Recall his comments on this point in the previous chapter. His concern that being bilingual has hurt his English literacy seems genuine.) Five years earlier his answer to this question was that most of his American middle school friends did not even know he was bilingual. Stephanie gushed that she 'felt great' being bilingual, and Valerie wrote that she felt 'enriched'. The twins' responses to this question when they were 12;10 and 10;10, respectively, were also generally positive.

When asked how he felt being bilingual around his Québec friends who spoke only French (Question 2), John (age 12;10) answered 'Weird, because I sound different'. John's answer to the same question when he was aged 18;1 was much longer ... and strikingly different. He answered in part: 'I speak well enough French to be perfectly integrated socially. In fact, my bilingualism and Americanism actually gave me an edge . . '.

John was clearly over the self-consciousness we observed when he was in middle school and trying to conceal his bilingualism.

Other strikingly different responses to the second survey were to Question 3, which asked how the children felt around their American friends when we (the parents) addressed them in French. Five years earlier, all three children answered 'humiliated' (John), 'embarrassed and kind of stupid' (Valerie), and 'real embarrassing' (Stephanie). Five years later, their answers to the same question were 'nothing special ... many people speak different languages' (John), 'Fine, but maybe a little embarrassed' (Valerie), and 'not too embarrassed' (Stephanie). Thus, John, at 18;1, seemed to have developed the most linguistic self-confidence about his (and his parents') bilingualism in a monolingual American venue, suggesting that he was largely identity-achieved in this area (Adams *et al.*, 1987). The twins were less embarrassed, but still somewhat self-conscious when we (the parents) spoke French around their American peers. Perhaps the twins will eventually develop the same measure of linguistic confidence as their brother displayed to this question. Indeed, a year and a half later, as I tap out these words, my sense is they would not answer this question the same way, and they would likely not indicate embarrassment at our speaking French to them around monolingual American English friends.

Valerie's response to Question 4, which asked how the children would feel if the parents spoke English to them around their Québécois friends, is telling. Five years earlier she indicated that she would be 'highly embarrassed because it would make me different'. As a 16 year old, she answered: 'Unabashed. English is my language. There is nothing to feel disconcerted about when Canada is a bilingual country'.

Here, we get a glimpse not only into Valerie's developing confidence about her bilingualism, but also into her perceptions of the differing linguistic norms of the two countries. She did not identify the U.S. as a bilingual country, even though she went through a French immersion program in a francophone part of Louisiana where up to half the residents still speak French. Plus, she had traveled throughout the American southwest and witnessed entire communities who spoke no English. Hers is a telling perception.

All three children's responses to the global Question 6, which asked if they feel perfectly bilingual, are the complete opposite of their answers five years earlier. John and Valerie both answered 'no', that they did not feel perfectly bilingual when they were ages 12;10 and 10;10, respectively. John complained of the presence of an English accent when he spoke French as being the reason he was not perfectly bilingual as a seventh grader. Five years later, both adolescents indicated that 'Yes', they felt perfectly bilingual, but added qualifiers about the degree of their perfection. Stephanie, on the other hand, who indicated that she was 'perfectly bilingual' when she was 10;10 had a different perspective five years later. She indicated that 'no' she did not feel perfectly bilingual 'because I know people more bilingual than myself'.

Accents

It is important to note once again that a goal of this study was not to measure the presence of accents (a phonological issue requiring a phonological measure), but to simply record 'perceptions' of accents (psychosociological construct), and how perceptions change. Quite simply, the re-occurring issue of accents among the children is interesting; especially in light of much research that indicates that those who acquire a second language prior to adolescence have little or no detectable foreign accent (Asher & García, 1969; Oyama, 1976; Seliger *et al.*, 1975; Tahta *et al.*, 1981). Clearly, according to the perceptions of the children's many native French teachers, their family and peers in Québec, and by their own self-assessments, John, Valerie and Stephanie all seem to have had identifiable English accents when they spoke French well into their adolescence.

John appears to have completely lost his identifiable American English accent in French only around age 14;2. The twins' American English tinged accents in French seemed to have disappeared completely by about age 17;3. Why is it important to note this? Because these are children who were reared in a French-speaking household since birth by two French-speaking parents, one of whom is a native Québécoise. Additionally, these children were immersed for months on end in a French-speaking social environment.

That there remained a perception by Québécois friends, teachers, and families, as well as the children themselves, of persistent accents into adolescence, seems to be contradictory to much existent linguistic research on this subject. Most scholarship suggests that simultaneous bilinguals reared in similar circumstances should speak their two languages with perfect, native like (no 'foreign" accent) fluency. Also, if the perceptions are correct that the twins had an identifiable American English accent later than their brother, this too would contradict some research which suggests that females tend to have less of a foreign accent in the L2 language (Tahta *et al.*, 1981; Watt & Milroy, 1999). Technically, though, there is no L2 language for infant bilinguals. Also, that John appears to have lost his accent in adolescence contradicts research that suggests that the capability to learn to speak a language without an identifiable accent decreases dramatically in adolescence (Anderson & Graham, 1994; Flege & Fletcher, 1992). As elaborated upon in Chapter 6, if true that the twins had more of a pronounced accent in French at age 16 than did their brother, this could be the result of five and a half years of French school immersion in Louisiana surrounded by peers who virtually all spoke French with a pronounced American English accent. Again, these are just observations and not empirically proven fact. Still, they're ideas worthy of consideration.

Concluding Thoughts on Bilingualism in Adolescence

So, then, what sort of conclusions can we draw regarding the effect of adolescence on the bilingual preferences of our children? Returning to the list of questions I raised in Chapter 8, we can state with confidence that the children's home language preferences in Louisiana shifted from predominately French to overwhelmingly English as they moved from pre-adolescence into early adolescence. The numbers, though, only tell part of the story. I recorded an interesting interchange between myself, John and Valerie when they were aged 9;3 and 7;3, respectively. Both were still in their linguistically un-self-conscious childhood, and we had just returned from Québec. In response to my question (in French) of how her day went, Valerie volunteered that she at times had trouble speaking in English. John, overhearing her, immediately jumped in and said, *'C'est vrai, lorsque je parlais anglais des fois j'ai dit 'oui, parce que', sans penser'.* (It's true, when I spoke English sometimes I said *'oui, parce que'* [yes, because] without thinking.) Their trouble shifting into English prior to adolescence contrasts sharply with their sudden and abrupt language shifts of just a few years later.

The second question I posed was whether the French-speaking gap between John and the twins in Louisiana narrowed as they moved through adolescence. The data indicate that this is indeed the case: the twins followed John's preference for English speaking in Louisiana as they too moved out of childhood. Actually, as is shown in the next chapter, controlling for age, the onset of the twins' preference for English was sooner and more pronounced than was their brother's.

Thirdly, I wanted to know if the greater amount of time spent in the U.S. meant that the children's preference for French in Québec would diminish relative to their preference for English in the U.S. Interestingly, this is not the case. Throughout this five-year period during summers immersed in French-speaking Québec, the children's language preference shifted from English to French in a remarkably short time. Within weeks they were speaking no English within the family. An important caveat here is that the children's French during the first weeks of total immersion in Québec was usually halting, and they often searched for words as they tried to express themselves in French. It took a few weeks of input from their environment and output (practice) on their part before they were speaking with the fluidity of a native French speaker. Still, what is remarkable is that they tried to speak French around our table though speaking English in the early days of summer would have been easier. Additionally, we noted that their French *proficiency* (as distinct from *preference*) seemed to *increase* over the five-year period, as is evidenced by the authors' observations of the children's greater command of the language and its idioms in fast-paced conversation with native French speakers. Again, it is important to note that this increased proficiency was more evident toward the end of the two-month Québec immersion experience. In a somewhat interesting anomaly, the children seem to have had more trouble shifting into French once arriving in the Québec milieu as their adolescence progressed (recall the increased linguistic self-consciousness), but once the shift was complete progressed to a point of greater proficiency toward the end of the summer than they had exhibited at the end of the previous summer. In the case of the twins, their reading and writing skills improved yearly as well, as is evidenced by their written French schoolwork, their teacher-assigned grades, and their SAT II French scores.

Fourthly, I was interested to see if the consistently high level of French speaking in Canada was a result of the parents' increasing preference for the language over the five-year period. This, the data indicate, was not the case, as the parents' French speaking remained constant while in Québec. This finding means that the children's growing preference for English in the U.S. – while maintaining high levels of French speaking in Canada – must be attributable to causes external to the family. Finally, the answer to the fifth question, which asked if the girls' school French immersion program affected their home French speaking as they moved into adolescence, is 'no'. Their levels of French speaking around the Louisiana dinner table fell to comparable levels as their brother – once they began the transition into adolescence.

Parental linguistic influence on the children decreased steadily as the children moved through adolescence. This is underscored by the fact that both the mother's and father's recorded dinnertime utterances continued to be predominately in French. The mother did speak increasingly more English in Louisiana over the four years considered. I'll be the first to admit that keeping to our initial resolution to speak only French in the household became an increasingly difficult task as the children moved into their teenage years. Looked at another way, the children's linguistic influence over us, the *parents*, was likely increasing, in the same way that the children had influence on our clothes and music. Still, we have tape recorded evidence of entire discussions with the children where the parents barely uttered a word in English, and the children uttered not one word in French. Simply put, these exchanges are but poignant reminders that parental linguistic influence (and perhaps *all* parental influence) had fallen off drastically. Instead, the cultural milieu of the children's peers – for whom English was the lingua franca – influenced the children to construct American self-identities that were monolingual. However, as the children moved toward late adolescence, we observed an increasing appreciation on their part for their bilingualism, and a growing self-confidence in their identities as bilinguals. This is evidenced by the spontaneity with which they once again began speaking French in monolingual American milieus.

Emerging identities and linguistic confidence

An individual's language development is dynamic, and as noted by Labov (2000), teenagers younger than 17 are still calibrating their speech based on the models of older teenagers. However, Labov postulates that by age 17, our linguistic systems are essentially in place, and we then begin a new process of modifying our systems. Thus, the linguistic story of these three youngsters is incomplete, and could still take surprising and divergent paths as they make linguistic adjustments as adults. As noted above, changes are already taking place: Valerie and Stephanie were both studying Spanish, and Valerie was studying German.

What are the wider implications of our findings? Of course, it is difficult to generalize from a case study of only three subjects to a broader population. However, what we found would be consistent with the literature that stresses that adolescence is the time of life that an individual seeks his or her own identity apart from parents and other authorities, and within the context of their peer groups (Erikson, 1968; Hill & Holmbeck, 1986; Steinberg & Silverberg, 1986; Steinberg, 1997). Perhaps our study has made it even clearer that how we speak is part of our identity, and adolescents look to their peers, not their parents, for linguistic models.

What could our findings suggest with regards to bilingual adolescents in the United States? Based on our observations and data, we submit that one point which seems perfectly clear to Suzanne and me is that even if tremendous effort is exerted to preserve a minority language, if that language is not cherished by the adolescent's peer group, he or she will likely not speak the language – even in the home. Thus, those who fear that English in the U.S. is somehow in danger of losing its pre-eminence seem to have it backwards: the preponderance of the research – including our own – indicates that the endangered species are all the non-English minority languages – especially among American adolescents. This fact is both an empirical and visceral one for me. From an empirical perspective, over the years I've been following the steadily decreasing numbers of Louisianans who speak French as a first language. Viscerally, I feel this decrease as a slow, inevitable withering away of part of my own noble culture and heritage.

Chapter 11
Taking the Measure of Bilingualism

Introduction

This chapter addresses the technical dimensions of measuring the children's and parents' bilinguality, and the children's biliteracy. Those not needing a detailed description of the study's quantitative measures can skip it. The chapter provides a statistical analysis of the author-developed Bilingual Preference Ratio (BPR) and the Edelman's measure of bilingual dominance. It also quantitatively analyzes the teacher responses to the Likert items on the French proficiency survey.

Measures of Bilingualism

Detailed analyses are provided for each of the following:

- Bilingual Preference Ratio (BPR) (defined in detail in Chapter 3): The monthly variation in this measure will be longitudinally examined for John and the twins from December 1994 to December 2000, and for the parents from January 1997 through December 2000. Comparisons are made between all family members.
- Edelman's Contextualized Measure of Degree of Bilingualism: Results from 20 administrations of Edelman's measure to each of the three children are analyzed in each of the following domains: home, neighborhood, and school. The children ranged in age from 9;9 to 11;0 (twins), and 11;9 to 13;0 (John). These ages correspond roughly to the period defined as early adolescence (Steinberg, 1993), which overlapped for both John and the twins since girls enter adolescence approximately two years earlier than boys (Berk, 1996; Malina, 1990).
- Children French Proficiency Surveys (administered five and a quarter years apart)
  - average scores reported for each child by administration;
  - t-values reported for paired mean comparisons of time 1 and time 2;

- bivariate correlations between average teacher scores and time1 / time2 for each child;
- bivariate correlations between time 1 and time 2 administration for each child.
• Teacher French Proficiency Surveys (10 teachers for twins, 5 for John)
  - average teacher values for each item are generated for each child;
  - average teacher values are correlated with child's responses at time 1 and time 2;
  - standard deviations and correlations are provided for teacher items by each child and across children;
  - bivariate correlations of average item value across children.

Bilingual Preference Ratios (BPRs)

The fluctuations between the children's Bilingual Preference Ratios (BPRs) are displayed graphically in Figure 2 (Louisiana context), Figure 3 (Québec context), and Figure 1 (monthly averages from December 1994 to December 2000). The parents fluctuating BPRs are presented in Figure 4 (Louisiana and Québec contexts) and Figure 1 (monthly fluctuations from January 1997 to December 2000). BPRs can range in value from 0 (no French spoken on audiotape) to 1.0 (only French spoken on audiotape). A value of 0.5, this author suggests, would indicate perfectly balanced bilingualism: an equal number of French and English words were spoken.

Table 1 provides descriptive statistics for each family member's BPR statistics.

The father had the overall highest average BPR (0.85) of any other family member, indicating that the large majority of the words (tokens) he uttered on audiotape were in French. His overall BPR was followed in descending order by the mother (0.77) and the twins (0.38). John had the smallest overall BPR (0.24) suggesting he had a much stronger preference for speaking English than French over the six years of the home audiotaping in Louisiana and Québec. I ran a series of paired t-tests to determine if there were any statistically significant differences between the family members' overall BPR averages. Only one pair of means was not statistically different: the mother's and father's ($t = -1.852$, $p = 0.07$). This indicates that there is not a statistically significant difference in the proportion of French to English which they spoke, and that both parents' global BPRs can be considered statistically the same.

Table 2 presents bivariate correlation coefficients between all family members' monthly BPRs.

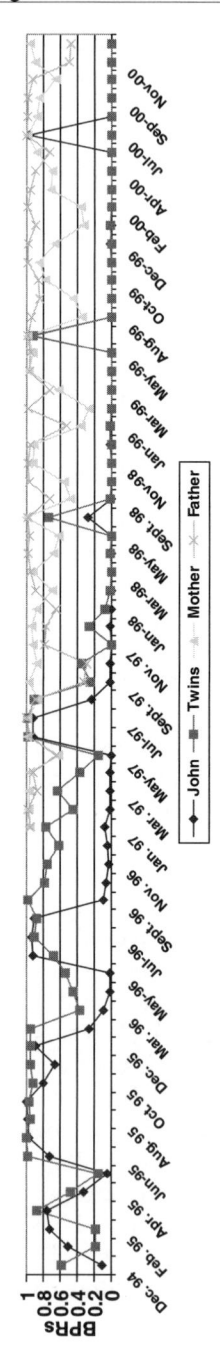

Figure 1 Monthly Bilingual Preference Ratios (BPRs) of all family members: December 1994 to December 2000

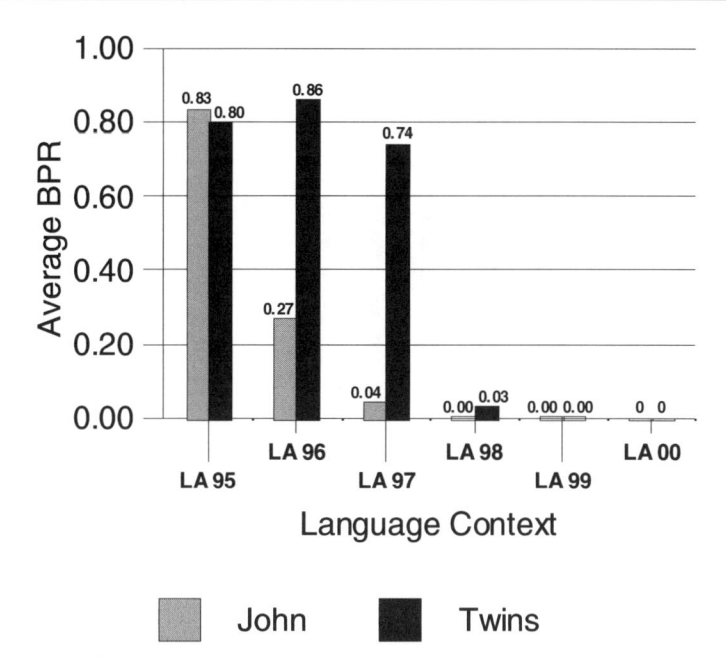

Figure 2 Children's Louisiana BPRs

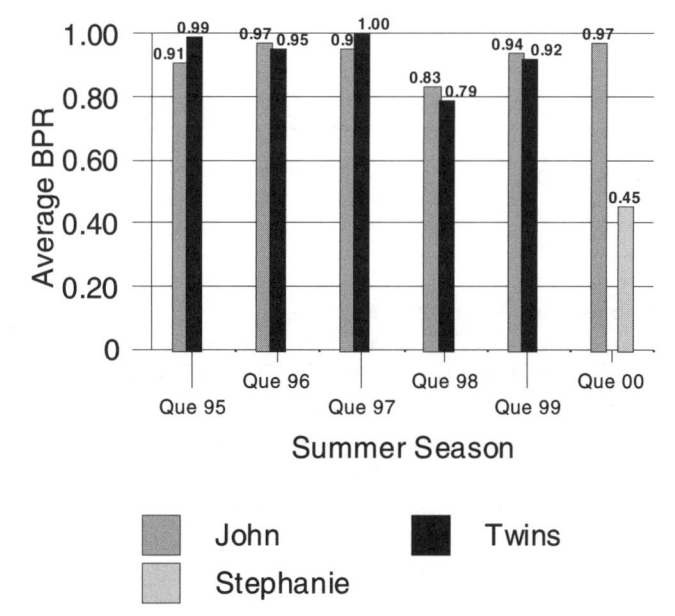

Figure 3 Children's summer Québec BPRs

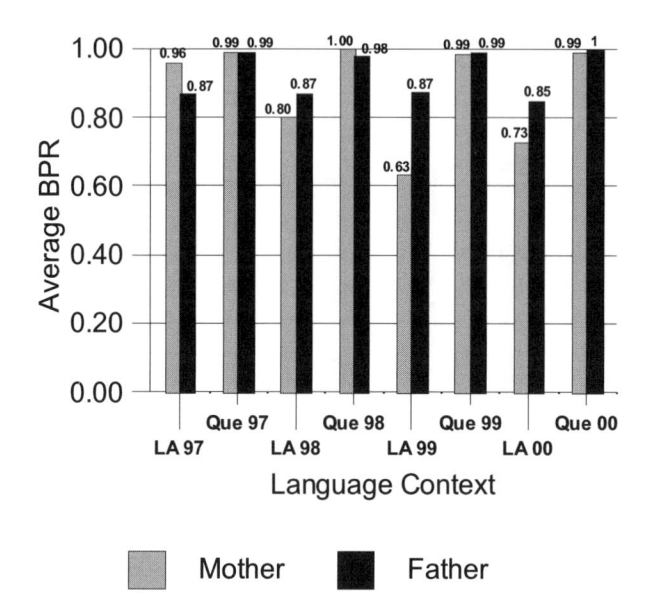

Figure 4 Parents language references: Québec and Louisiana

Table 1 Descriptive statistics of family members Bilingual Preference Ratios (BPRs)

	N	Minimum	Maximum	Mean	Std. Deviation
John	68	0.00	1.00	0.2404	0.3699
Twins	68	0.00	1.00	0.3751	0.3960
Mom	44	0.26	1.00	0.7723	0.2209
Dad	44	0.29	1.00	0.8534	0.1849

These Pearson product moment correlation coefficients can be used to quantitatively gauge whether or not family members' changing language preferences are co-varying with each other. The Pearson's correlation coefficient is appropriate for this purpose given the relatively large number of values (N, or number of monthly BPR coefficients) of each family member– 68 for John and the twins, and 44 for both parents. There is a strong correlation ($r = 0.733$, $p < 0.001$) between the BPRs of John and his twin sisters. In other words, their monthly BPRs rise and fall together in very close unison. This corroborates the trends seen in Figure 1, and empirically establishes the strong, statistically significant relationship between their changing language preferences. The next largest correlation was between

Table 2 Correlations between Bilingual Preference Ratio (BPRs) of family members

		Twins	Mom	Dad
John	Pearson correlation	0.733**	0.357*	0.244
	Sig. (2-tailed)	0.000	0.017	0.110
	N	68	44	44
Twins	Pearson correlation		0.491**	0.134
	Sig. (2-tailed)		0.001	0.385
	N		44	44
Mom	Pearson correlation			−0.018
	Sig. (2-tailed)			0.909
	N			44

* Correlation is significant at the 0.05 level (2-tailed).
** Correlation is significant at the 0.01 level (2-tailed).

the mother's and twins' BPRs, and is somewhat smaller ($r = 0.491$, $p < 0.01$). Still, this indicates a moderate correlation between the mother's and twins' BPRs, an interesting finding given the noticeably smaller, though still statistically significant correlation between the mother's and son's BPRs ($r = 0.357$, $p < 0.05$). Could the mother be conversing more with the twins than with either the son or the father, influencing the twins' language preferences during their mutual interactions? We do see that the mother spoke progressively less French in Louisiana with each succeeding year (see Figure 4), unlike the father. Perhaps she was speaking this English with the children – hence the moderately sized correlation.

Surprisingly, the father's BPRs did not correlate significantly with any other family member. The reason is a lack of variance. As can be seen in the Table 1 descriptive statistics for the BPRs, the standard deviation of the father's BPRs is the smallest (S.D. = 0.18) of any family member, indicating very little variation in his changing language preferences compared to either the mother (S.D. = 0.22), or most significantly, the children (John's S.D. = 0.37; twins' S.D. = 0.40).

Thus, there is little variation in the father's BPRs to significantly co-vary with the other family members' shifting BPRs. Looked at another way, the father's choice of language is the most consistent in the family. This is evidenced by his larger, average global BPR of 0.85. So even though the mother and father statistically have the same average BPR, the father's is the most consistently high. Given that I took charge of the tapings, I knew when the recordings started, and was likely the most conscious of my speaking during the dinnertime sessions. This suspicion is somewhat corroborated on videotape not expressly shot for use in this project, when I spoke much more English than I did on audiotape at about the same time.

Correlation between John's and the Twins' Home Language Preferences (BPRs)

A statistical approach for indirectly measuring the effect of the twins' school French immersion program on their home language preferences is to correlate their BPRs with John's, adjusting for age. In this sense, John, who had only one semester of French immersion, becomes a control. Figure 5 graphically shows the fluctuating children's BPR's by age, beginning with age 9;7 through 13;7 (the last month a BPR was generated for the twins).

The twins were enrolled in a French immersion program throughout this age range. As can be seen, at most age intervals, John had a higher BPR than the twins. The 43 cases are highly correlated ($r = 0.793; p < 0.000$), indicating that the children's BPRs fluctuate very closely together, controlling for age. This high correlation suggests once again that the external variables influencing the children's language preferences were influencing them in the same way at the same age. Since John was not in an immersion program for most of this age range, we can conclude that the variable 'French immersion program' had little impact on home language preference.

The graphic in Figure 5 also indicates that the twins' BPR fell faster and further than John's did during the same age range. The twins' BPR began falling from its pre-adolescent plateau at age 10;4, whereas John's BPR began its steady descent a month later, when he was age 10;5. The girls' BPRs were consistently much lower than John's from age 10;4 until there was a convergence with his at age 10;11. Thereafter, the children's BPRs fluctuated together in remarkable symmetry till the end of the project. Indeed, the correlation between the BPRs of John and the twins during the 28 months beginning when the children were aged 10;11 is a remarkably high $r = 0.960$, $p < 0.001$: an almost perfect positive correlation!

The strong relationship between John and the twins' undulating BPRs, whether adjusting for date or age, is particularly telling when we consider that the twins spent up to three hours per day immersed in French within their Louisiana school environment. It appears that, unfortunately, we do not see any obvious boost to their home French speaking as a consequence

Taking the Measure of Bilingualism 171

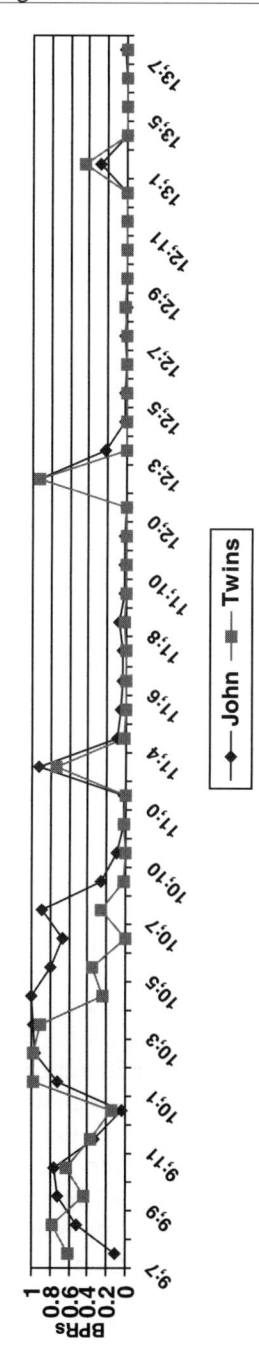

Figure 5 Bilingual Preference Ratios (BPRs) of John and twins: Superimposed by age, ages 9;7 through 13;7

of their school French immersion, a stated goal of at least one of Louisiana school system's immersion programs (Boudreaux, 1998), and probably an implicit goal in all the state's French immersion programs. Indeed, at times, the twins' French speaking sank to even lower levels than their brother's.

Why so counter-intuitive a finding? Since the twins chronologically lagged behind John by a period of two years, the symptoms of early adolescence first appear in John's behavior – including a significant decrease in French speaking at home. Thus, the twins were exposed to John's changed attitudes and speech, both of which were not conducive to their continuing high level of French speaking at home (recall his taunts of, 'English! English! English!). John, on the other hand, was not exposed to these negative factors at the same age, but on the contrary, had two younger sisters who were still speaking mostly French at home as he moved into early adolescence. His French speaking still fell off, but much more gradually than the plunge the twins' French speaking took at approximately the same age John was when his BPR in Louisiana began a descent from which it never recovered. Nevertheless, though the twins' French immersion program did not seem to encourage French speaking outside of class, it is still important to note, as we did in Chapter 6, that the program did have an obvious and dramatic positive effect on their reading and writing of the French language.

Edelman's Contextualized Measure of Degree of Bilingualism

Tables 3–5 provide descriptive statistics for the Edelman's coefficients generated for each child in three areas (home, school, and neighborhood) during 20 administrations of this measure of bilingual dominance over a 27-month period. Figures 6–8 graphically display each child's Edelman's coefficient in each domain over the 20 administrations of the measure.

As can be seen, the home domain is the context with the largest average coefficient for each child (average of 20 administrations), suggesting that the children were more French dominant in this domain than in either the school or neighborhood domains. That is, in a 45-second period they could name proportionally more words in French than in English that related to their home environment than they could name about either their neighborhood or school environments. This is confirmed by running a series of paired t-tests which reveal that there is indeed a statistically significant difference between John's average Edelman's coefficients for the home and school ($t = 3.142$, $p < 0.01$), but not the home and neighborhood. There

Table 3 Descriptive statistics for John's Edelman's coefficients

	N	Minimum	Maximum	Mean	Std. Deviation
Home	20	0.24	0.62	0.4370	0.1191
School	20	0.19	0.61	0.3590	0.1060
Neighborhood	20	0.22	0.64	0.3955	0.1216
Average	20	0.25	0.59	0.3972	0.0942

Table 4 Descriptive statistics for Stephanie's Edelman's coefficients

	N	Minimum	Maximum	Mean	Std. Deviation
Home	20	0.33	0.60	0.4465	0.0853
School	20	0.27	0.54	0.4200	0.0713
Neighborhood	20	0.25	0.61	0.3935	0.0925
Average	20	0.32	0.54	0.4200	0.0646

Table 5 Descriptive statistics for Valerie's Edelman's coefficients

	N	Minimum	Maximum	Mean	Std. Deviation
Home	20	0.32	0.68	0.4890	0.0950
School	20	0.30	0.50	0.4195	0.0559
Neighborhood	20	0.27	0.64	0.4450	0.1021
Average	20	0.35	0.54	0.4512	0.0519

is also a statistically significant difference between Stephanie's average Edelman's coefficients between the home and neighborhood domains ($t = 2.617$, $p < 0.05$), but not the home and school domains. For Valerie, there is a statistically significant difference between the average coefficients for home and school ($t = 3.083$, $p < 0.01$), but not home and neighborhood. Thus, we have corroborative evidence that French speaking in the home environment, which was probably stressed as much during this 27 month period as during any other time in the family's history, had a decidedly greater influence on the children's French speaking than the French they were exposed to in the contexts of the neighborhood or the school. It is still important to note that no child was overall French dominant (> 0.50) in any domain.

Bivariate correlation coefficients were generated for all three domains for each child (not reported in a table). There were no statistically significant relationships between any of Valerie's three domains. That is, the

Figure 6 John: Edelman's coefficients of bilingual dominance, ages: 10;8–13;1

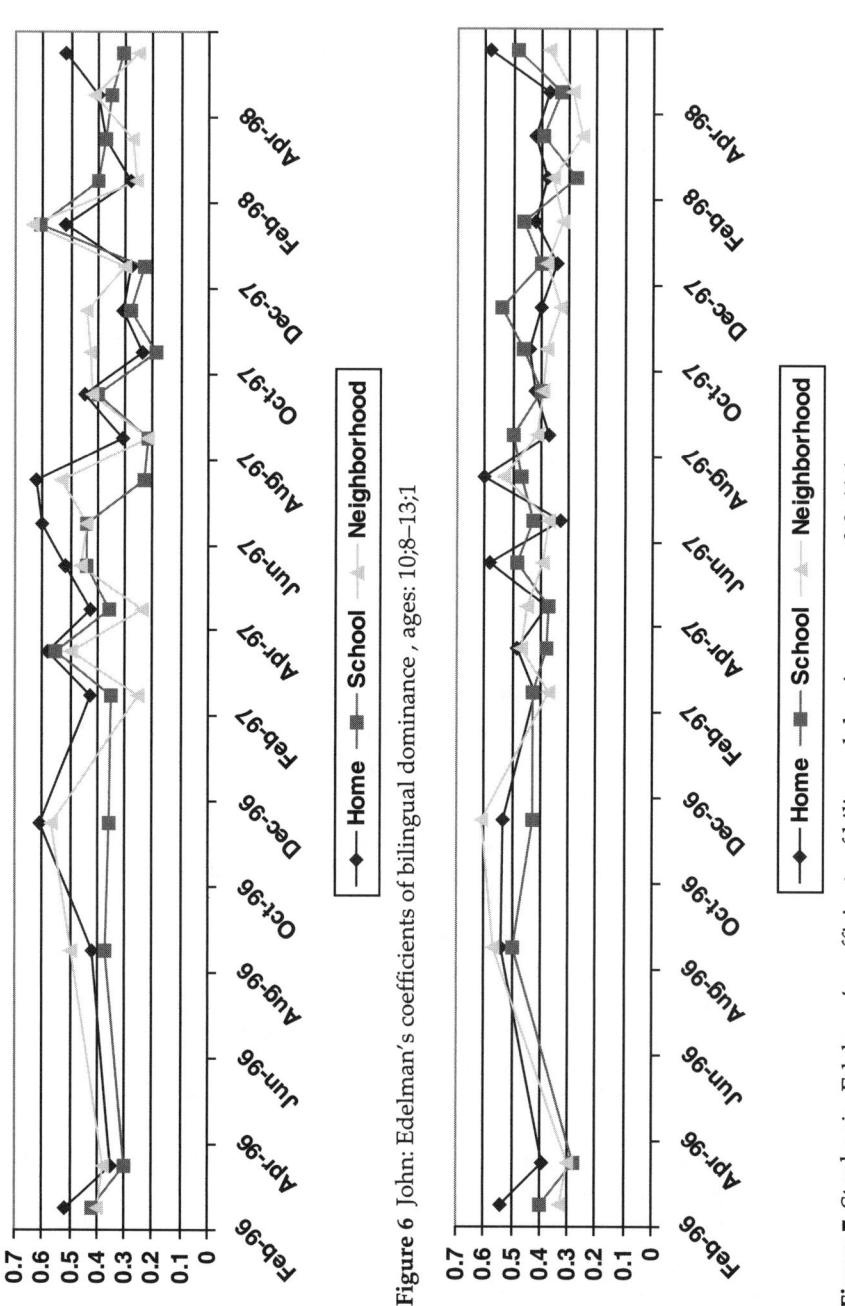

Figure 7 Stephanie: Edelman' coefficients of bilingual dominance, ages: 8;8–11;1

Taking the Measure of Bilingualism 175

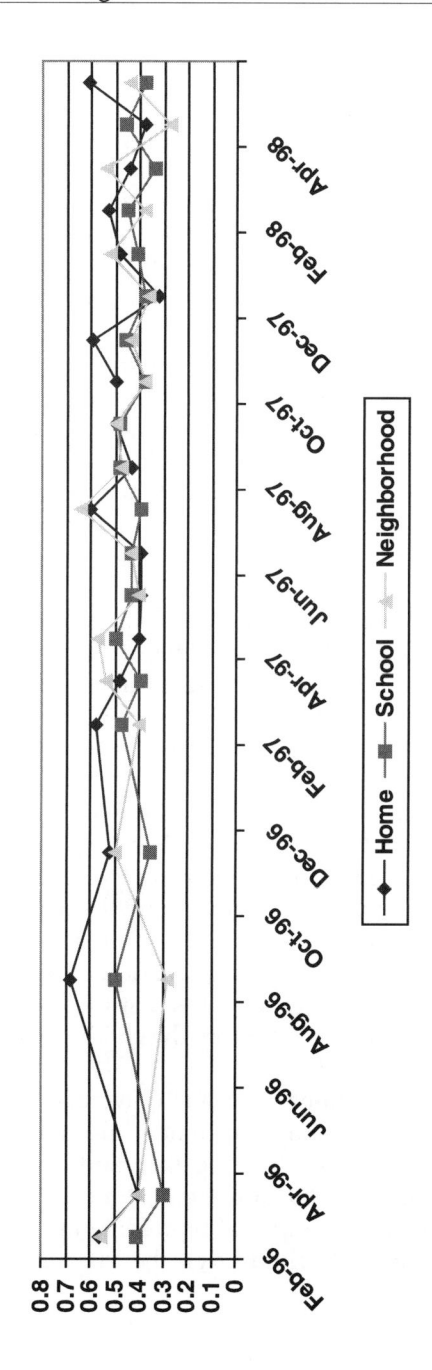

Figure 8 Valerie: Edelman's coefficients of bilingual dominance, ages: 8;8–11;1

three domains do not significantly co-vary together. However, the two domains of home and neighborhood were significantly correlated for both John ($r = 0.534$, $p < 0.05$) and Stephanie ($r = 0.484$, $p < 0.05$). In other words, when the Edelman's coefficient for a given administration tended to be high for the home domain for John and Stephanie, it also tended to be high in the neighborhood domain for these two. Recalling how the Edelman's coefficient is created, this means that when the two siblings named a proportionally larger number of French to English words in the home domain, they also tended to name a proportionally larger number of words in the neighborhood domain. The school domain, however, was not significantly correlated with the other two domains for either John or Stephanie.

It is not easy to interpret why these relationships – or lack of relationships – hold. Theoretically, it would seem that all three domains should be correlated: on days that the children are thinking and speaking more in French, it would be logical to expect that they would name a proportionately greater number of items in French in each domain. That the home and neighborhood domains are moderately correlated for John and Stephanie – but not the school domain – may suggest the greater influence of English in these domains of the children's lives at this pre-adolescent state in their lives. Indeed, John's average Edelman's coefficient in the school domain is significantly and substantively smaller (0.359) than it is in either the home (0.437) or neighborhood domains (0.396).

Tables 6-8 present the correlations between the children's coefficients in each domain.

As can be seen, the only area where there are statistically significant relationships between the children's Edelman's coefficients are in the home domain. John's home coefficients are moderately positively correlated with Stephanie's ($r = 0.551$, $p < 0.05$), and the twins' home coefficients are even more highly correlated ($r = 0.593$, $p < 0.01$). In other words, John's and Stephanie's, and Stephanie's and Valerie's' home coefficients fluctuate meaningfully together. This suggests that the linguistic influences on the children in the home were affecting the children in the same way over this 27-month period of time.

Table 9 gives the correlations between the average Edelman's coefficient for each child, which is the simple arithmetic mean derived by adding the coefficients at each administration together, and dividing by three. This average could be considered a sort of global measure of language dominance. Figure 9 shows the graphical representation of the average Edelman's coefficient for each child over the 20 administrations of this measure.

Table 6 Bivariate correlations between Edelman's home coefficients for each child

		Stephanie	*Valerie*
John	Pearson correlation	0.551*	0.178
	Sig. (2-tailed)	0.012	0.452
	N	20	20
Stephanie	Pearson correlation		0.593**
	Sig. (2-tailed)		0.006
	N	20	20

* Correlation is significant at the 0.05 level (2-tailed)
** Correlation is significant at the 0.01 level (2-tailed)

Table 7 Bivariate correlations between Edelman's school coefficients for each child

		Stephanie	*Valerie*
John	Pearson correlation	−0.173	0.080
	Sig. (2-tailed)	0.467	0.738
	N	20	20
Stephanie	Pearson correlation		0.247
	Sig. (2-tailed)		0.294
	N	20	20

Table 8 Bivariate correlations between Edelman's neighborhood coefficients for each child

		Stephanie	*Valerie*
John	Pearson correlation	0.368	0.107
	Sig. (2-tailed)	0.111	0.652
	N	20	20
Stephanie	Pearson correlation		0.160
	Sig. (2-tailed)		0.501
	N	20	20

Table 9 Bivariate correlations between average Edelman's coefficients for each child

		Stephanie	Valerie
John	Pearson correlation	0.379	0.300
	Sig. (2-tailed)	0.099	0.198
	N	20	20
Stephanie	Pearson correlation		0.534*
	Sig. (2-tailed)		0.015
	N	20	20

* Correlation is significant at the 0.05 level (2-tailed)

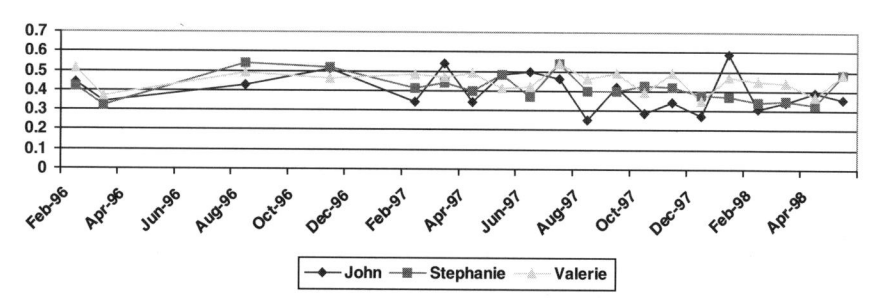

Figure 9 John, Stephanie, and Valerie: Average Edelman's coefficients of bilingual dominance, John: ages 10;8–13;1; twins ages 8;8–11;1

John's average Edelman's coefficients are not statistically significantly related to either of his sisters' averages, though it approaches significance with both of them (it is hard to achieve statistical significance with an N of only 20). The twin's average coefficients, however, are moderately correlated ($r = 0.534$, $p < 0.05$). This suggests that the environmental factors influencing the twins' language dominance were influencing them in a more similar fashion than these same influences were affecting their brother. This is logical, since the twins spent much time together in the same classrooms, with the same friends, and at play at home in the same bedroom. This moderate correlation is yet additional justification for calculating the twins' BPR's as a unit rather than separately.

French Proficiency Surveys

Table 10 provides descriptive statistics for the French Proficiency Surveys, including the average teacher French proficiency scores, and total

Taking the Measure of Bilingualism

Table 10 French Proficiency Survey scores: Descriptive statistics

	Minimum	Maximum	Mean	Total score	Std. Deviation
John: Self Report 1	1.00	4.00	3.1000	31.0	1.2867
John: Self Report 2	2.00	5.00	4.1000	41.0	1.1005
Average teacher score: John (N=5)	2.20	4.60	3.8200	36.6 (average)	0.9016
Stephanie: Self Report 1	2.00	5.00	4.3000	43.0	0.9487
Stephanie: Self Report 2	4.00	5.00	4.1000	41.0	0.5270
Average teacher score: Stephanie (N=10)	3.10	4.50	4.0600	40.4 (average)	0.5661
Valerie: Self Report 1	2.00	5.00	3.6000	36.0	0.8433
Valerie: Self report 2	2.00	5.00	3.7000	37.0	0.9487
Average teacher score: Valerie (n=10)	3.10	4.60	4.0600	40.6 (average)	0.5461

teacher proficiency scores for Stephanie (N=10), Valerie (N=10) and John (N=5). Also presented are the average self-reported scores of the children on the same measure at Time 1 (February 1998) and Time 2 (May 2003).

Figures 10-12 chronologically display the total French Proficiency ratings given by each child's teacher.

As can be seen, John's five average teacher ratings steadily decreased over time as he moved into adolescence. The twins' ratings, though they fluctuated, tended to increase over time, perhaps representing their increasing French proficiency as a consequence of their French immersion program.

Self-reported French proficiency scores

Table 11 provides results from paired *t*-tests of the children's average French Proficiency scores at Time 1 and Time 2.

As can be seen, only John's average scores from the first survey administration to the second survey administration are significantly different (t = −2.74, $p < 0.05$). This suggests that there is a meaningful difference in the higher scores he assigned himself on the French Proficiency Survey

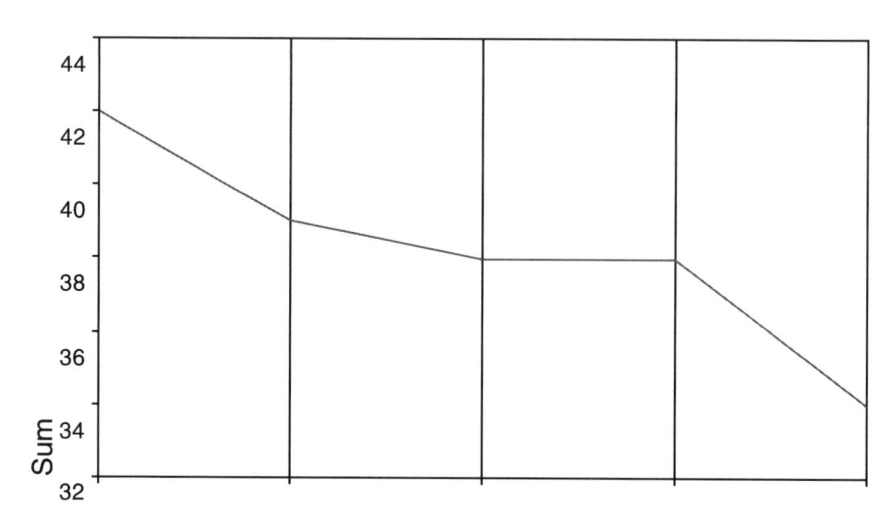

Time 1 Through Time 5

Figure 10 John's teacher French Proficiency Survey scores, ages 10-0–12;10

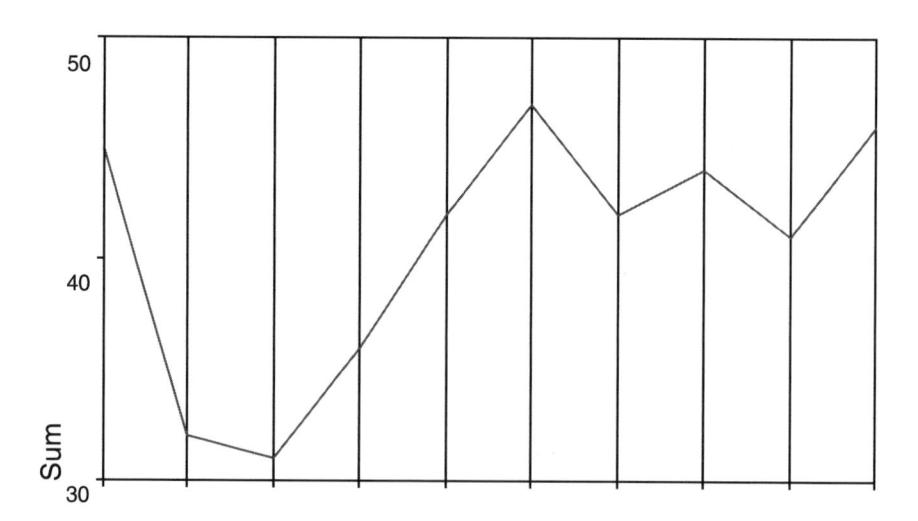

Time 1 Through Time 10

Figure 11 Stephanie's teacher French Proficiency Survey scores, ages 8;1–12;0

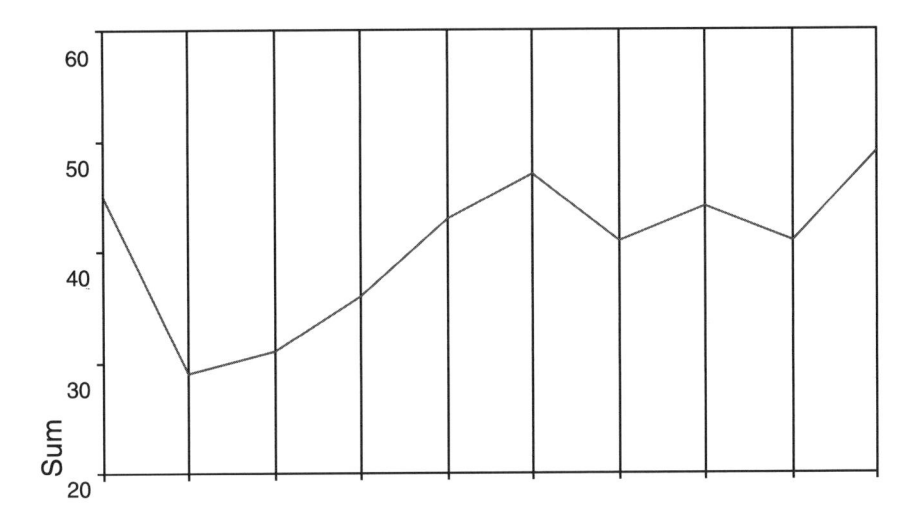

Taking the Measure of Bilingualism 181

Time 1 Through Time 10

Figure 12 Valerie's teacher French Proficiency Survey scores, ages 8;1–12;0

Table 11 Paired samples *t*-test comparisons of average self-report scores on children's French Proficiency tests at Time 1 (T1) and Time 2 (T2)

Paired Differences	Mean	Std. Deviation	Std. Error Mean	95% Confidence interval of the difference Lower	Upper	t-value	df	Sig. (2-tailed)
Pair 1 John (T1) – John (T2)	–1.0000	1.1547	0.3651	–1.8260	–0.1740	–2.739	9	0.023
Pair 2 Stephanie (T1) – Stephanie (T2)	0.2000	0.9189	0.2906	–0.4574	0.8574	0.688	9	0.509
Pair 3 Valerie (T1) – Valerie (T2)	–0.1000	1.1972	0.3786	–0.9564	0.7564	–0.264	9	0.798

Table 12 Correlations between John's average French Proficiency Survey scores at Time 1 and Time 2, and average teacher scores

		John Time 1	John Time 2	Average teacher scores
John Time 1	Pearson correlation		0.541	0.898**
	Sig. (2-tailed)	.	0.106	0.000
	N	10	10	10
John Time 2	Pearson correlation			0.692*
	Sig. (2-tailed)			0.027
	N			10

* Correlation is significant at the 0.05 level (2-tailed)
** Correlation is significant at the 0.01 level (2-tailed)

during the second administration, providing additional evidence that he truly perceived himself as being much more French proficient at age 18;1 than at age 12;10. The twins' views of their level of French proficiency did not change in a statistically meaningful way. They were enrolled in a French immersion program during the first survey administration at age 10;10, when they assigned themselves higher scores than John did at the same time. It is also possible John rated himself lower in French Proficiency at Time 1 due to his having already moved into early adolescence, and was more susceptible to peer influences that did not value bilingualism.

Subsequently, however, John spent four summers living and working full time at a French-speaking summer camp, where his immersion experience resulted in a significant improvement in all levels of his French proficiency. Additionally, at age 18;1 during the second survey administration, he may have been further removed from the earlier noted negative American peer influences than were his sisters.

Bivariate correlation coefficients were generated between the children's self-reported scores on the French Proficiency Surveys at Time 1 and Time 2, and the average of the teachers' scores on the same survey. These correlations were generated to detect meaningful relationships between how the teachers and children viewed the children's bilingualism. Table 12 gives the correlations between John's self-reporting on the 10-item survey, and the average of his teachers.

As can be seen, there is a very strong and statistically significant correlation between how John rated himself at age 12;10, and the average of how his five French teachers and camp counselors rated him when he ranged in age from 10;0 to 12;10 ($r = 0.898$, $p < 0.000$). This strong relationship suggests that John's perceptions of his French proficiency tracks almost perfectly with how his teachers rated him, providing justification for both the validity and reliability of the instrument. It also suggests that John was both honest and accurate in the assessment of his abilities in French. There is a smaller, though still statistically significant relationship between John's self-reported proficiency at Time 2 and the average of his teachers' assessments ($r = 0.692$, $p < 0.05$), indicating a certain continuity in John's developing French proficiency over the period. However, there is no statistically significant relationship between John's self-reported French proficiency at Time 1, when he was 12;10, and his self-reported French proficiency at Time 2, when he was age 18;1. This suggests that there was indeed a meaningful change in how John perceived and rated his French proficiency as he was on the cusp of young adulthood, compared to when he was in early adolescence.

Table 13 gives the correlation coefficients between Stephanie's self-reported scores on the 10 item French Proficiency Survey at Time 1, Time 2, and the average of her 10 French teachers and camp counselors.

As with her brother, there is a statistically significant correlation between Stephanie's self-reported French proficiency at Time 1, when she was 10;10, and the average scores of her 10 teachers and camp counselors ($r = 0.749$, $p < 0.05$). This, once again, is indicative of both the reliability and

Table 13 Correlations between Stephanie's average French Proficiency Survey scores at Time 1 and Time 2, and average teacher scores

		Stephanie Time 1	*Stephanie Time 2*	*Average teacher scores*
Stephanie Time 1	Pearson correlation		0.259	0.749*
	Sig. (2-tailed)	.	0.469	0.013
	N	10	10	10
Stephenie Time 2	Pearson correlation			0.211
	Sig. (2-tailed)			0.558
	N			10

* Correlation is significant at the 0.05 level (2-tailed)

validity of the instrument, as well as Stephanie's honesty and objective accuracy in reporting her level of French proficiency at age 10;10. No other correlations, however, even approach statistical significance. Stephanie's original assessment of her French proficiency at age 10;10 doesn't correspond to how she rated herself five years later at age 16;1.

Table 14 shows the correlation coefficients between Valerie's self-reported scores on the French proficiency survey at Time 1, Time 2, and the average of her French teachers and camp counselors.

The findings for Valerie are harder to interpret, as the only significant correlation is between her Time 2 self-reported French proficiency, and the average reported scores of her various French teachers ($r = 0.746$, $p < 0.05$). When I correlated all three children's Time 1 self-reported French Proficiency Surveys, only John's and Stephanie's were correlated ($r = 0.701$, $p < 0.05$). Thus, though John rated himself as significantly lower than either of his sisters, his item responses fluctuate meaningfully with Stephanie's. We would expect to find this relationship with identical twins the same age, but inexplicably, do not. Recall that the only twin with whom John had a significantly correlated Edelman's coefficient were in the home domain with his sister Stephanie, which was interpreted to mean that home influences were influencing their French speaking in the same way over that 15-month period of time. Still, Valerie's and Stephanie's home Edelman's coefficients were even more highly correlated ($r = 0.593$, $p < 0.01$).

Table 14 Correlations between Valerie's average French Proficiency Survey scores at Time 1 and Time 2, and average teacher scores

		Valerie Time 1	Valerie Time 2	Average teacher scores
Valerie Time 1	Pearson correlation		0.111	0.323
	Sig. (2-tailed)	.	0.760	0.362
	N	10	10	10
Valerie Time 2	Pearson correlation			0.746*
	Sig. (2-tailed)			0.013
	N			10

* Correlation is significant at the 0.05 level (2-tailed)

Given this interesting anomaly, I correlated the children's Time 2 self-reported results on the French Proficiency Survey. Surprisingly, none of the children's results were correlated with any of their siblings. This means that their responses to each of the 10 Likert questions do not co-vary meaningfully together. One child may have rated himself/herself high on say, ability to use correct grammar, while another could just have easily as rated themselves low on this item. Perhaps these findings taken together suggest that the children's evolving French proficiency (or their perceptions of this proficiency) differ in meaningful ways – even for twins who share the same genotypes and linguistic environments. Could the children's differing competencies on individual measures of their French proficiency simply reflect the differences in their own unique personalities? The empirical findings of this chapter suggest that this could indeed be the case.

Chapter 12

Lessons Learned, Broader Implications and Guidelines for Parents

As can be seen through the pages of this book, we've achieved our lofty goal of rearing perfectly fluent French-English bilingual children who are also functionally biliterate. Indeed, upon meeting and conversing with our children, a Québécois may mistake our children for native Québécois speakers. This mistaking of nationality is almost certainly likely to happen in a conversation with John, who uses so many idiomatic Québécois expressions that he speaks pretty much just like a Québécois.

All three children can read and write in both languages. Indeed, even though the twins spent most of their elementary school years being instructed primarily in French, by all measures – grades, work samples, placement tests, and standardized tests – they perform better, and in most cases much better, than the majority of American students on subjects assessed in English. On the flip side, though their brother attended only one semester of French immersion in Louisiana (as a fourth grader), and six weeks in a Québécois classroom as a fourth and fifth grader, he can express himself in writing in French, though he much prefers to read the language. John spontaneously reads novels written on an adult reading-level in French and English alike. Our children turn in sterling performances on English-assessed academics despite the fact that we deprived them of English in our home for most of their childhood, to the extent of strongly discouraging their watching English-speaking TV.

The End of One Journey and the Beginning of Another

As of this writing the twins were high school seniors and John was a university sophomore. Since the children were attending school and university away from the immediate family, the home dimension of our family project is largely completed. These young adults are essentially beyond any significant linguistic influence we, the parents, might still have over them. As we learned from observing John, his bilinguistic self-perception and bilingual language preferences changed from ages 16;0 to 18;0 as he moved toward linguistic identity achievement. The bilinguistic self-perceptions of the twins, too, were maturing and solidifying over this same two-year period from ages 14;0 to 16;0. Now, as twelfth graders, both girls were enrolled in a Spanish III immersion class, and in Valerie's case, she was pursuing her second year of a fourth language (German). The twins were clearly moving beyond bilingualism. I have to believe that the mastery of two languages, and having souls straddling two cultures, have fueled the twins' interest and thirst to learn and master yet more languages – and experience yet new cultures.

How Do We Know?

As a trained social scientist, I assiduously recorded fieldnotes and audio-taped family conversations over many years of this project. I also devised and implemented several longitudinal measures to assess the children's developing bilingualism and biliteracy. My wife Suzanne and I were able to observe and document their functioning in several language contexts. A careful analysis of these data allowed me to determine how the children's various milieus were influencing their bilingualism and biliteracy. Due to the unusual, varied, and complex circumstances of our project, as well as the careful application of scientifically validated methods and measures, this study illuminates more clearly how children – especially in early through late adolescence – acquire and use their languages. It was a privilege and marvel to observe and record.

The Power of Society

While for the first 10 years or so Suzanne and I had much direct linguistic influence on our children, and we were able to mold their attitudes and encourage them to speak the minority home language, we lost this power when our children reached adolescence. The power of the peer group to influence individuals is undeniable and extremely well documented (Bankston & Caldas, 1996, 2002; Caldas & Bankston, 1997; Bankston *et al.*, 1997; Eckert, 1989; Erikson, 1968; Steinberg, 1997). This influence extends to many behaviors, including, as we've seen in this study, language usage (Heller, 1999; Ochs, 1993; Tarone & Swain, 1995). A major finding of this study is that during adolescence, the children's peer groups had much more influence on the children's languages preferences and movement toward minority language fluency than did we, the parents. But we also noted the power of extra-family linguistic influences on our children well before they entered adolescence.

Our experience of rearing three bilingual children who speak, read, and write two languages has been a challenge, and has at times required a great deal of discipline, effort, and expense. We had a plan to achieve specific objectives. We implemented and adhered to our plan over a 19-year period, modifying our strategies when necessary. For example, after the first year and a half of the 'one parent, one language approach' in anglophone Louisiana, we sensed that John was being exposed to much more English than French in his daily life. He was being showered by English in eight hours of day care from Monday through Friday, by American television, by relatives, in shopping centers, at parks, and increasingly through play with neighborhood children. He was also only hearing English from his father, who loved him and liked to speak with him. We knew that John needed more French input, and thus decided that both Suzanne and I should both only speak the minority language, French, in the home (a conclusion reached by other researchers as well). Still, when John began speaking not long after the change in our plan, he spoke more English than French.

Thus, though John understood our French perfectly well, when he did begin speaking he preferred to speak the majority societal language, English. Thus, we sensed at about year three that we needed to immerse our children in an all-French-speaking environment – Québec in our case. We felt that in order for John and his newborn twin sisters to attain the level of fluency we desired, the children needed to experience a setting where everyone spoke French in the same way that they had been experiencing a totally English-speaking societal context. The little experiment we conducted when John was three years old confirmed our intuition about the importance of societal immersion for language preference: when he returned from just two weeks of total French immersion in Québec, he spoke much more French than before he left.

When the children were old enough to stay full time at a summer camp with their peers, we felt that this was probably an optimal (though expensive) immersion strategy available to us to move the children toward fluency in French, because they would have no recourse to English. Our data support the efficacy of periodically cutting the children off from English. At about this same time we also began to realize the importance of media, and started buying and renting French videocassettes, buying and checking out French books, buying French comic books, and ultimately, acquiring French TV via satellite. Moreover, we diligently and devotedly employed these various media, to the extent of denying English

TV in our U.S. home for more than a year, and limiting access to American TV for about three years. We also made every effort (sometimes clownishly) to link French in our family with our shared French heritage. This strategy seemed to work for a while – at least until early adolescence. Then, it became a largely useless and even counter-productive strategy. However, we felt it was very important to elevate the status of the minority home language in the children's minds. Children need to be proud of their home language when it differs from what everyone around them is speaking. There are already too many factors conspiring to squelch the speaking of the minority tongue without adding the additional factor of shame. Whereas as adolescents the children expressed displeasure in our speaking French to them around their peers, we never had the sense that it was French *per se* that embarrassed them, but that we weren't speaking to them in the language that everyone else's parents were speaking.

Importance of Societal Immersion

As the children aged, we began to accumulate evidence supporting the importance of societal immersion to ensure their achieving native-like fluency in French. We came to this conclusion as we observed the children become completely fluent and literate in American English at approximately the same pace as their American peers (though they were initially slower to speak than the average child). Indeed, they were achieving at academically more advanced levels than their American classmates from as early as pre-school. On measures of kindergarten readiness they mostly scored better than average on teacher administered instruments. We did have moments of doubt about the possible deleterious effects of depriving the children of English in our home. These fears proved completely unfounded. Indeed, we cannot rule out that the children's bilingualism is at least in part responsible for the higher cognitive functioning evidenced by all three children on virtually every standardized measure of intelligence, creativity, and achievement on which they have been formally and informally assessed. Moreover, the children progressed on a largely normal developmental schedule in English and thrived in their American schools in spite of the fact that we were speaking much more French than English in our home during their childhood. Therefore, we knew that the children were acquiring their English fluency largely as a result of immersion in English-speaking environments outside of our Louisiana home, including day care, school, and friendship peer groups. Also, at least until the children were aged 9;7 and 7;7, respectively, they listened to what was probably an average amount of American TV programming in our home.

We've come to have a very healthy respect for the power of the media to influence our children's language usage and attitudes.

To ensure the same level of fluency in French, after a few years of reflection we made the momentous decision to invest in a modest cottage in Québec. This summerhouse would provide a base that would allow the children to be immersed for up to two months per year in a totally francophone milieu. We would now be able to provide a measure of societal French-immersion that would be a counter-weight to the societal American immersion experience of the children during the regular school year. We acquired a second-hand TV, and tuned it to a French-speaking station, forbidding our children from ever watching the one English speaking station we were able to receive. Actually, it took much less effort to enforce the 'no English TV' rule in Québec than it did in the U.S. – for the children it just seemed 'natural' to watch French TV in a French-speaking environment.

Adolescence

As the children approached and entered adolescence, we had to modify our plan yet again in the face of perfectly normal adolescent opposition. We could no longer control the children's media as before. They begged us to allow them to watch American TV. They pleaded for us to discontinue speaking French to them while they were around their friends in Louisiana – even though their friends were French–English bilinguals! Forcing the issue would have simply provoked the children even more, unnecessarily souring our otherwise good relationships with them. Quite frankly, it just didn't feel 'natural' to enforce the French-only rule among adolescents who insisted they didn't want to stand out from their friends as 'freaks'.

However, fortunately, at this same time the children adopted the same attitude with their French-speaking peers in Québec. They not only did not want us speaking English around their Québécois peers, they did not even want us speaking English within the confines of our Québec cottage far from the ears of their peers! When I would inadvertently slip up and speak a few words of English, the children would ask, 'Pourquoi parles-tu en anglais, papa?' (Why are you speaking English, Dad?) Such is the power of society to coerce linguistic conformity. This was precisely what we had hoped for. Our big investment was paying off royally.

Thus, after approximately age 11, it was the children's peer groups, and not we, the parents, that furthered and perfected our project goal of rearing perfectly fluent bilingual children. It was John's Québécois peers who so influenced his manner of speaking French that he sounded very much like any other Québec teenager. Ironically, but perfectly explainable, it was the twins' bilingual American peers in their school French immersion program who perhaps contributed most to their slightly more pronounced American English accents (as least based on my perceptions and those of teachers and family) when speaking Québécois French through about age 15 or 16. Likewise, the immersion students' application of English syntax to French sentence structure may have influenced the way the twins' spoke French for the period of time they were enrolled in the program. It took a couple more years of exposure to their Québec peers before the twins, too, appeared to have lost much if not all of the influence of American English on their Québécois French (at around age 17;2). During the summer of 2004 while working as a counselor at the Québec French summer camp, Valerie told me that another Québécois counselor mistook her for a native of France. This piece of evidence, among others, suggested that she was perfectly fluent, but may not have spoke exactly like a Québécois.

This whole issue of accents is quite subjective, I've learned, and this study did not incorporate an objective measure of this attribute of speech. However, documenting people's perceptions of accents proved an interesting dimension to the study, and it was in fact through studying the responses of the children, their teachers, their peers, their Québec family, and us (the parents) that I've come to a new appreciation of how we perceive accented speech, and how in the children, their perceptions of their accents changed over time. Recall how John, oblivious to how he spoke French at age 9, was suddenly consumed with self-consciousness about how he spoke the language around his peers at age 11. Then, after two months of total immersion with his French-speaking peers during the impressionable age of 14, he was not only not self-conscious any more, but came out of that experience seeming to speak just like his friends! Gender may have also played a role in John's speaking the vernacular of his Québécois peers with such fluidity, as linguists have noted that males are more likely to speak non-standard versions of a language than are females, ostensibly to be 'cool'. John fitted in very well with his Québécois friends, in part, it seems, because he was 'cool'.

Implications for Parents

What have we learned from our experience that we can share with other parents, especially immigrants to the U.S. and Canada, or anglophone or francophone Canadians who are interested in rearing bilingual and/or biliterate children? One important discovery for us, that seems applicable as well to other families in our situation, was the importance of language immersion in fostering fluency in the children. It seems that an essential element to ensuring that our children learned to speak fluent French like native Québécois was our ability to periodically sever them from any contact with English. In other words, we immersed them in situations where they could only speak French, and where they were even cut off from communication with us, their parents. Moreover, it seemed that the ideal immersion situation was one in which the children were surrounded by native French speaking peers who did not have the ability to communicate with the children in English.[1] Our experience, in combination with other sociolinguistic research, has convinced me that societal immersion in both of a child's languages is necessary to becoming as fluently bilingual as possible.

As I already acknowledged, the results from a case study are not directly generalizable to larger populations. Still, the results from our case study help illuminate why some strategies and educational programs to help children become bilingual and biliterate might be more effective than others.

Lessons from a School French Immersion Program

Our children's school language immersion programs worked, and worked well. Moreover, learning to read and write in the minority tongue, French, did not detract from literacy in the majority tongue, English. In fact, the children's biliteracy may have helped them in both of their languages.

From pre-k through first grade the twins only studied English in school. Then, from second grade through seventh grade Valerie and Stephanie were immersed in both English and French academics, but with more formal instruction in French than in English. They both went on to study French in their American high schools, where they did quite well. Still, in spite of years of formal training in reading and writing French, Valerie and Stephanie probably did not, in the estimation of Suzanne and me, learn to write as well as an average native francophone student of the same age. However, let me be clear that we believe that our twins achieved a remarkable level of French literacy, and attribute much of their skill to their excellent French teachers. The question then arises: after all of their obvious advantages, why is it that a francophone Québécois or French child of average academic standing, but who's only ever been educated in French, may write a more grammatically correct essay in French than either Valerie or Stephanie? I believe the answer to this question is the same answer to the question of why they speak French so spontaneously and fluently:

authentic immersion. The twins were only ever exposed to what I'd term authentic, French academic immersion for the six weeks we enrolled them in a Québec elementary school. As many good things as I can say about their Louisiana school French immersion experience, I cannot classify it as 'authentic' academic immersion in the same way as the twins' Québec school experience was authentic. 'Authentic' academic French immersion, in my estimation, is not just having a native French-speaking teacher in front of the class speaking only French. Authentic also means being surrounded by native French-speaking children who spontaneously speak to each other in French, and then use their French reading and writing skills in their everyday lives. Recall the great pragmatist philosopher John Dewey's insight into how we learn: by doing. If we use a written and spoken language in the course of our everyday affairs, then we're going to become very proficient and expert in its usage.

What are the implications of our findings about school immersion programs for other parents seeking to ensure that their children become as literate as possible in a second or minority language? First, I'm convinced that foreign language immersion programs work, and for many parents this is an ideal way to ensure your child learns to read, write, and speak his or her second or home language fluently. Your child may not learn to read, write, and speak exactly like a native speaker, but they will in all likelihood become functionally bilingual and biliterate. Still, if your goal like ours is to rear children as biliterate as possible, then I would recommend seeking out educational immersion experiences that are as authentic as possible. As my children entered early adolescence, and this 'truth' became increasingly clear to me, I began seeking (unsuccessfully) opportunities to study and teach abroad in a francophone country for a year or more, so that I could enroll my children in an authentic French immersion academic setting.

Fortunately, learning languages is a process, and as Yogi Berra, the famous New York Yankees manager observed, 'It ain't over till it's over'. I didn't begin seriously learning to speak, read, and write in French until I was older than my children currently are as I craft these words (and I'd like to think that I'm still learning). In spite of my late start, I'd like to think that I am fairly literate (but far from perfect) in French. Still, I think my daughters are probably more literate than I am, a fact I credit to their Louisiana French immersion and high school French programs. All three of my children may, as part of their university coursework, be able to study abroad with francophones in francophone institutions. Perhaps, one of them, following the example of their father, will even marry into a francophone family. This was the secret of their father's bilingualism.

What We Accomplished

We appear to have reared perfectly fluent French-English bilinguals. All three children attained a measure of biliteracy, though at least to this point, they may not have acquired the ability to write in French as well as an average francophone student who only ever attended francophone schools. It is harder to determine how developed their French reading skills are. But given that they spontaneously read French novels written on an adult level for the sheer pleasure of reading, these skills seem to be very highly developed relative to francophone students of the same age. We may therefore have achieved our objective of rearing children who read at levels comparable to or perhaps even higher than francophone children their age. That John would spontaneously choose to read *The Lord of the Rings* in French after having so little formal instruction in French is telling. Indeed, I have taught perfectly normal American children whose native tongue is English, and who were seniors in high school, yet who had very little interest in reading anything at all. I truly believe that reading often to our children when they were still toddlers, and providing reading material in French and English throughout the children's lives, contributed greatly toward their internalizing a love of reading in general. Likewise, I attribute the children's love of reading in French to our emphasis on French literacy from very early in their lives, as well as the grammatical foundation laid down in their French immersion programs. Recall that John began reading French comic books immediately after only one semester of his Louisiana school French immersion program.

Authentic Societal Language Immersion

Though I couldn't orchestrate a long-term 'authentic' French immersion *educational* experience for my children, we were able to provide authentic French *societal* immersion for extended periods of time during summer vacations. In analyzing our data, I have to attribute the high degree of our children's spoken French language proficiency and fluency to this fact. As can be seen in references throughout this book, the ideal French language immersion situation for our children meant, in my estimation, *no recourse to English*. Period. Their immersion experience began with birth, when their mother wrapped them in the cadences of Québécois French. Yet as much French as was spoken in our family when the children were toddlers, as young children they still did not speak with the proficiency of a French-speaking child who is totally immersed in Rousseau's mother tongue. However, when we could finally expose our children to an entire society of French speakers over an extended period of time, they ultimately learned to speak French pretty much like native francophone Québécois. *They had no choice.*

There are no indications that the children's bilingual abilities are evidence of some special precocity on either their part, or our part. After 19 years of careful, systematic observation of these three individuals acquiring two languages simultaneously from birth, an analysis of the data strongly suggests that language immersion with native speakers of the tongue (other than simply the mother) was the ideal and perhaps only method for ensuring that our children learned to speak their languages with spontaneous, un-self-conscious, native-like phonology and control. This does not imply that our methods would work with every child, or that other methods could not be equally or even more effective with other children. However, for our children to have acquired the high level of bilingualism that we set for them at the beginning of our project, it seems that total societal language immersion was required for extended periods of time with their peers.

An argument could be raised that the circumstances of our family project are so unique, that we cannot generalize any of our findings beyond our family's experience. After all, we had resources not available to some families, or access to school language immersion programs not available to every student. It is true that we provided opportunities for our children that perhaps some less fortunate families could not provide their children. However, what is important to consider is *how* we invested the resources in our children. Our very largest expenditures were associated with providing the societal language immersion experiences that were otherwise beyond our reach: purchasing a small summer home in Canada, traveling to and from our summer home, and putting our children in a French-speaking summer camp. In other words, we had the resources to 'create' the laboratory conditions within which the children learned their languages. The laboratory was expensive. This fact by itself, however, does not mean that our findings are somehow less applicable, or that the means we employed are somehow superior. Much of the social capital that we invested in our children, i.e., meaningful interaction with them through activities such as reading and conversation, cost not a penny. Oftentimes the greatest expense wasn't monetary, but rather was time and discipline. Even the Louisiana French immersion program was in a state-funded public school that didn't charge tuition. However, even in families where less social capital in children is invested, the importance of societal immersion for acquiring fluency in a language is no less important. Indeed, authentic societal language immersion may be even more important for ensuring that children from at-risk, disadvantaged, or monolingual families acquire fluency in the second or minority language. Still, we know many of the twins' peers who are functionally bilingual and biliterate in French and English, yet who do not even have one French-speaking parent, and have never been totally immersed in a French speaking society. They may not speak French with the fluency of Valerie and Stephanie who've been speaking French outside of their French immersion classrooms for their entire lives, but these young Louisianans understand French perfectly well, and are able to express themselves in speaking and writing the language if called upon to do so.

Input=Output

French in, French out. Spanish in, Spanish out. English in, English out. Our experience has been that what our children heard (input), our children spoke (output). While my project has convinced me of the truth of this axiom, not all researchers seem to agree – and I'm not really sure why. For example, some have suggested that language immersion programs (input) in general are not effective. To quote Crawford (1998) from the ERIC website, 'There is no credible evidence to support the "time on task" theory of language learning, the claim that the more children are exposed to English, the more English they will learn'. Crawford was referring primarily to regular education programs in the United States that enroll non-English-speaking immigrants. He was critical of immersing non-English-speaking students directly into an English-speaking curriculum. His views are part of a heated debate about how the United States should educate the growing millions of non-English-speaking children flooding the country's school systems. Since the project of this book was about rearing bilingual children from birth in a family where both languages were spoken, our situation was not the same as a monolingual child learning the societal language for the first time at, say, 10 years old.

However, our study, like others, does very much address the issue of the 'time on task' theory of learning. Perhaps I am misunderstanding Crawford's point of view and those who share it, but did we not all learn our maternal language(s) as a direct result of simply being exposed to it (them)? Our parents were not interpreting for us what they were saying. They simply said it, and we learned it. The more they said something (repetition/input) the quicker we learned it. And we learned it like they said it. When we hear a four-year-old child cursing, where do we usually lay the blame? We hold the parents accountable, of course, or the child's environment. Let's not forget Louisiana's school English immersion policy first implemented in the 1920s, which took monolingual French-speaking children in the first grade and proceeded to almost extinguish their spontaneous French speaking with constant English input. Of course, it didn't hurt the state's English-only goal to allow teachers the freedom to humiliate the young francophone children for speaking their mother tongue.

Ultimately, we learned to speak the way our peers, or those who surround us speak, thus accounting for the differences in our dialects and accents. This central linguistic principle accounts for the children's phonology (the way they speak) in both French and English. The more the children were exposed to Québécois French (input), the more their accents morphed to reflect first the accent of their Québécois mother, and then the accent of their Québécois peers (output). When native French speakers from France heard our children speak French when they were around four to eight years old they remarked how the children spoke like Québécois (output). This is because of the influence of their mother's Québécois accented speech (input). Since John was exposed to even more Québécois French than his sisters as a consequence of longer periods of time immersed in a Québécois peer group as a teenager (input), he spoke more like a Québécois than his siblings (output). The twins were not only exposed to less Québécois French than John, they were exposed to much more English-accented French in their Louisiana school French immersion program (less than optimal input) – thus, the tenacity of their American accent when they spoke Québécois French (output). My interpretation of what happened is that it took a little longer for their Québécois milieu to sort of undo the influence of their Louisiana French immersion program. Even the children's speaking Cajun English (output) for several months as youngsters was a consequence of immersion in schools with country Cajun children (input). When the children transferred to suburban schools and were immersed in peer groups who did not speak English like Cajuns, but rather like popular American teen-speak (input), the children's accents seemed to morph yet again to reflect this new linguistic reality (output).

Admittedly, our having enrolled the three children in a Québécois school is not completely analogous to immersing a non English-speaking immigrant directly into the regular education program in an American school, because our children could already speak French. However, it was their first immersion in an all-francophone academic environment, and the experiment gives some insights into what academic and cultural immersion can be like for some students. Our daughters, especially Stephanie (age 7;1) were completely hostile to our plan, to the point of almost crying on the morning of that first day when we dragged the children from our familiar mountain cottage to the car for the tense trip to their new, completely unfamiliar school. This is a predictable response to the unknown. Some might decry our coercion as 'child abuse'. We feel our 'coercion' was quickly justified.

Though the twins went to their new Québécois school pouting, within three days they were totally integrated into their new Québécois peer groups, telling us they loved their new school and their new friends. Recall that the children had only been in a Louisiana partial school French-immersion program for one semester at this point, but were required to complete all of the academic tasks of their Québécois classmates who had only ever been in francophone schools. By the end of the experience all three children were indicating they wanted to return to the all-French-speaking school during their next summer vacation (which they did)! Cultural immersion is an initially scary and uncomfortable prospect, and of course language and academic immersion all the more so. But the intimidation for our children was temporary, and our children did indeed adapt, and learn. We attribute this 'genuine' immersion experience to significantly furthering our children's French fluency and confidence in a way our home environment could not do.

Our children eventually performed well in their francophone studies, and consequently felt good about their French reading, writing, and speaking abilities. Gardner and Tremblay (1995) singled out an individual's self-satisfaction as being a crucial motivator in determining whether or not they will associate pleasure with their performance in a second language. What's an important lesson from our experiment for other parents wanting to further their child's second language skills? If you have the chance, consider similar opportunities to immerse your child in academic environments with his or her peers where their academic performance won't be a part of their permanent academic record (unless you want it to be). Whereas such an opportunity might not be formal schooling *per se*, it could be a summer enrichment program put on by a local school board or university. The advantage of such a program is that your child learns to read and write the target language while perfecting their speaking skills with motivated peers. Many of Louisiana's French immersion students take advantage of a summer French immersion program put on by the Université-Sainte-Anne in Nova Scotia, where they study only in French at this francophone university for three weeks. In what seems a sort of revenge for Louisiana's once punishing Cajuns for speaking French at school, students at Sainte Anne are only permitted to speak French. After one warning for slipping up and speaking English, they're kicked out of the university for a second offence.

I've come to believe in the importance of immersion – whether familial, academic, or societal – as a powerful language-learning tool. Now, learning a language through immersion can cause some uncomfortable, and perhaps even humbling and humiliating moments for the learner. This was certainly the case for this book's author as he learned French, and provided entertainment for those native French speakers who observed in silent amusement his bumbling efforts. But these awkward moments quickly pass. I recall the day that a non-English-speaking student from the Dominican Republic took a seat in my 11th grade American History class. If Amarylis (whose name I still recall after almost 20 years) was receiving LEP (Limited English Proficient) assistance at the time, I was unaware of it. Our high school had very few immigrant students, and no teacher was permanently assigned to work with LEP students. What I do recall was that Amarylis was soon speaking with me in English, and turning in her assignments just like every other student. Indeed, it was not long before she was outperforming most of the native English-speaking students in my class. She learned English quickly because in addition to having a strong desire to succeed academically (like many immigrants), she was totally immersed in both English academics and English-speaking peer groups. Also, like any 16 year old, this student had a strong desire to integrate into and conform to her peer groups – including linguistically. Again, though not completely analogous to John's immersion with his summer camp peers when he too was an adolescent (because he could already speak French), John's 'peer immersion' experience expedited his French fluency. What makes Amarylis' experience so telling is that her American peer groups took someone who spoke almost none of the target language, and still managed to make her a fairly fluent speaker of the language after only one academic year. Another factor which both John and Amarylis had in common were parents that were very concerned for their children's academics: Amarylis' parents wanted her to be a doctor. The lesson to be learned here is that if you're really concerned about your child's not only becoming bilingual, but achieving high academic marks in the process, then you should become very involved in his or her education.

No Language Penalty

Now, a central biliteracy issue, as Hornberger (2003) succinctly puts it, is 'the degree to which literacy knowledge and skills in one language aid or impede the learning of literacy knowledge and skills in the other' (p. 4). Every member of my family was concerned, or at least a little apprehensive at some point in our project, that Valerie and Stephanie's French immersion program could somehow cost them when the time came to take a college entrance exam. Indeed, this issue greatly concerned Suzanne, who taught fourth grade French immersion students. Suzanne was so concerned that her students might miss a question on Louisiana's high stakes fourth grade exit exam that she introduced her students to the English terminology that her students might see on the test. In retrospect, it seems that our having immersed our children in French at home, and our enrolling Valerie and Stephanie in academic French for most of their elementary school years, didn't hurt them academically in English.

Though just a bit premature to close the book on this point yet, we suspect that based on their initial ACT, SAT and other standardized high school test scores, that neither girl has been inordinately handicapped as a result of being deprived of essential information delivered in English. In fact, we cannot discount an academic 'boost' as a result of their studying in two, and now even in three and four languages. I discovered that Louisiana students in French immersion programs like my twins outscored their peers who only had instruction in English (Caldas & Boudreaux, 1999). Thus, not only did the twins' school French immersion program not seem to hurt their or their classmates' academic performance in English, it may actually have boosted their English performance. Just the day before I wrote these words at the close of their first semester as high school seniors, one of my daughters related to me that her English teacher gushed that she (my daughter) deserved an 'A++++' in her English class. This is a teacher with a Ph.D. in English.

What's the Best Bilingual Program?

Based on my observations and research, I have become an advocate of the kind of foreign language immersion program attended by my daughters, which provided about 60% of instruction in the minority tongue (French) and 40% in the societal language (English). While in their suburban school French immersion program they became solidly literate in French while learning to read and write English on a pace that equaled or exceeded their monolingual cohort. Moreover, I watched the girls' friends become bilingual and biliterate as well. However, before giving a global endorsement to all bilingual education programs, there are a few important points to note about the program the girls attended which may not be typical of all foreign language immersion programs.

There is a plethora of research that suggests that obtaining a very good education in general is in part a product of the clientele with whom the education is received. Valerie and Stephanie were surrounded with other high achieving, socioeconomically advantaged students for five years of their school French immersion experience. These students came from homes where education was highly valued. Indeed, I attended a couple of standing-room only meetings of the 'Friends of Immersion', a parents' group who provided all kinds of support, monetary and otherwise, to Lafayette's French immersion program. These parents were involved to the hilt. I'm not suggesting that an immersion program with lower socioeconomic status students would not be a good program, because my own research indicates that students in poverty have disproportionately benefited from Louisiana's French immersion programs. What I would advise as a researcher and former public school teacher is that parents shopping for the best bilingual education program for their child should shop carefully. There is research out there to support or detract from just about every kind of bilingual program available (Baker, 2001). I suggest that parents adopt the time-honored strategy of *CAVEAT EMPTOR* (buyer beware). Visit the school which houses the program you're interested in, talk to parents whose children are enrolled in the program, and even sit in and observe a bilingual classroom in session if you can. These programs work, but they may not all work to the same degree or in the same way.

Parents deciding on an immersion program for their child can learn from research conducted on successful Canadian immersion programs as well. In Canada, however, bilingual education takes on an added complexity since there are two dominant societal languages – not one. Indeed, given Canada's official bilingual status, and its national and provincial efforts to promote bilingualism, this country has been the source of much high quality research on the effectiveness of school language immersion programs. One study (Tucker, 1986) identified several characteristics of a successful Canadian language immersion program that American parents may find instructive. These characteristics were: the L1 language has high status, the children in the program are middle-class, participation is voluntary, parents are very involved in the program, and instruction in both languages begins immediately. Valerie and Stephanie's Lafayette, Louisiana immersion program met every one of these characteristics.

Suggestions for Immigrants to the United States and Canada

My research has convinced me that English-speaking and French-speaking peer groups are possibly even more important than schools in ensuring that non-English-French-speaking immigrants to the U.S. and Canada learn to speak these two North American languages fluently. In other words, if you're a non-native English speaker to the U.S. who wants your child to achieve a very high level of fluency in English, which every immigrant I've ever met has greatly desired, choosing a very good educational program may have the added benefit of placing your child in a very good peer group. This sphere of friends and acquaintances within which your child will be immersed will ensure your child learns English effortlessly and fluently. Peers, in combination with a good bilingual education program (whose quality is in part a function of the quality of its students), will help accomplish the lofty, loving bilingual and biliterate goals you have set for your children. I share more information on rearing your child to speak your home language below.

So, How Do You Ensure Fluency in Your Child's Minority Tongue?

Many of the suggestions I now offer to parents apply to situations like my own family, where one or both parents are bilingual. However some of my advice also applies to monolingual immigrant families. Where it's necessary, I'll try to make a distinction between the two family situations. Given that the influence of American English was so strong while our children were in Louisiana, even while the twins were enrolled in a French immersion program, the biggest challenge throughout our project was rearing children who spoke, wrote, and read French. We had to expend much time and energy to accomplish this dimension of our project. Our children learned the societal language of the U.S. effortlessly because they were socially and academically immersed in it. We were swimming upstream by trying to teach a minority language in a majority language environment.

How did we teach the minority language? We successfully accomplished this by speaking mostly French in the home, and by providing a constant stream of reading material, videocassettes, audiocassettes and French satellite programming. As a consequence of our simply speaking French to our children, they were speaking our home tongue at roughly the same time they began speaking English, though without the same facility. Still, much of our direct parental influence over our children, including linguistic influence, ended in adolescence. Even with our very best, concerted efforts, we have to attribute the children's adolescent francophone peer groups with finishing the job of bringing our children to the level of French fluency we established for them even before they were born. One implication of this fact is that during the time that you, the parent, do have so much influence, you should be using it. Discipline yourself to speak the non-societal language in the home as much as possible. It's not easy – but it works.

If it were possible to summarize 19 years of research in one statement, it would be something like this: our findings suggest that it takes language immersion in families, classrooms, communities, and peer groups dominated by native speakers of the target language for an individual to acquire a high level of fluency in reading, writing, and speaking the language. When Valerie (16;2) and John (17;2) told us that fellow campers in their all-French-speaking camp were surprised to learn that they spoke English, this was to us the best assessment possible that they had achieved the level of bilingualism for which we had been striving.

Now, I would like to offer advice learned in the crucible of experience to immigrant families in any country desiring that their children become fluent speakers, readers, and writers of both the societal and home languages. First, if you are able to, associate with communities dominated by families who speak the societal language with native-like proficiency. Since your children will eventually speak the country's language like the peers who surround them, do all within your power to ensure that your children are immersed in schools with peer groups who speak the variety of the societal language you want your children to learn. In this way, your child will learn the societal language effortlessly – without your help – while learning the skills necessary to achieve academically (the literacy half of the equation).

If your child is at least two years old when you immigrate, he or she is likely already a native speaker of your home language, unless you're rearing them bilingually as we did. In the case of simultaneous bilinguals, they may not speak any language intelligibly until sometime after two years of age. So please don't worry unnecessarily if your bilingual child's language seems underdeveloped at age two – their tiny but busy brains have twice as much to assimilate as monolingual children. Anyway, as with us and the French language, your job then becomes one of ensuring that your child continues to develop proficiency in the home language, and ultimately learns to read and write the language (if biliteracy is your goal). To these ends, I reiterate yet again that you must speak the minority home language as often as possible with your child. You should also read to your children in the home language, and if possible, make periodic trips to milieus where your home language is the dominant language. In this way, your children will realize that your home language is cherished and used by many people in the same way that their 'second' language is. For Hispanic Americans desiring to rear bilingual Spanish-English children, I would recommend reading the book *Guia Para Padres Y Maestros De Ninos*

Bilingues by Ada and Baker (2001) which is replete with useful information on how to successfully accomplish this.

If you have access to after-school or weekend programs which teach reading and writing skills in your home or minority language, you may want to enroll your child. Koreans in Los Angeles utilize such programs as these to ensure their children learn Korean (Zhou & Logan, 2003). If your home language is offered as a course in your child's school, which is more likely at the secondary than elementary level, encourage your child to take the course.

Use summertime vacations (since children will normally not miss school) as opportunities to immerse your children in their home or minority languages. Returning to the home country for total societal immersion may be the best way to ensure your child's continuing and developing fluency in the minority language, as it was for ours. If you, the parent, cannot accompany your child, perhaps the child could stay with trusted friends or relatives for some period of time. In this way, your children may have no choice but to speak the minority language, as our children sometimes had to speak French in Canada. There may be summertime academic enrichment programs in your home country in which you can enroll your children, exposing them to an authentic academic immersion experience.

The Power of Media

With the widespread and inexpensive availability of satellite TV, you may be able to locate stations that broadcast in the minority language you want your child to learn. If so, you've got a powerful weapon in your arsenal of language-learning tools. Children love TV. Use this natural attraction to your (and their) linguistic advantage. Tune in the minority language station and leave it there. If your children are like mine were (and are), they'll quickly develop an affinity bordering on addiction for certain shows. Once they're glued to the set, you'll be maximizing language input effortlessly. Your children will now be absorbing the language like sponges, and will eventually be spontaneously speaking words and phrases that they've heard on TV in their expanding knowledge of the home language.

The caveat about extended exposure to the TV is the quality of the programming. Recall that Suzanne and I sometimes winced at what our children were seeing and hearing on French and Canadian stations. Let me add, though, that the sometimes racy programming that they watched (racy, anyway, by our standards) doesn't seem to have harmed them. They've become decent young adults who actually like studying and reading (and watching a little TV, too). Thus, significant exposure to TV doesn't seem to have hurt their attention spans, either.

Another powerful media tool available to parents is showing your children films in the minority language on VHS or DVD recorders. We eventually acquired quite a library of high interest French-speaking videocassettes that the children devoured through constant viewing and re-viewing. I documented the acquisition of several specific words and phrases that my children picked up from watching their favorite videocassettes. Whereas we were fortunate enough to shop in Canada where we could find large stocks of French films, families today often don't have to travel any further than their local video store to buy or rent many DVDs which have an option to watch the film in more than the language in which it was shot. Though not every film is dubbed in another language, and your family's tongue might not be one of the languages into which a film has been translated, many blockbuster Hollywood films have been dubbed in French, German, or Spanish. Since many DVDs will have subtitles available in several popular languages, you can also further the child's literacy in the minority tongue by activating the subtitle feature. If your child is as curious as my children were (and still are), they'll actually make a game of trying to decipher the subtitles.

I think that our project demonstrates clearly that one can indeed raise perfectly fluent bilingual-biliterate children, though the children may spend much of their time in a monolingual environment. Ample research documents children successfully acquiring two languages at the same time, even though they may have only limited exposure to one of the two languages either inside or outside of the home (De Houwer, 1991; Fantini, 1985; Okita, 2002; Saunders, 1982, 1988). The job of bilingual parents is to maximize exposure to the minority tongue. Thinking back on it, one of the most difficult tasks in our project was simply forcing ourselves to speak the home language – French – while immersed in a totally English-speaking environment. From my point of view, any determined bilingual parent can rear children who at least speak the minority home language if they're willing to impose the self-discipline necessary to sometimes run counter to popular linguistic pressure. Of course, for immigrant parents who speak only the minority tongue, there is no other option but to speak the minority tongue at home, and their children will of necessity learn to understand and speak their parents' native language. The issues facing these parents are slightly different than they are for parents who speak both the minority and majority languages. For monolingual immigrant parents desiring to rear bilingual children the more important concerns are likely to center on ensuring that their children become competent readers, writers, and speakers of the majority language, since the children will often be getting ample minority language input at home. Still, what I have said about learning to read and write the minority tongue applies equally to monolingual immigrant and bilingual families. If the children are not exposed to written forms of the minority language and are not encouraged to learn it, they probably won't.

Now, in addition to self-discipline our bilingual project was aided in part by some planning, enthusiasm, research, family stability, and even some luck. As we've pointed out, bringing our children to Québec for societal immersion in the home tongue helped immensely. Obviously, not every family who desires to rear bilingual children may be able to make annual 2000-mile pilgrimages to further their family goal of bilingualism. But then 2000 miles do not separate every family's two languages, and not all families want or need to achieve the high levels of bilingualism and biliteracy we established for our project. We do believe that our experience and others' certainly prove, beyond any doubt, that rearing functionally bilingual children (though perhaps not biliterate children) can be accomplished simply by systematically speaking to your child in two languages from early in their lives. Moreover, this method costs not a penny.

Those Americans wishing to rear bilingual English-Spanish speaking children, and living within reasonable traveling distance of the Mexican border, do not need to travel nearly as far as we did to find total linguistic/cultural immersion in the minority language. Indeed, many of these interested parents do not even need to leave the U.S. at all, making the task of rearing Spanish-English bilinguals in the U.S. a considerably easier one than rearing French-English bilinguals. Still, I'm not going to sugar coat the fact that for many families the task of rearing fluent, competent bilingual-biliterate children is an endeavor that will require much effort. However, if the experience of our project is generalizable to other families at all, we can attest that as we reflect back on our 'family project', our efforts now seem small in relation to the huge payoff. Indeed, we are now already looking toward the future and hoping for bilingual grandchildren one day. Moreover, we are volunteering to offer our assistance based on many years of research and 'hands on' experience.

Note
1. The findings reported in our 2000 study empirically make this point the best (Caldas & Caron-Caldas, 2000).

Bibliography

Ada, A.F. and Baker, C. (2001) *Guia Para Padres Y Maestros De Ninos Bilingues*. Clevedon: Multilingual Matters.

Adams, G.R., Abraham, K.G. and Markstrom, C.A. (1987) The relations among identity development, self-consciousness and self-focusing during middle and late adolescence. *Developmental Psychology* 23, 292–7.

Alexander, K. and Alexander, M.D. (1998) *American Public School Law*. New York: West/Wadsworth.

Anderson, P.J. and Graham, S.M. (1994) Issues in second language phonological acquisition among children and adults. *Topics in Language Disorders* 14, 84-100.

Anti-bilingualism wins in Massachusetts (2003, November 6). NewsMax wires. Retrieved on-line at http://www.newsmax.com/archives/articles/2002/11/6/81114.shtml.

Armsden, G. and Greenberg, M.T. (1987) The inventory of parent and peer attachment: Individual differences and their relationship to psychological well-being in adolescence. *Journal of Youth and Adolescence* 16, 427–54.

Asher, J. and García, G. (1969) The optimal age to learn a foreign language. *Modern Language Journal* 38, 334–41.

Association of Catholic Principals of Montreal (1969, June) A brief to the commission of inquiry on the position of the French language and on language rights in Quebec. Montreal.

Baddley, A.D. (1986) *Working Memory*. Oxford: Clarendon Press.

Bachman, L. (1990) *Fundamental Considerations in Language Testing*. Oxford: Oxford University Press.

Baetens Beardsmore, H. (1982) *Bilingualism: Basic Principles*. Clevedon: Multilingual Matters.

Baker, C. (2001) *The Foundations of Bilingual Education and Bilingualism*. Clevedon: Multilingual Matters.

Balkan, L. (1970) *Les effets du bilinguisme français-anglais sur les aptitudes intellectuelles*. Bruxelles: Aimav.

Bankens, B. and Akins, D. (1989) French immersion comparative data Stanford 7-plus achievement test at Prien elementary school (Research report No. 90-017-422-04) Calcasieu Parish School Board, Lake Charles, LA.

Bankston, C. and Caldas, S.J. (1996) Majority Black schools and the perpetuation of social injustice: The influence of de facto segregation on academic achievement. *Social Forces* 75 (2), 535–55.

Bankston, C.L. and Caldas, S.J. (2002) *A Troubled Dream: The Promise and Failure of School Desegregation in Louisiana.* Vanderbilt University Press.

Bankston, C.L. and Zhou, M. (1995) Effects of minority-language literacy on the academic achievement of Vietnamese youths in New Orleans. *Sociology of Education* 68, 1–17.

Bankston, C., Caldas, S.J. and Zhou, M. (1997) The academic achievement of Vietnamese American students: Ethnicity as social capital. *Sociological Focus* 30, 1.

Barker, V, Giles, H., Noels, K., Duck, J., Hecht, M. and Clément, R. (2001) The English-only movement: A communication analysis of changing perceptions of language vitality. *Journal of Communication* 51 (1), 3-37.

Ben-Zeev, S. (1977) Mechanisms by which childhood bilingualism affects understanding of language and cognitive structures. In P.A. Hornby (ed.) *Bilingualism: Psychological, Social and Educational Implications* (pp. 29–55). New York: Academic.

Berk, L.E. (1996) *Infants, Children, and Adolescent* (2nd edn). Boston: Allyn & Bacon.

Berman, R.A. (1979) The re-emergence of a bilingual: A case study of a Hebrew-English speaking child. *Workings Papers on Bilingualism* 18, 157–79.

Berndt, T.J. (1979) Developmental changes in conformity to peer and parents. *Developmental Psychology* 15, 608–16.

Bialystok, E. (1988) Levels of bilingualism and levels of linguistic awareness. *Developmental Psychology* 24, 560–7.

Bialystok, E. (2001) *Bilingualism in Development: Language, Literacy, and Cognition.* Cambridge: Cambridge University Press.

Bianculli, D. (1992) *Teleliteracy: Taking Television Seriously.* New York: Continuum.

Blum-Kulka, S. (1994) The dynamics of family dinner talk: Cultural contexts for children's passages to adult discourse. *Research on Language and Social Interaction* 27, 1-50.

Boudreau, A. (1996) Les mots des jeunes Acadiens et Acadiennes du Nouveau-Brunswick. In L. Dubois and A. Boudreau (eds) *Les Acadians et leur(s) langue(s)* (pp. 137–50). Moncton, N.-B.: Les Éditions d'Acadie.

Boudreaux, N. (1998) A formative evaluation of the French immersion program in the Cecilia schools of Saint Martin Parish. (Unpublished Masters Thesis)

Boudreaux, N. and Caldas, S.J. (1998a, March). A comparison of French immersion and non-immersion LEAP test results. Paper presented at the 1998 annual meeting of the Louisiana Educational Research Association, Shreveport, LA.

Boudreaux, N. and Caldas, S.J. (1998b, April) Foreign language immersion: A key to success on standardized tests. A paper presented at the 1998 annual meeting of the American Educational Research Association, San Diego, CA.

Boudreaux, R. (1995, March 26). Acadiana may be more French than we think. *The Sunday Advertiser*, p. D-1.

Brasseaux, C.A. and Conrad, G.R. (1992) *The Road to Louisiana: The Saint Domingue Refugees*. University of Southwestern Louisiana (Lafayette): Center for Louisiana Studies.

Briller, B. and Miller, S. (1984) Assessing academic achievement. *Society* 21 (6), 6-9.

Burt, M. and Dulay, H. (1978) Some guidelines for the assessment of oral language proficiency and dominance. *TESOL Quarterly* 12, 177–92.

Butler, S.R., Marsh, H.W. and Sheppard, M.J. (1985) Seven-year longitudinal study of the early prediction of reading achievement with kindergarten children. *Journal of Educational Psychology* 77, 349–61.

Caldas, S.J. (1998) How to suppress childhood bilingualism… And bring it back to life again. *Learning Languages* 4, 15–23.

Caldas, S.J. (2004) From the mouth of babes … A review of *Cross-linguistic structures in simultaneous bilingualism* (by Susanne Döpke, ed.) *Contemporary Psychology: APA Review of Books* 49 (1).

Caldas, S.J. and Bankston, C.L. (1997) The effect of school population socioeconomic status on individual student academic achievement. *Journal of Educational Research* 90, 269–77.

Caldas, S.J. and Bankston, C.L. (1999a) Black and white TV: Race, television viewing, and academic achievement. *Sociological Spectrum* 19, (1), 39-61.

Caldas, S.J. and Bankston, C.L. (1999b) A multilevel examination of student, school, and district-level effects on academic achievement. *Journal of Educational Research* 93 (4), 91–100.

Caldas, S.J. and Boudreaux, N. (1999) Poverty, race, and foreign language immersion: Predictors of academic achievement. *Learning Languages* 5 (1), 4–15.

Caldas, S.J. and Caron-Caldas, S. (1992) Rearing bilingual children in a monolingual culture: A Louisiana experience. *American Speech* 67, 290–6.

Caldas, S.J. and Caron-Caldas, S. (1996, April) A case study in family french-immersion and academic achievement. A paper presented at the annual meeting of the American Educational Research Association, New York, NY.

Caldas, S.J. and Caron-Caldas, S. (1997) Cultural influences on French/English language dominance of three bilingual children. *Language, Culture and Curriculum* 10, 139–55.

Caldas, S.J. and Caron-Caldas, S. (1999) Language immersion and cultural identity: Conflicting influences and values. *Language, Culture and Curriculum* 12, 42–58.

Caldas, S.J. and Caron-Caldas, S.C. (2000) The influence of family, school and community on 'bilingual preference': Results from a Louisiana/Quebec case study. *Applied Psycholinguistics* 21, 365–81.

Caldas, S.J. and Caron-Caldas, S.C. (2001, April) The language preferences of adolescent bilinguals: allegiance and opposition. Paper presented at the 2001 annual meeting of the American Educational Research Association, Seattle, WA.

Caldas, S.J. and Caron-Caldas, S. (2002) A sociolinguistic analysis of the language preferences of adolescent bilinguals: shifting allegiances and developing identities. *Applied Linguistics* 23, 490–514.

Caldas, S.J. Caldas, S.C., Caldas, J.T., Caldas, S.V. and Caldas, V.S. (1998, April). Language immersion and cultural identity: Do real Americans speak only English? A paper presented at the 1998 annual meeting of the American Educational Research Association, San Diego, CA.

Carringer, D. (1974) Creative thinking abilities of a Mexican youth. The relationship of bilingualism. *Journal of Cross-cultural Psychology* 5 (4), 492–505.

Campbell, R.N. (1984) The immersion education approach to foreign language teaching. In *Studies on Immersion Education: A Collection for United States Educators* (pp. 114-43). Sacramento: California State Department of Education.

Castellanos, D. (1992) A polyglot nation. In S.J. Crawford (ed.) *Language Loyalties: A Source Book on the Official English Controversy* (pp. 13–18). Chicago: University of Chicago Press.

Caussinus, M. (2004) La motivation influence-t-elle le passage de compétence à performance dans le processus d'apprentissage du Français langue etrangère? Doctoral dissertation, University of Louisiana.

Center for Applied Linguistics. (2003) *Directory of Two-Way Bilingual Immersion Programs in the U.S.* Retrieved September 1, 2003, from http://www.cal.org/twi/directory.

Chall, J.S., Jacobs, V.A. and Baldwin, L.E. (1990) *The Reading Crisis: Why Poor Children Fall Behind*. Cambridge, MA: Harvard University Press.

Christian, D. (1994) *Two-way Bilingual Education: Students Learning Through Two Languages*. Santa Cruz: National Center for Research on Cultural Diversity and Second Language Learning.

Clément, R. and Kruidenier, B.G. (1985) Aptitude, attitude and motivation in second language proficiency: A test of Clément's Model. *Journal of Language and Social Psychology* 4, 21–37.

Cohen, A.D. (1989) Attrition in the productive lexicon of two Portuguese third language speakers. *Studies in Second Language Acquisition* 11 (2), 135–49.

Coleman, J.S., Campbell, E.Q., Hobson, C.J., McPartland, J. Mood, A.M., Weinfeld, F.D. and York, R.L. (1966) *Equality of Educational Opportunity*. Washington, DC: U.S. Government Printing Office.

Corson, D. (1992) Bilingual education policy and social justice. *Education Policy* 7, 45–69.

Cowan, N. (1995) *Attention and Memory: An Integrated Framework*. Oxford Psychology Series, 26, Oxford University Press.

Crain-Thoreson, C. and Dale, P.S. (1992) Do early talkers become early readers? Linguistic precocity, preschool language, and emergent literacy. *Developmental Psychology* 28, 421–9.

Crawford, J. (1992) *Hold Your Tongue*. New York: Addison-Wesley.

Crawford, J. (1998) Ten fallacies about bilingual education. Retrieved from ERIC on-line at http://www.cal.org/ericcll/digest/crawford01.html.

Crocker, L. and Algina, J. (1986) *Introduction to Classical and Modern Test Theory*. New York: Holt, Reinhard and Winston.

Daigle, J.O. (1984) *A Dictionary of the Cajun Language*. Ann Arbor, MI: Edwards Brothers, Inc.

Davies, M.M. (1989) *Television is Good for your Kids*. London: Hilary Shipman.

De Houwer, A. (1990) *The Acquisition of Two Languages From Birth: A Case Study*. Cambridge: Cambridge University Press.

Deuchar, M. and Quay, S. (2000) *Bilingual Acquisition: Theoretical Implications of a Case Study*. Oxford: Oxford University Press.

Diaz, R. (1983) Thought and two languages: The impact of bilingualism on cognitive development. In E.W. Gordon (ed.) *Review of Research in Education* (Vol. 10, pp. 23–54). Washington, DC: American Educational Research Association.

Dodson, C.J. (1985) Second language acquisition and bilingual development: A theoretical framework. *Journal of Multilingual and Multicultural Development* 6, 326–46.

Dolbec, M. (2003, 10 Juillet). La France adopte le 'courriel' québécois. *Le Soleil*, A–5.)

Döpke, S. (1992) *One Parent, One Language. An Interactional Approach.* Amsterdam and Philadelphia: John Benjamins.

Döpke, S. (ed.) (2000) *Cross-linguistic Structures in Simultaneous Bilingualism.* Amsterdam/Philadelphia: John Benjamins.

Dörnyei, Z. (2001) *Motivational Strategies in the Language Classroom.* Cambridge: Cambridge University Press.

Dubois, S. and Horvath, B.M. (2003) The English vernacular of Creoles of Louisiana. *Language, Variation and Change* 15, 255–88.

Durkheim, E. (1951) *Suicide: A Study in Sociology* (translated by George Simpson and John A. Spaulding.) New York: The Free Press.

Eckert, P. (1989) *Jocks and Burnouts: Social Categories and Identity in the High School.* New York: Teachers College Press.

Edelman, M. (1969) Contextualized measure of degree of bilingualism, *Modern Language Journal* 53, 179–82.

Edwards, J. (1994) *Multilingualism.* New York: Routledge.

Elkind, D. and Bowen, R. (1979) Imaginary audience behavior in children and adolescents. *Developmental Psychology* 15, 33–44.

Enright, R.D., Lapsley, D.K. and Shukla, D. (1979) Adolescent egocentrism in early and late adolescence. *Adolescence*, 14, 687–95.

Erikson, E.H. (1968) *Identity: Youth and Crisis.* New York: Norton.

Facts on File (1996, Aug. 22) *House Passes English Bill.* Author. Vol. 56, 596.

Fantini, A.E. (1985) *Language Acquisition of a Bilingual Child: A Sociolinguistic Perspective.* Clevedon: Multilingual Matters.

Feagin, J.R., Orum, A.M. and Sjoberg, G. (eds) (1991) *A Case for the Case Study.* Chapel Hill, NC: The University of North Carolina Press.

Ferdman, B.M. (1990) Literacy and cultural identity. *Harvard Educational Review* 60 (2), 181–204.

Fisher, D. (1990, March) Family communication and the sexual behavior and attitudes of college students. *Journal of Youth and Adolescence* 16, 481–95.

Fishman, J.A. (1985a) Language, ethnicity and racism. In J.A. Fishman, M.H. Gernter, E.G. Lowy, and W.G. Milan (eds) *The Rise and Fall of the Ethnic Revival: Perspectives on Language and Ethnicity* (pp. 3-13). Berlin: Mouton Publishers.

Fishman, J.A. (1985b) Language maintenance and ethnicity. In J.A. Fishman, M.H. Gernter, E.G. Lowy and W.G. Milan (eds) *The Rise and*

Fall of the Ethnic Revival: Perspectives on Language and Ethnicity (pp. 57–76). Berlin: Mouton Publishers.

Fishman, J. (2001) *Can Threatened Languages be Saved?* Clevedon: Multilingual Matters.

Flege, J.E. and Fletcher, K.L. (1992) Talker and listener effects on the perception of degree of foreign accent. *Journal of the Acoustical Society of America* 91, 370–89.

Foley, D.E. (1990) *Learning Deep in the Capitalist Heart of Tejas Culture*. Philadelphia: University of Pennsylvania Press.

Franklin, B. (1932) *The Autobiography of Benjamin Franklin* (compiled and edited, with notes, by J. Bigelow). New York: Walter J. Black, Inc.

Gaines, J.H. (1996) The talking drum. *Journal of Black Psychology* 22, 202–22.

Galindo, D.L. (1995) Language attitudes towards English and Spanish varieties: A Chicano perspective. *Hispanic Journal of Behavioral Sciences* 17, 77–100.

Gardner, R.C. (1985) *Social Psychology and Second Language Learning: The Role of Attitudes and Motivation*. London: Edward Arnold.

Gardner, R.C. and Lambert, W.E. (1972) *Attitudes and Motivation in Second-Language Learning*. Rowley, MA: Newbury House Publishers.

Gardner, R.C. and Tremblay, P. (1995) On motivation, research agendas and theoretical frameworks. *Modern Language Journal* 78 (3), 359–68.

Gawlitzek-Maiwald, I. (2000) 'I want a chimney builden': The acquisition of infinitival constructions in bilingual children. In S. Döpke (ed.) *Crosslinguistic Structures in Simultaneous Bilingualism* (pp. 123–48). Amsterdam/Philadelphia: John Benjamins.

Genesee, F. (1987) *Learning Through Two Languages: Studies of Immersion and Bilingual Education*. New York: Newbury House.

Genesee, F., Nicoladis, E. and Paradis, J. (1995) Language differentiation in early bilingual development. *Journal of Child Language* 22, 611–31.

Giles, H. and Powesland, P.F. (1975) *Speech Style and Social Evaluation*. London: Academic Press.

Giles, H., Williams, A., Mackie, D.M. and Rosselli, F. (1995) Reactions to Anglo- and Hispanic-American-accented speakers: Affect, identity, persuasion, and the English-only controversy. *Language and Communication* 15, 107–120.

Gordon, M.M. (1964) *Assimilation in American Life*. New York: Oxford University Press.

Grissmer, D.W., Flanagan, A., Kawata, J. and Williamson, S. (2000) Improving student achievement: What NAEP state test scores tell us. Retrieved 8/25/03 from http://rand.org/publications/MR/MR924/index.html

Grosjean, F. (1982) *Life with Two Languages: An Introduction to Bilingualism.* Cambridge: Harvard University Press.

Gut, U. (2000) Cross-linguistic structures in the acquisition of intonational phonology by German-English bilingual children. In S. Döpke (ed.) *Cross-linguistic Structures in Simultaneous Bilingualism* (pp. 201–26). Amsterdam/Philadelphia: John Benjamins.

Hakuta, K. (1986) *The Mirror of Language.* New York: Basic Books.

Hakuta, K. (1999) The debate on bilingual education. *Developmental and Behavioral Pediatrics* 20, 36–7.

Heller, M. (1999) *Linguistic Minorities and Modernity: A Sociolinguistic Ethnography.* New York: Longman.

Henry, J. and Bankston, C. (1999) Cajun ethnicity: Structural or symbolic? *Sociological Spectrum* 19, 223–48.

Hill, J.P. and Holmbeck, G.N. (1986) Attachment and autonomy during adolescence. In G. Whitehurst (ed.), *Annals of Child Development* (Vol. 3, pp. 145–89). Greenwich, CT: JAI Press.

Hornberger, N.H. (1998) Language policy, language education, language rights: Indigenous, immigrant, and international perspectives. *Language in Society* 27, 439–58.

Hornberger, N.H. (2003) Continua of biliteracy. In N.H. Hornberger (ed.), *Continua of Biliteracy: An Ecological Framework for Educational Policy, Research and Practice in Multilingual Settings* (pp. 3–34). Clevedon: Multilingual Matters Ltd.

Hornik, R.C. (1978) Television viewing and the slowing of cognitive growth. *American Educational Research Journal* 15, 1–15.

Hornik, R.C. (1981) Out-of-school television and school: Hypotheses and methods. *Review of Educational Research* 52, 193–214.

Hudson, L. and Gray, W. (1986) Formal operation, the imaginary audience, and the personal fable. *Adolescence* 21, 751–65.

Ianco-Worrall, A. (1972) Bilingualism and cognitive development. *Child Development* 43, 1390–1400.

Jarvis, L.H., Danks, J.H. and Merriman, W.E. (1995) The effect of bilingualism on cognitive ability: A test of the level of bilingualism hypothesis. *Applied Psycholinguistics* 16, 293–308.

Jespersen, O. (1922) *Language. It's Nature, Development and Origin.* London: George Allen and Unwin Ltd.

Jones, C.P. and Adamson, L.B. (1987) Language use in mother-child and mother-child-sibling interactions. *Child Development* 58, 356–66.

Klein, D. (2003) A positron emission tomography study of presurgical language mapping in a bilingual patient with a left posterior temporal cavernous angioma. *Journal of Neurolinguistics* 16, (4/5), 417–27).

Klein, D., Zatorre, R.J, Milner, B., Meyer, E. and Evans, A.C. (1994) Left putaminal activation when speaking a second language: Evidence from PET. *NeuroReport* 17 (5), 2295–7.

Klein, D., Milner, B., Zatorre, R.J., Meyer, E. and Evans, A. (1995) The neural substrates underlying word generation: a bilingual functional-imaging study. *Proceedings of the National Academy of Sciences*. USA. Vol. 92, 2899–903.

Klein, D., Milner, B., Zatorre, R.J., Zhao, V. and Nikelski, J. (1999) Cerebral organization in bilinguals: A PET study of Chinese-English verb generation. *NeuroReport* 10 (13) 2841–6.

Klein, D., Zatorre R.J., Milner B. and Zhao, V. (2001) A cross-linguistic PET study of tone perception in Mandarin Chinese and English speakers. *NeuroImage* 13, 646–53.

Katz, S.R. (1996) Where the streets cross the classroom: A study of Latino students' perspectives on cultural identity in city schools and neighborhood gangs. *The Bilingual Research Journal* 20, (3&4), 603–31.

Labov, W. (2000) *Principles of Linguistic Change. Volume II: Social Factors*. Oxford: Basil Blackwell.

Lambert, W.E. and Tucker, G.R. (1972) *The St. Lambert Experiment*. Rowley, MA: Newbury House Publishers.

Landry, R. and Allard, R. (1991) Can schools promote additive bilingualism in minority group children? In L. Malavé and G. Duquette (eds) *Language, Culture and Cognition* (pp. 198-231). Clevedon: Multilingual Matters.

Lanza, E. (1992) Can bilingual two-year-olds code switch? *Journal of Child Language* 19, 633–58.

Lanza, E. (2000) Language contact: A dilemma for the bilingual child or for the linguist? In S. Döpke (ed.) *Cross-Linguistic Structures in Simultaneous Bilingualism* (pp. 123–48). Amsterdam/Philadelphia: John Benjamins.

Lanza, E. (1997) *Language Mixing in Infant Bilingualism*. Oxford: Clarendon.

Lapsley, D.K., Jackson, S., Rice, K., Shalid, G. (1988) Self-monitoring and the 'new look' at the imaginary audience and personal fable: An ego-developmental analysis. *Journal of Adolescent Research* 3, 17–31.

Leopold, W. (1949) *Speech Development of a Bilingual Child: A Linguist's Record, Vol 4: Diary from Age 2*. Evanston, IL: Northwestern University Press.

Linn, R.L. and Gronlund, N.E. (2000) *Measurement and Assessment in Teaching*. Columbus, OH: Merrill/Prentice Hall.

Louisiana Department of Education (1996) District Composite Report. Baton Rouge.

Lowy, E.G., Fishman, J.A., Gertner, M.H., Gottesman, I. and Milan, W.G. (1985) Ethnic activists view the ethnic revival and its language consequence. In J.A. Fishman, M.H. Gernter, E.G. Lowy and W.G. Milan (eds) *The Rise and Fall of the Ethnic Revival: Perspectives on Language and Ethnicity* (pp. 283–301). Berlin: Mouton Publishers.

Macedo, D. (2000) The colonialism of the English only movement. *Educational Researcher* 29 (3), 15–24.

Makin, L., Campbell, J. and Jones Diaz, C. (1995) *One Childhood, Many Languages*. Sydney: Harper Educational.

Malina, R.M. (1990) Physical growth and performance during the transitional years (9 to 16). In R. Montemayor, G.R. Adams and T.P. Gullotta (eds) *Advances in Adolescent Development: Vol. 2. From Childhood to Adolescence: A Transitional Period?* Newbury Park, CA: Sage.

Mazel, J. (1979) *Louisiane: Terre d'aventure*. Paris: Laffont.

McAndrew, M. and Lamarre, P. (1996) The integration of ethnic minority students fifteen years after bill 101: Linguistic and cultural issues confronting Quebec's French language schools. *Canadian Ethnic Studies* 28, (2), 40–63.

McCollum, P. (1993, April). Learning to value English: Cultural capital in a two-way bilingual program. Paper presented at the annual meeting of the American Educational Research Association, Atlanta, GA.

McKay, S.L. and Wong, S.C. (1996) Multiple discourses, multiple identities: Investment and agency in second-language learning among Chinese adolescent immigrant students. *Harvard Educational Review* 66, 577–608.

Medved, M. (1992) *Hollywood vs. America: Popular Culture and the War on Traditional Values*. New York: Harper-Collins.

Moyer, A. (2004) *Age, Accent and Experience in Second Language Acquisition*. Clevedon: Multilingual Matters.

Nicoladis, E. and Genesee, F. (1996) A longitudinal study of pragmatic differentiation in young bilingual children. *Learning Languages* 46 (3), 439–64.

Nicoladis, E. and Genesee, F. (1998) Parental discourse and codemixing in bilingual children. *International Journal of Bilingualism* 2 (1), 85–99.

Noels, K. and Clément, R. (1989) Orientations to learning German: The effects of language heritage in second language acquisition. *The Canadian Modern Language Review* 45 (2), 245–57.

Ochs, E. (1993) Constructing social identity: A language socialization perspective. *Research on Language and Social Interaction* 26 (3), 287–306.

Ochs, E. and Schieffelin (1989) Language has a heart. *Text 9*, 7–25.

Okita, T. (2002) *Invisible Work: Bilingualism, Language Choice and Childrearing in Intermarried Families*. Amsterdam and Philadelphia: John Benjamins.

Oxford, R. and Shearin, J. (1994) Language learning motivation: Expanding the theoretical framework. *Modern Language Journal* 78 (1), 12–26.

Oyama, S. (1976) A sensitive period in the aquisition of a nonnative phonological system. *Journal of Psycholinguistic Research* 5, 261–85.

Ozmon, H.A. and Craver, S.M. (2002) *Philosophical Foundations of Education*, 7th edn Englewood Cliffs, NJ: Prentice-Hall.

Pan, B.A. (1995) Code negotiation in bilingual families: 'My body starts speaking English'. *Journal of Multilingual and Multicultural Development* 16, 315–27.

Paradis, M. (1996) *Evaluation de L'aphasie chez les bilingues*. Paris: Hachette.

Peal, E. and Lambert, W. (1962) Relation of bilingualism to intelligence. *Psychological Monographs* 76, 1–23.

Petersen, J. (1988) Word-internal code-switching constraints in a bilingual child's grammar. *Linguistics* 26, 479-93.

Phinney, J.S. (1993) Multiple group identities: Differentiation, conflict, and integration. In J. Kroger (ed.) *Discussions on Ego Identity* (pp. 47–73). Hillsdale, NJ: Erlbaum.

Pierce, B.N. (1995) Social identity, investment, and language learning. *TESOL Quarterly* 29, 9–31.

Portes, A. and Schauffler, R. (1994) Language and the second generation: Bilingualism yesterday and today. In R.G. Rumbaut and S. Pedrazgo (eds) *International Migration Review*, Vol. 28 (pp. 640–61). New York: Wadsworth.

Portes, A. and Schauffler, R. (1996) Language acquisition and loss among children of immigrants. In S. Pedraza and R.G. Rumbaut (eds) *Origins and Destinies: Immigration, Race, Ethnicity in America* (pp. 432–43). New York: Wadsworth.

Postman, N. (1985) *Amusing Ourselves to Death: Public Discourse in the Age of Television*. New York: Penguin Books.

Potter, W.J. (1987) Does television hinder academic achievement among adolescents? *Human Communication Research* 14, 27–46.

Prado, W. (1958) Appraisal of performance as a function of the relative-ego-involvement of children and adolescents. Unpublished doctoral dissertation, University of Oklahoma.

Putnam, R.D. (2001) *Bowling Alone: The Collapse and Revival of American Community*. New York: Simon & Schuster.

Rampton, B. (1995) *Crossing: Language and Ethnicity Among Adolescents*. New York: Longman.

Reynold, D. (1928) In Bieler Jahrbuch – *Annales Biennoises* II, 105.

Rioux, R. (1994) L'enseignement du français aux étudiants franco-américains ou les étudiants franco-américains devant leur(s) langue(s). In L. Dubois and A. Boudreau (eds) *Les Acadians et leur(s) langue(s)* (pp. 253–65). Moncton, N.-B.: Les Éditions d'Acadie.

Rodriguez-Fornells, A., Rotte, M., Heinze, H.J., Nösselt, T. and Münte, T.F. (2002) Brain potential and functional MRI evidence for how to handle two languages with one brain. *Nature* 415 (6875), 1026–29.

Romaine, S. (1995) *Bilingualism*. Oxford: Basil Blackwell.

Ronjat, J. (1913) *Le Dévelopment du langage observé chez un enfant bilingue*. Paris: Librairie Ancienne H. Champion.

Rotheram-Borus, M.J. (1989) 'Ethnic differences in adolescents' identity status and associated behavior problems'. *Journal of Adolescence* 12, 361–74.

Saunders, G. (1982) *Bilingual Children: Guidance for the Family*. Clevedon: Multilingual Matters.

Saunders, G. (1988) *Bilingual Children: From Birth to Teens*. Clevedon: Multilingual Matters.

Savic, S. (1980) *How Twins Learn to Talk*. (trans. Vladislave Felbabov). New York: Academic.

Schickendanz, J.A., Chay, S., Gopin, P., Sheng, L.L., Song, S. and Wild, N. (1990) Preschoolers and academics: Some thoughts. *Young Children* 46 (1), 4–13.

Schiff, S. (2003, July 7) Making France our best friend. *Time Magazine* 162 (1), 70–3.

Scott, L.F. (1956) Television and school achievement. *The Phi Delta Kappan* 38, 25–8.

Scott, S. (1973) The relation of divergent thinking to bilingualism: Cause or effect? Unpublished research report. McGill University.

Seliger, H., Krashen, S. and Ladefoged, P. (1975) Maturational constraints in the acquisition of second languages. *Language Sciences* 38, 20–2.

Sinka, I. (2000) The search for cross-linguistic influences in the language of young Latvian-English bilinguals. In S. Döpke (ed.) *Cross-linguistic Structures in Simultaneous Bilingualism* (pp. 149–74). Amsterdam/Philadelphia: John Benjamins.

Snow, C.E. (1991) Language proficiency: Towards a definition. In G. Appel and H.W. Dechert (eds) *A Case for Psycholinguistic Studies* (pp. 63–89). Amsterdam: John Benjamins.

Snow, M.A. (1990) Language immersion: An overview and comparison. In A.M. Padilla, H. Fairchild and C. Valadez (eds) *Foreign Language Education* (pp. 109–26). Newbury Park, CA: Sage Publications.

Stanovich, K.E. (1986) Mathew effects in reading: Some consequences of individual differences in the acquisition of literacy. *Reading Research Quarterly* 21, 360–406.

Statistics Canada (1996) *Profile of Census Divisions and Subdivisions in Quebec.* Catalogue 95-186-XPB, Volumes I through IV.

Steinberg, L. (1993) *Adolescence* (3rd edn) New York: McGraw-Hill.

Steinberg, L. (1997) *Beyond the Classroom.* New York: Simon & Schuster.

Steinberg, L., Silverberg, S. B. (1986) The vicissitudes of autonomy in early adolescence. *Child Development* 57, 841–51.

Swain, M. and Lapkin, S. (1985) *Evaluating Bilingual Education: A Canadian Case Study.* Clevedon: Multilingual Matters.

Tahta, S., Wood, M. and Loewenthal, K. (1981) Foreign accents: Factors relating to transfer of accent from the first language to a second language. *Language and Speech* 24 (3), 265–72.

Tarone, E. and Swain, M (1995) A sociolinguistic perspective on second language use in immersion classrooms. *The Modern Language Journal* 79, 166–78.

Tashakkori, A. and Teddlie, C. (1998) *Mixed Methodology: Combining Qualitative and Quantitative Approaches.* Thousand Oaks, CA: Sage.

Thomson, D. (1995) Language, identity, and the nationalist impulse: Quebec. *Annals of the American Academy of Political and Social Science* 538, 69–83.

Tomasello, M., Mannle, S. and Kruger, A.C. (1986) Linguistic environment of 1- to 2- year old twins. *Developmental Psychology* 22, 169–76.

Tomiyama, M. (2000) Child second language attrition: A longitudinal case study. *Applied Linguistics* 21, 304–32.

Trosset, C. (1986) The social identity of Welsh learners. *Language in Society* 15 (2), 165–92.

Trudgill, P. (2001) *Sociolinguistics: An Introduction to Language and Society* (4th Edn). Harmondsworth: Penguin.

Tucker, G.R. (1986) Implications of Canadian research for promoting a language competent American society. In J.A. Fishman (ed.) *The Fergusonian Impact* (Volume 2: Sociolinguistics and the Sociology of Language: 361–9). Berlin: Mouton de Gruyter.

Turnbull, M., Lapkin, S. and Hart, D. (2001). Grade 3 immersion students' performance in literacy and mathematics: Province-wide results from Ontario (1998–99). *The Canadian Modern Language Review* 58, 10–26.

U.S. Bureau of the Census (1996) *Statistical Abstract of the United States.* Table 878, p. 562. Washington, DC: U.S. Government Printing Office.

U.S. Census Bureau (1990) *Census of Population and Housing: Louisiana.* STF-3A Magnetic Computer Tape. Washington: Bureau of the Census.

U.S. Census Bureau (2000) *Census of Population and Housing*. Washington, DC: Government Printing Office.

U.S. Census Bureau (2004) Facts for features. Public information office. Retrieved April 28, 2004 from the World Wide Web: http://www.census.gov/Press-Release/www/releases/archives/facts_for_features_special_editions/001702.html.

U.S. English (May, 2001) U.S. English incorporated: Toward a united America. Retrieved May 8, 2001, from the World Wide Web: http://www.us-english.org/inc/

Valdez-Menchaca, M.C. and Whitehurst, G.J. (1992) Accelerating language development through picture book reading: A systematic extension to Mexican day care. *Developmental Psychology* 28, 1106–14.

van der Linden, E. (2000) Non-selective access and activation in child bilingualism: The lexicon. In S. Döpke (ed.) *Cross-linguistic Structure in Simultaneous Bilingualism* (pp. 201–26). Amsterdam, Philadelphia: John Benjamins.

Wardaugh, R. (2002) *An Introduction to Sociolinguistics* (4th edn). Oxford, UK: Blackwell.

Wartenburger, I., Heekeren, H.R., Abutalebi, J., Cappa, S., Villringer, A. and Perani, D. (2003) Early setting of grammatical processing in the bilingual brain. *Neuron* 37 (1), 159–71.

Watt, D. and Milroy, L. (1999) Patterns of variation and change in three Newcastle vowels: Is this dialect leveling? In P. Foulkes and G. Docherty (eds) *Urban Voices* (pp. 25–46). London: Arnold.

Weisgerber, L. (1966) Vorteile und gefahren der zweisprachigkeit. *Wirkendes Wort* 16 (2), 73–89.

West's Louisiana Statutes Annotated (1977) *Treaties and Organic Laws, Early Constitutions, Volume 3, U.S. Constitution and Index* p. 696. St. Paul, MN: West Publishing Co.

Whitehurst, G.J., Arnold, D.S., Epstein, J.N., Angell, A.L., Smith, M. and Fischel, J.E. (1994). A picture book reading intervention in day care and home for children from low-income families. *Developmental Psychology* 30, 679–89.

Williams, T.H. (1969) *Huey Long*. New York: Knopff.

Woman ordered to speak English (1995, August 29). *The Daily Advertiser*, p. A–5.

Zentella, A.C. (2004) *Foreword*, in S.R. Schecter and R. Bayley (eds). *Language as Cultural Practice: Mexicanos en el Norte*. Marhwar, NJ: Lawrence Erlbaum.

Zhou, M. and Bankston, C.L. (1998) *Growing Up American: How Vietnamese Children Adapt to Life in the United States*. New York: Russell Sage Foundation.

Zhou, M. and Logan, J.R. (2003) Increasing diversity and persistent segregation: challenges of educating minority and immigrant children in urban America. In S. Caldas and C. Bankston (eds) *The End of Desegregation?* (pp. 185-99). Huntington, NY: Nova Science Publishers.

Appendices

Appendix 1: French Proficiency Survey

Pourriez-vous prendre quelques minutes pour répondre à ce petit questionnaire? Pour un projet universitaire, nous ramassons systématiquement des informations au sujet de l'acquisition du français par nos enfants. S'il vous plaît soyez aussi honnête et objectif que possible.

Répondez à question 1-7 en comparant l'enfant avec un enfant *francophone du même âge* avec des abilités académiques moyens. 1=très inférieur 5=très comparable

(1) Abilité de comprendre le professeur dans la classe	1 2 3 4 5
(2) Abilité de répondre au professeur dans la classe	1 2 3 4 5
(3) Abilité de communiquer avec les autres étudiants dans la classe	1 2 3 4 5
(4) Abilité d'exprimer ses idées au professeur	1 2 3 4 5
(5) Abilité d'utiliser la grammaire correcte	1 2 3 4 5
(6) Expression orale générale	1 2 3 4 5
(7) Expression écrite générale	1 2 3 4 5

Pour #8 & #9, 1=beaucoup 5=pas du tout

(8) Présence d'un accent américain	1 2 3 4 5
(9) Présence de mots anglais dans sa conversation	1 2 3 4 5

Pour #10, 1=incapable 5=très capable

(10) Abilité de fonctionner à son niveau dans une école d'un pays *francophone*.	1 2 3 4 5

Commentaires (optionel):

Appendix 2: French Proficiency Survey

(Translated from French. Completed by children's Québec and Louisiana French, French summer camp, and French immersion teachers)

Could you take a few minutes to respond to this questionnaire? For a university project, we are systematically collecting information on how our children are acquiring French. Please be as honest and objective as possible.

Respond to questions 1-7 by comparing the child with a francophone child of the same age with average academic ability. 1=very inferior 5=very comparable

(1) Ability to understand the teacher in the class   1 2 3 4 5
(2) Ability to respond to the teacher in the class   1 2 3 4 5
(3) Ability to communicate with other students in the class   1 2 3 4 5
(4) Ability to express ideas to the teacher   1 2 3 4 5
(5) Ability to use correct grammar   1 2 3 4 5
(6) General oral expression   1 2 3 4 5
(7) General written expression   1 2 3 4 5

For #8 & #9, 1=much 5=not at all
(8) Presence of an American accent   1 2 3 4 5
(9) Presence of English words in conversation   1 2 3 4 5

Pour #10, 1=incapable 5=very capable
(10) Ability to function on level in a school in a francophone
     country   1 2 3 4 5

Comments (optional):

Appendix 3: Children's French Proficiency Survey. (Administered in French)

S'il vous plaît soyez aussi honnête et objectif que possible. Imagine que tu entres dans une école française avec des élèves qui ne parlent que le francais. Réponds à question 1-7 en comparant toi-mème avec un enfant *francophone du mème âge* avec des abilités académiques moyens. 1=très inférieur 5=très comparable

(1) Abilité de comprendre le professeur dans la classe   1 2 3 4 5
(2) Abilité de répondre au professeur dans la classe   1 2 3 4 5
(3) Abilité de communiquer avec les autres étudiants dans
    la classe   1 2 3 4 5
(4) Abilité d'exprimer tes idées au professeur   1 2 3 4 5
(5) Abilité d'utiliser la grammaire correcte   1 2 3 4 5

(6) Expression orale générale 1 2 3 4 5
(7) Expression écrite générale 1 2 3 4 5

Pour #8 & #9, 1=beaucoup *5=pas du tout*
(8) Présence d'un accent américain 1 2 3 4 5
(9) Présence de mots anglais dans ta conversation 1 2 3 4 5

Pour #10, 1=incapable 5=trPs capable
(10) Abilité de fonctionner à ton niveau dans une école d'un pays *francophone*. 1 2 3 4 5

Commentaires (optionel):

Appendix 4: Children's French Proficiency Survey

(Translated from French) Please be as honest and objective as possible. Imagine that you are entering a French school with students who speak only French. Respond to questions 1-7 by comparing yourself with a francophone child of the same age who is academically average.

1=very inferior 5=very comparable

(1) Ability to understand the teacher in the class 1 2 3 4 5
(2) Ability to respond to the teacher in the class 1 2 3 4 5
(3) Ability to communicate with other students in the class 1 2 3 4 5
(4) Ability to express ideas to the teacher 1 2 3 4 5
(5) Ability to use correct grammar 1 2 3 4 5
(6) General oral expression 1 2 3 4 5
(7) General written expression 1 2 3 4 5

For #8 & #9, 1=much 5=not at all
(8) Presence of an American accent 1 2 3 4 5
(9) Presence of English words in conversation 1 2 3 4 5

Pour #10, 1=incapable 5=very capable
(10) Ability to function at your level in a school in a francophone country 1 2 3 4 5

Comments (optional):

Appendix 5: Bilingual Self-Perception Survey

(This is a sample. The original [also in English] had more space for answers)

(1) How do you feel being bilingual compared to Americans who speak only English?
(2) How do you feel being bilingual when around your Québec friends who speak only French?
(3) How do feel around your American friends, when your parents address you in French? Why?
(4) How would you feel around your Québec friends if your parents addressed you in English?
(5) In general, do you feel fortunate to speak two languages? Why?
(6) Do you feel like you're perfectly bilingual? If you answered 'no', why not?
(7) If you spoke French exactly like a Québécois, how would that change your feelings when with your friends in Québec?
(8) On a scale of 1-5, '1' equals a strong French accent, and '5' equals no French accent. To what degree do you think you have a detectable accent when you speak English?   1 2 3 4 5
(9) On a scale of 1-5, '1' equals a strong English accent, and '5' equals no English accent. To what degree do you think you have a detectable accent when you speak French?   1 2 3 4 5

Index

Authors

Ada, Alma, 5, 204
Adams, Gerald, 150, 158
Alexander, Kern, 18
Anderson, P.J., 160
Armsden, Gay, 129
Asher, James, 159

Baetens Beardsmore, Hugo, 27
Bachman, L., 39
Baddley, Alan, 99
Baillargeon, M., 38
Baker, Colin, 10
Balkan, L., 13
Bankston, Carl, 8, 15, 106, 187
Barker, Valerie, 10
Ben-Zeev, Sandra, 13
Berk, Laura, 96, 147, 164
Berndt, Thomas, 99
Bialystok, Ellen, 13, 14
Bianculli, David, 93, 94
Blum-Kulka, Shoshana, 25
Boudreau, Annette, 134
Boudreaux, Nicole, 21, 85, 172
Brasseaux, Carl, 17, 50, 88
Briller, Bert, 93
Brown, Roger, xiii
Burt, M., 26
Butler, S.R., 70

Caldas, Stephen, 14, 19, 21, 27, 40, 43, 68, 80, 93, 106, 107, 108, 187, 200
Caron, Jacques, 55-56
Caron, Michel, 56
Castellanos, Diego, 11
Caussinus, Marylise, 16
Chall, Jeanne, 70
Cheramie, David, 84
Christian, Donna, 20, 21

Clément, Richard, 66
Cohen, Andrew, 124
Coleman, James, 40
Corson, David, 20
Cowan, Nelson, 99
Crain-Thoreson, Catherine, 90
Crawford, Jim, 16, 17, 18, 196
Crocker, L., 28

Daigle, Jules, 19
Davies, Maire Messenger, 93
De Houwer, Annick, xiii-xiv, 1, 23, 26, 42, 205
Deuchar, Margaret, xiii-xiv, 1, 23, 24, 27
Dewey, John, 38, 193
Diaz, R., 13
Dodson, C., 27
Dole, Bob, 10
Döpke, Susanne, xv, 3, 14, 27, 39, 42, 43
Dörnyei, Zoltan, 66
Dubois, Sylvie, 52, 88
Durkheim, Emile, 45

Eckert, Penelope, 89, 112, 116, 117, 118, 132, 143, 147, 187
Edelman, Martin, 26, 27
Edwards, John, 11
Elkind, David, 122, 127
Enright, Robert, 9, 150
Erikson, Erik, 107, 163, 187
Esters, Irvin, 19

Fantini, Alvino, 1, 23, 27, 205
Feagin, Joe, 23-24
Ferdman, Bernardo, 106
Fishman, Joshua, 16, 46, 50, 106
Flege, James, 160

Index

Foley, Douglas, 112, 113, 115
Franklin, Benjamin, 10, 13

Gaines, Joseph, 12
Galindo, D. Letticia, 107, 115
Gardner, Robert, 30, 36, 37, 77, 198
Gawlitzek-Maiwald, Ira, 42
Genesee, Fred, 14, 20, 27
Giles, Howard, 128, 134
Gordon, Milton, 11
Grosjean, François, 27
Gut, Ulrike, 26, 42, 47, 70

Hakuta, Ken, 12, 13
Heller, Monica, 106, 119, 134, 187
Henry, Jacques, 50
Hayakawa, Samuel, 10
Hill, John P., 118, 163
Hornberger, Nancy, 20, 199
Hornik, Robert, 93
Hudson, L., 127

Ianco-Worrall, Anita, 14, 55

Jarvis, L, 13
Jespersen, Otto, 12
Jones, Christopher, 47

Katz, Susan, 107
Klein, Denise, 15

Labov, William, 162
Lambert, Wallace E., 13, 20
Landry, R, 21
Lanza, Elizabeth, xiv-xv, 25, 27, 29, 42, 43
Lapsley, Daniel, 9, 150
Leopold, Werner, 1, 27
Linn, Robert, 28
Locke, John 13
Lowy, Esther, 19

Macedo, Donaldo, 107, 134
Makin, Laurie, 12
Malina, Robert, 106, 164
McAndrew, Marie, 67, 119
McKay, Sandra, 107, 134
Medved, Michael, 93
Meisel, Jurgen, xiii

Moyer, Alene, 4

Nicoladis, Elena, 27, 43
Noels, Kimberly, 16

Ochs, Elinor, 113, 115, 118, 128, 139, 187
Okita, Toshie, 1, 2, 45, 90, 205
Oyama, Susan, 159
Oxford, R, 16, 78

Pan, B.A., 25
Paradis, Michel, 25
Peal, E., 13
Petersen, Jennifer, 27
Phinney, Jean, 107, 115
Pierce, B.N., 127
Portes, Alejandro, 8, 11, 12, 107
Postman, Neil, 93
Potter, W., 93
Putnam, Robert, 45

Rampton, Ben, 127, 135, 135
Rioux, R., 113
Rodriguez-Fornells, Antoni, 14
Romaine, Suzanne, 1
Rotheram-Borus, Mary Jane, 107

Saunders, George, 1, 23, 27, 42, 58, 106, 205
Savic, S., 47
Schickendanz, Judith, 91
Scott, L.F., 93
Seliger, Herbert, 159
Sinka, Indra, 58
Snow, Catherine, 26
Snow, Marguerite, 21, 73
Stanovich, Keith, 90
Steinberg, Lawrence, 40, 70, 90, 106, 118, 121, 129, 141, 147, 157, 163, 164, 187

Tahta, S., 161
Tanton, John, 10
Tarone, Elaine, 187
Tashakkori, Abbas, 22
Thomson, Dale, 108
Tomasello, Michael, 47
Tomiyama, Machiko, 107, 124

Trosset, Carol, 135
Trudgill, Peter, 131
Tucker, G. Richard, 201
Turnbull, Miles, 13

Valdez-Menchaca, M., 91
van der Linden, 42, 43
Vihman, Marilyn, xiii

Wardaugh, Ronald, 26, 33
Wartenburger, Isabelle, 14, 15
Watt, Dominic, 160
Whitehurst, Grover, 91
Williams, T. Harry, 17

Zentella, Ana Celia, xiv, 5
Zhou, Min, 15, 204

Subjects

Academic performance
– belief (or fear) it is hindered by bilingualism, 12, 137-138, 158, 189, 200
– link with household climate, 80, 199
– link with multilingualism, 13, 14-16, 21, 187, 200
Acadian exile, 17
Acadiana, 18, 50
– origin of name, 49
Acadie, 49, 54
Accents, 4, 36, 45, 50, 52, 53, 58, 59, 66, 67, 81, 110, 111, 127, 140, 155, 157, 197
– association with attractiveness, 128, 134
– discussion of, 159-160
– influenced by non-native speaking immersion program students, 72, 81, 84, 85, 89, 160, 191, 197
– loss of, 130-131, 133, 145, 157
– self-consciousness of, 122-123, 153, 155, 156
– subjective nature of, 82, 88, 191
Adolescence, 21
– bilingual identity development, 107, 127
Adolescent opposition, 6, 67, 114-116, 136, 139, 141, 189
Anglicisms, 84, 134
Arbitrariness of language, 14, 55
Assimilation, 11, 15, 77
Audiotape recordings, 59, 68, 102, 120, 123, 139-140, 141-143, 150, 134-165
– as methodology employed in study, 25-26

Bilingual dominance, 26, 27, 29, 30
Bilingual education, 16, 200-201
– debate, 196
– two-way programs, 20
Bilingual identity, 128, 139, 145, 146, 147, 149, 152, 186-187
– *See also* Social identity
Bilingual preference, 83
– analyzed over course of adolescence, 107
– explanation of concept, 26-27, 30, 108
Bilingual preference ratio (BPR), 108, 123, 126, 135, 140-142, 154
– description of measure, 26-29
– statistical analysis of results, 165-172
Bilingual proficiency, 26-27
Bilingual self-perception survey, 36, 133, 148, 152
– description of 31-32
– results presented and discussed, 152-159
Bilingualism, balanced, 28, 165, 193
Biliteracy, 67, 75, 80, 82, 83, 84, 87, 91, 92, 144, 145, 186, 192, 193, 194, 198-200, 203-204, 206
– influenced by television, 93-94
– promoted by library visitations, 105
– reading strategies employed, 90-91
– *See also* Literacy, Reading

Cajuns, culture of, 110-112
– linguistic humiliation, 18-20, 111, 197
– resurgence of interest in language, 19
Case studies, xiii
– as research methodology, 23-24
Cinema, as important bilingual educational strategy, 100-101

Index

CODOFIL (Counsel for the Development of French in Louisiana), 19-20, 38
Code switching, *See* Language mixing
Cognitive ability (and functioning), boosted by multilingualism, 13-15
– *See also* Academic performance
Comic books, importance for second language literacy, 37
Community, influences on language usage, 45, 53-54, 107
– linguistic norms, 45, 50, 59, 161
Context, *See* Language context, Social context
Creoles, 17, 50, 53, 88, 116, 151
Cross linguistic structures, 43, 70, 116-117, 134-135
Cursing, *See* Profanity

Degree of bilingualism, 26, 29
Discipline (scolding), 54-56, 71
Dreams, 65
DVD's, use as bilingual education strategy, 205

Edelman's Contextualized Measure of Degree of Bilingualism, 28, 30, 154, 156
– statistical analysis of results, 172-178
'English-only' movement, 10-11
Entertainment, as important bilingual–biliteracy strategy, *See* Cinema, Comic books, Games, Hobbies, Media, Television, Videocassettes
Ethnicity, link with language, 46, 50, 73, 108, 148, 163, 189
Ethnography, 60

Fieldnotes, as methodology employed in study, 24-25, 187
Flashcards, 91
Fluency, 26, 74, 125, 131, 140, 141, 145, 160, 186, 188, 189, 190, 192, 194, 195, 198, 199, 202, 203, 206
Franco-centric curriculum, 73
French immersion programs, *See* Immersion programs
'French-only rule'
– as applied to cinema, 100

– as applied to television, 95
– in home, 73
French proficiency survey, 75, 79, 81, 82, 84, 125, 127
– description of, 30-31
– results from children's version, 85-87, 152
– results from teachers' surveys, 87-88
– statistical analysis of results, 178-185
'Frenchies,' the peer group, 112, 120, 125, 135, 136

Games, as language tools, 104

Hegemony, of English, 9, 133-134
Hobbies, and influence on language choice, 49
– as complications to 'French-only' rule, 101-102
Homework, 70-71, 78

Identity, 9
– achievement, 150, 158, 186-187
– development in bilinguals, 107, 128, 162
– of family, 108
– reconfiguration of, 115, 139
– social construction of, 118, 126-127, 139
– *See also* Bilingual identity, Social identity
Illocutionary competence, 39
Integrative motivation, 36, 37, 77
Imaginary audience, 127, 151
Immersion programs, 135-136, 192-193, 195-196, 200-201
– authentic academic immersion, 77-78, 193
– establishment in Louisiana, 20
– in Canada, 201
– in suburban school, 79
– influence on out-of-school language usage, 68
– link with academic performance, 14, 64, 75, 80, 199-200
– partial, 73, 199
– 'sink or swim', 78

Koreans, 204

Lafayette, Louisiana, demographics 111
Language attrition, 124
Language context, 27, 108
Language, developmental delay, 42, 47, 70, 203
Language immersion, importance for learning a second tongue, 35, 36, 39, 46, 47, 58, 62, 131, 189
– See also Societal immersion
Language immersion programs, See immersion programs
Language inhibitory functions, 14
Language input=output, 7, 47, 59, 99, 196-197, 204
Language minorities, 60
Language mixing, 42, 43, 61-62, 92, 102, 119, 120, 153
Language preference, 26, 64, 108, 117, 118, 121, 132, 138, 187
Language proficiency, 26, 67
– as distinct from language preference, 108
Language revival, 16
Language shift, 117-119, 126-127, 142, 148, 151, 161
Language systems, 43, fused, 43
Library usage, as biliteracy learning tool, 104-105
Linguistic anguish, 68, 123
Linguistic conformity, 115-116, 190
– resisting, 203
Linguistic friction, 62-64, 113, 118, 124
Linguistic humiliation, 18-19
Linguistic norms, of United States, 107, 144
Linguistic self-confidence, 77, 145, 148-152
Linguistic self-consciousness, 59, 62, 65, 66, 68, 71, 123, 161
– associated with early adolescence, 114-116, 191
– lack of, 109, 145, 149-150
– See also Accents
Literacy, 80, 145
– See also Biliteracy
Long, Huey, 17

Media, importance of for language acquisition, 8, 50-51, 188-190, 202
– parental control of, 109, 114
– See also Television, Videocassettes
Melting Pot, 11
Mixed methods, 22
Multilingualism, 187
Music, as language learning strategy, 96, 105

Native Americans, 11
Nova Scotia, 49, 73

'One parent, one language approach', 3, 39, 41, 42, 188

Parallel monolingualism, 68, 150
Participant observation, as methodology employed in study, 22, 24
Peer influences, on academics, 75, 77
– on bilingual self-perception, 153-155
– on language acquisition xiv, 6, 8, 43, 197, 199, 201-203
– on language usage (choice), 21, 65, 68, 77, 85, 98, 114, 119, 124, 127, 130-132, 135, 137, 139, 143, 145-146, 148, 151, 163, 187, 190
Pennsylvania German, 11, 13
Positron emission tomography, 15
Pragmatic competence, 39
Pragmatic differentiation, 43
Pre-adolescence, influence on language usage, 62, 66, 67
– influence on language attitudes, 66, 103
Profanity, 14, 55-57, 196

Québec, 'silent revolution', 57
– sovereignty movement, 36, 37, 60-61, 133

Reading
– church missals, 92
– for pleasure, 83, 91-92, 194
– French comic books, 91
– French novels, 130, 144, 186, 194
– parental strategies, 90-91, 194, 204
Reading readiness measures, 70

Index

Repetition, as important language learning strategy, 100-101, 196
— *See also* 'Time on Task' theory, Videocassettes
'Residual effect', 125, 135, 140
Richard, Zachary, 36, 112

School, success, 70
Social capital, 195
Social class, of children's peers, 112-113, 201
— and school success, 39-40, 201
Social context (or milieu or environment or atmosphere), 29, 34, 44, 50, 51, 162-163, 187, 188, 197-198
— *See also* Language context
Social identity, 113, 139, 163
Societal language immersion, 38, 66, 150, 151, 190, 198, 199, 206
— importance for language choice, 46, 62, 64
— importance for language fluency, 61, 189, 192, 193, 194, 195, 203, 204
Sociolinguistic competence, 39
Speech screening test, 70
Summer camp (as language tool), 58-59, 66, 131, 140, 145, 150, 182, 188, 195
— as aid to promoting biliteracy, 66-67, 82, 124

Technology terms, as complications to the 'French-only rule', 101-103
— *See also* Hobbies
Television, as bilingual educational strategy, 94-95, 204
— influence on biliteracy and reading, 92
— influence on language usage, 42, 52, 75, 98
— parental control of, 95-98, 114, 186, 188-190
— sexuality on, 96, 204
— watching in Canada, 98
Tests (assessments), 186, 189, 200
'Time on Task' theory, 196

Université Sainte-Anne, 198
'US English', 10

Vacations, as tool to promote home language usage, 64, 204
Videotape recordings, 29, 48, 67
Videocassettes (VHS), 46, as aid in promoting biliteracy, 100
— as bilingual educational strategy, 99-100, 205
— importance of repetitive viewing, 99, 100
Vietnamese, 15

Xenophobia, 8, 10-11, 17-18